The Fire of Liberty in Their Hearts

The Fire of Liberty in Their Hearts

THE DIARY OF JACOB E. YODER OF THE
FREEDMEN'S BUREAU SCHOOL, LYNCHBURG, VIRGINIA

1866-1870

Edited by Samuel L. Horst

The Library of Virginia
Richmond —1996

Library of Congress Catalog Card Number: 96-077910

Standard Book Number: 0-88490-181-5

Library of Virginia, Richmond, Virginia
© 1996 by The Library of Virginia
All rights reserved.
Printed in the United States of America

This book is printed on acid-free paper meeting requirements of the American Standard for Permanence of Paper for Printed Library Materials.

Jacket illustration: Jacob Yoder and an unidentified colleague stood behind their pupils in Lynchburg, sometime in the early 1870s. (Courtesy of the editor)

Jacket design: Paris Ashton-Bressler, Virginia Department of General Services, Office of Graphic Communications.

Illustration on page xi courtesy of the editor.

CONTENTS

FOREWORD

The Jacob Eschbach Yoder diary is important as an account of the Reconstruction era, as the record of a young man coming of age in mid-Victorian America, and as a document of educational training and philosophy in the nineteenth century. Opening with an eyewitness account of the social ferment of the post–Civil War era in the South, the diary also records Yoder's personal struggles to overcome private doubts and achieve self-mastery, and his search for manhood through professional accomplishment and economic independence. Yoder's training in Pennsylvania and his commitment to the education of the freedmen in Lynchburg as both a teacher and an administrator provides an interesting overview of the philosophy and practice of education in the nineteenth century.

When he began keeping his diary on 28 April 1866 in Reconstruction Lynchburg, Jacob Yoder understood that he was a witness to a profound moment in the transformation of southern, and American, society. His diary recounts his attempts to understand black and white attitudes toward the old Virginia that had been swept away, and the hopes and fears of citizens about the new world being formed around them. Although Yoder generally found whites hostile to his educational mission, he also recorded long-lost voices of the Reconstruction era, such as a German former Confederate whom Yoder found "liberal and reasonable" (14 June 1866). Likewise, Yoder interviewed an Irish overseer who thought the "abolition of slavery no harm to the country," although he expressed patently racist views about black suffrage and equality (23 June 1866). Yoder spoke with several former slaves who recounted aspects of their experience in bondage, and he quickly became aware of the diversity of opinion in Lynchburg's black community about the future course of Reconstruction.

He did not approve of, or understand, all that he saw and heard. Several times he commented on "the mode of worship of the colored people," whose "noisy worship," dancing, and singing he could not appreciate (10 June 1866, 14 June 1866). Nevertheless, his eyewitness account of African American life in Lynchburg testifies to the freedmen's immediate grasp of the meaning of freedom through education, social organization, and religion. From the banner reading "We Are Free," carried in a grand procession (5 June 1866), to the tableau entitled "Emancipation" in the exercises at the Camp Davis school (21 June 1866), Yoder noted the public manifestations of a social revolution.

Yoder's accounts of public life and events are embedded within a much more private and personal narrative of his own coming-of-age. After his return to Pennsylvania on 30 June 1866, Yoder's inner struggles with his own morality and religious views became especially pronounced. Forming a distinct section of his diary, the entries during his Pennsylvania sojourn reveal a young man searching mightily for his place in the world, and to define his manhood. His religious upbringing and moral training weighed heavily on Yoder, and his often-tortured musings tell us much about becoming a man in mid-nineteenth-century America. After much soul-searching, Yoder finally accepted education as his true calling, a decision already apparent when his diary abruptly ends on 8 April 1867.

Throughout his trials in Pennsylvania, Yoder's thoughts were often drawn back to Virginia and the overall issues of Reconstruction. He corresponded with his black and white friends in Lynchburg and commented often on national Reconstruction politics. The fulfilment of both his personal journey for manhood and his public quest for position and security came soon after his return to Virginia in the autumn of 1868 as the administrator of the Lynchburg area's Freedmen's Bureau schools. The Yoder of the diary that resumes on 15 November 1869 was a more sober, professional man facing the realities of the end of Reconstruction in Lynchburg. The clipped, businesslike diary entries reveal Yoder as an industrious, and more circumspect, Yankee struggling to preserve African American education in changing times. Yoder would marry and spend the rest of his life in Lynchburg as an administrator in the black public school system, the once-zealous young man now reconciled to the realities of southern life. The transformation of Jacob Yoder into a community stalwart contradicts the stereotype of the carpetbagger thrown out after Reconstruction, but also serves as a metaphor for the declension of the Reconstruction era.

Library of Virginia   GREGG D. KIMBALL

Thursday.

May 3rd 1866.

There is in many respects after all a great difference between freedom and slavery. The slave could not go any where without a pass. Any one person must gradually become a free woman or a freeman; yet it is not uncommon to find men and women that have quite exalted ideas of freedom. Their very looks show the fire of liberty in there hearts.

One thing the Colored kerkple are to dull to see, that Andrew Johnson is their It is a real pity that they can not see who their true friends are. Papers of S pronounce Tom Elliott the most respectable and intelligent man among the Colored people, for chiming his tone of report to Gen. Steedman to suit that of the white people

A Letter to Rev. R. A. Vancourt.

Dear Friend

This is not the first time my thoughts have been with you since my arrival While my labors hardly allow me to correspond with friends their

Tues. May 9. 1866.

Wednes-
day Wrote to Daniel H. Steck and Geo.
W. Sisson. Read another article on
the war of races. Made another
report. Had a pleasant rain.

Thursday May 10. 66.
All the schools small on account of
the holiday. The people in Dixie celebrate
this day in memory of the Death
of Gen. Stonewall Jackson. They
honor this christian hero with
many honors. Processions formed
in the morning and went out the
burial Places. There on the graves
of friends and Confederate soldiers
they placed their floral wreaths.
First in the morning they
went to the cemetery where the
soldiers are principally are buried.
The first wreathes were placed
on Union grave by mistake.
As soon as they discovered the
error if such it was, they removed
them. After school that part of
the Freedmen's living in Camp Davis
went to see the Union Graves. These

INTRODUCTION

Jacob Eschbach Yoder was one of the many northern schoolteachers who went south to assist in educating the newly freed African American population in the years immediately following the Civil War. Impelled by a religious fervor stemming from his upbringing in the Mennonite faith and especially by the educational ideals he had absorbed from his mentor, James Pyle Wickersham, Yoder left his native Pennsylvania early in 1866 to become an instructor and administrator of the Freedmen's Bureau school in Lynchburg, Virginia. Perhaps sensing that he was engaged in a historic enterprise, Yoder kept a diary recording his thoughts and experiences. Though incomplete, the manuscript provides valuable information about his work and personal development as well as useful insights into life in Reconstruction-era Virginia. Yoder's diary reveals that he was a product of his times and held the same preconceived ideas about African Americans as did most of his northern contemporaries. While he believed that African Americans should be given all of the rights of citizenship and should be educated so that they could participate in the economic and political life of the nation, he never overcame his reluctance to accept blacks as his social equals.

Unlike most northern educators who taught in the post–Civil War South, Yoder married another Freedmen's Bureau schoolteacher and settled in the same community in which his school had been located. When the Freedmen's Bureau program ended in 1870, Yoder accepted a position in Lynchburg's new public school system, ultimately becoming principal of the city's all-black high school and administrator of Lynchburg's black schools, serving the black community for the rest of his life. His diary was preserved by his descendants after his death in 1905. In 1971, the Yoder family presented the manuscript and associated papers to the Virginia State Library, now the Library of Virginia.

I. Childhood and Youth

Jacob Eschbach Yoder was born on 22 February 1838. He was the eighth of the sixteen children of Jacob Maurer and Anna Eschbach Yoder. At the time of his birth, his family was living near Gilbertsville in Montgomery County, about forty miles northwest of Philadelphia.[1]

Yoder descended from Swiss Mennonite pioneers who had immigrated to the United States by way of the German Palatinate and settled in Pennsylvania in the 1720s. Many other German settlers in the area were members of the Reformed or Lutheran Churches. Jacob and his family attended the Boyertown Mennonite Church, which held services once a month. On the other Sundays each month, the family probably went to the Hereford Mennonite Church located six miles from Boyertown. Individual members of the family likely attended other churches in the area as well, including the nearby Falkner Swamp Reformed Church.[2]

It is not known how Jacob acquired his early education, but most likely he attended one of the church schools offered at the Boyertown Mennonite Church and the Hereford Mennonite Church. It was customary for Mennonite children to be educated at such schools "when instruction for the young was no more given at home." Sometimes conducted by the Mennonite minister, these schools ran four months a year, six days a week, six hours a day and included secular as well as religious education. The state of Pennsylvania had established a free public school system in 1834 but apparently no school opened in Boyertown, in neighboring Berks County, two miles away from Yoder's home, until 1866. It seems likely that Jacob subsequently attended the Mount Pleasant Seminary, a private school founded in Boyertown in 1842, for in later years he conducted a correspondence with the school's first principal, Jacob Whitman, who was well-known locally as a teacher of the sciences.[3]

Jacob's father died on 24 June 1854 and was buried in the Boyertown Mennonite Church cemetery. His will, written two months before his death, provided for the payment of expenses, a widow's dowry of one-third of the estate for his wife, and equal division of the remainder of his assets among the eleven surviving children. In 1862, when the estate was finally settled, twenty-four-year-old Jacob received $624.00, a sizable inheritance for such a large family. Nevertheless, he still faced the necessity of making his own way in the world. Two years earlier, in 1860, he had decided to train as a teacher, thus choosing to follow educational pursuits rather than a career in some more lucrative field.[4]

Abandoning his family's farming life, young Jacob Eschbach Yoder enrolled at Millersville Normal School in Lancaster County on 1 April 1860. Millersville's

Yoder's training at Millersville Normal School, the first state institution for teacher education in Pennsylvania, inspired him to go south and teach former slaves. (Library of Virginia)

dynamic young principal, James Pyle Wickersham, who would eventually become a nationally known educational leader, had founded the school as a county teachers' institute in 1855. Four years later Millersville became the first state normal school in Pennsylvania and was viewed by many as a model school.[5] Yoder was attracted to Millersville by Wickersham's outstanding reputation and took copious notes in the inspiring educator's classes.

For reasons that are not completely clear, Yoder left Millersville in the autumn of 1863 and began teaching school, probably at Mount Pleasant Seminary in Boyertown. Indeed, his fragmentary diary shows that he was still teaching there early in 1864. He may have left school to avoid a call to military service, thereby postponing his education until the war had ended and teaching instead. The tenets of the Mennonite faith required members to avoid military service. Yoder may well have subscribed to those beliefs, even though he was evidently not a member of the Mennonite Church.

If he did not believe in military service, Yoder may have preferred to leave Millersville since James P. Wickersham took an active role in raising a regiment that included more than one hundred students and teachers at his normal school. On 9 July 1863, just after the Battle of Gettysburg, Wickersham received a commission as colonel of the 47th Regiment of the Pennsylvania Volunteer Emergency Militia. Yoder's name appears on the muster rolls for Company I, 48th Pennsylvania Regiment, which was recruited between 2 and 8 July 1863. Company I was mustered in on 28 July 1863 and discharged a month later on 26 August.

Whether or not Yoder actually served during that period is not known, but he did not return to Millersville Normal School until the war's end in April 1865.[6]

Along with the issue of actively supporting the Union, Millersville Normal School's principal influenced his students, and Yoder in particular, in more than just the art of teaching. He also imbued them with the importance of undertaking the education of the South's newly freed slaves. James P. Wickersham articulated his vision in a major address before the National Teachers' Association meeting at Harrisburg, Pennsylvania, on 16 August 1865. Speaking about the reconstruction of the South, Yoder's mentor enumerated the actions he thought were needed to secure the fruits of liberty to the former slaves. Wickersham expressed apprehension about the possibility of the southern aristocracy's return to power, for he viewed slavery as the source of the nation's problems and feared that the former slaveholders would effectively reenslave the freedmen. Civil rights should be provided to all, Wickersham held, and the preparation of freedmen for the rights of citizenship required education. Wickersham was strongly committed to a system of free schools for all in the South to secure the American state.[7] Yoder and many of his fellow Millersville classmates would heed Wickersham's call to educational work among the South's freedmen.

II. Freedman Education —1866

The Pennsylvania Freedmen's Relief Association (PFRA) had begun in March 1862 as the Port Royal Relief Committee, dedicated to providing relief and educational activities among freedmen on the Union-occupied Sea Islands of South Carolina. As the PFRA it expanded its work into Washington, D.C., and Union-occupied Alexandria, Virginia, and after the war into Lynchburg (among other Virginia areas), where the American Baptist Home Mission Society of the Northern Baptist Church had already begun educational work with the freedmen. Several of James P. Wickersham's Millersville students signed on to teach in Lynchburg under the auspices of the PFRA. The first, Jacob W. Shoemaker from Westmoreland County, Pennsylvania, interrupted his studies in May 1865 to take up an appointment as the city's initial PFRA superintendent. He was soon joined by Jacob Eschbach Yoder.[8]

Unlike the American Baptist Home Mission Society, which emphasized religious instruction along with general educational activities, the Quaker-sponsored Pennsylvania Freedmen's Relief Association was more secular and less concerned with indoctrination, conversion, and proselytizing. Although Yoder had enrolled at Millersville for the fall term of 1865–1866, he, like Shoemaker, interrupted his education and went to Lynchburg by March 1866 to become principal of the

SEA-ISLAND SCHOOL, No. 1.—ST. HELENA ISLAND. ESTABLISHED APRIL, 1862.

TEACHERS { MISS LAURA M. TOWNE, " ELLEN MURRAY, MRS. HARRIOT W. RUGGLES.   Supported by the Pennsylvania Branch.

EDUCATION AMONG THE FREEDMEN.

Pennsylvania Branch of the American Freedman's Union Commission.

An 1864 pamphlet solicited contributions for a school of the Pennsylvania Freedmen's Relief Association, the organization that sponsored Jacob Yoder in Lynchburg. (Library of Congress)

Camp Davis School. There he worked closely with his former classmate Shoemaker. The arrival in Lynchburg of teachers such as Yoder was the result of the PFRA's decision to direct most of its efforts to freedmen's education rather than to physical relief.[9]

Before the Civil War Lynchburg had enjoyed a growing economy with new businesses opening and manufacturers producing at peak levels. The James River and Kanawha Canal, six major turnpikes, and three railroads converged at Lynchburg, making the town an important transportation hub connecting the farming counties of the Southside and central Virginia with the markets in Richmond and the tidewater. Between 1851 and 1860, for example, Lynchburg's tobacco inspections grew from 5,810 to 9,801 hogsheads, while the Virginia and Tennessee Railroad between 1857 and 1859 increased its deliveries of grains from

20,065 tons to 21,383, and of livestock from 7.3 million tons to 8.6 million tons. Although Lynchburg's late antebellum financial boom was largely based on tobacco trading and manufacturing, the city also boasted iron foundries, grist mills, clothing manufacturers, furniture makers, and fertilizer processors, among many other businesses. At the same time, however, Lynchburg's population declined from a total of 8,071 to 6,853, demonstrating that Lynchburg's economic growth was not dependent on a concomitant population growth.[10]

Until June 1864, the fighting in the Civil War did not touch Lynchburg directly. As part of Union general Ulysses S. Grant's plan to take Richmond, General David Hunter was ordered to cut Confederate rail connections north of the James River, as well as those at Lynchburg. By 10 June, Hunter and his troops were headed for Lynchburg with Confederate forces gathering to oppose him. Between 16 and 18 June several skirmishes between Hunter's troops and those of Confederate general Jubal A. Early occurred near Lynchburg on Otter Creek and at Diamond Hill, but on 18 June after some light fighting, Hunter began his withdrawal from the area as the Confederate reinforcements had proved too strong to defeat. Although the town itself was not directly touched by battle, at war's end in April 1865 its economy had been damaged by four years of conflict and the Confederacy's collapse. The newly freed slaves joined the rest of the townspeople in facing an uncertain future.[11]

A railroad and manufacturing town in the Virginia piedmont region, the city of Lynchburg was largely untouched by the Civil War, as evidenced by this 1870s photograph taken from across the James River. (Library of Virginia)

Union soldiers pose at Camp Davis in 1865, the first location of Jacob Yoder's Freedmen's Bureau school. (Courtesy Jones Memorial Library, Lynchburg, Virginia)

After the war Lynchburg's black population increased rapidly as former slaves gravitated into the city to enjoy their newly acquired freedom and to avail themselves of government rations available through the Freedmen's Bureau. During and after the war, many blacks who went to Lynchburg settled in makeshift dwellings. Yoder's Freedmen's Bureau school enabled the children from these families to join with those from black families already living in Lynchburg to pursue an education.[12]

Yoder's Camp Davis school settled into a one-story frame building only recently abandoned by the Confederate military. The camp, named after Confederate States of America president Jefferson Davis, consisted of numerous, hastily constructed, single-story wooden barracks arranged in rows and was occupied by Union military personnel and Yoder's school. The camp stood in a wooded area on the southern outskirts of town near present-day Miller Park, bordered roughly by what are today Pierce, Kemper, Twelfth, and Sixteenth Streets.[13]

Yoder faced the task of educating five times as many students in Lynchburg as had attended his Boyertown, Pennsylvania, school during the war. By May 1866, enrollment at the Camp Davis School had reached 322 with an average attendance of 228 students. Three teachers assisted Yoder, as well as PFRA superintendent Shoemaker, who instructed a class of twenty-four prospective teachers. Yoder also had charge of a night school that averaged 23 students. The young principal viewed his educational task as a part of a grand enterprise and seldom

African Americans ran many of their own schools during Reconstruction, although some fell under Jacob Yoder's supervision as superintendent for the Lynchburg region. (Library of Congress)

complained about the meager physical facilities of the school building and the lack of basic school equipment.[14]

As an avid reader of freedmen's aid societies' literature and of the *Independent* —"that always noble sheet"—the leading religious weekly of his time, Yoder reveled in the speeches and sermons of Henry Ward Beecher, the prominent anti-slavery reformer and Congregationalist clergyman. Yoder had learned from Wickersham, if he had not already known it before, that freedmen's education was a national cause. Beecher reinforced this conviction and did something more. His arguments persuaded Yoder that freedmen's education was a work of God. In accepting Beecher's thesis, Yoder had moved a long way from his background in the sectarian Anabaptist view of discipleship, which adhered to nonparticipation in civic affairs, to a belief in a Christian national citizenship, which required everyone actively to better the lot of those less fortunate for both God and the nation.[15]

Lynchburg's white citizens generally looked askance at the northern teachers and viewed their work as subversive of the established southern racial order. In his diary, Yoder observed, "It is too plain that this people still love Slavery with some blind madness. They have only accepted the result of this war, because they must. Many hate every measure that is intended to elevate them [African Americans]. Education is their only passport to distinction. Therefore the whites so bitterly oppose it."[16]

Yoder, and other northerners like him, had their own doubts about the "experiment" in black education. Whereas Yoder believed that the freedmen deserved a chance to prove that they were entitled to the rights of free men, he was not entirely sure they could succeed. "When I meditate on the magnitude and responsibility of my labors, this thought comes in my mind: 'Who is sufficient for these things?' To effect the popular education of this people is no less difficult than it is desirable. They are immensely poor; profoundly ignorant; remarkably vicious," he wrote to Falkner Swamp Reformed Church minister Robert A. Vancourt early in May 1866. He blamed slavery for most of the freedmen's plight, however, and noted that "it is not an unimportant reward for us to know that we are laboring in a cause for the accomplishment of which thousands of the North's noblest hearts are praying." Stressing the requirement for immediate action to help the freedmen, Yoder told Vancourt, "At no future period will education be so much needed as it is at present; nor will they at any other time lay hold of the pearl of great prize in the same good earnest they do now. Of course, the assistance if they are to have any must come from the North; and at this time persons coming from there and showing their friendly feelings for them command a powerful influence among them. Now their enthusiasm is aroused. Let it be suppressed without feeding it, and it will never be so active again." Yoder also found another reason for the freedmen's desire for education, though "not a very laudable one in itself. They delight in doing any thing, that, in ante bellum days they were disallowed, and the white people allowed, to do. So some will *now* learn just for the sake of doing it."[17]

Images of Freedmen's Bureau schools, such as this Richmond classroom in 1866, appeared in the northern press, emphasizing the role of northern philanthropy in the postwar South. (Valentine Museum, Richmond, Virginia)

On 29 June 1866, the teachers at the Camp Davis School and their principal, Yoder, left Lynchburg for their homes in the North. Yoder hoped that he would be able to return to Lynchburg. Superintendent Shoemaker's health was poor and, because Yoder had assumed some of Shoemaker's duties—principally letter writing—he evidently hoped to secure the PFRA superintendent position there for the coming school year. He failed to obtain the position, however, perhaps because of his youth and lack of experience, writing in his diary on 9 July that he had been to Philadelphia to learn the decision of the "Board of Education" but found that his trip had been for "naught."[18]

Jacob Yoder spent the summer of 1866 at home attempting to improve his educational skills and to find another position for the next school year. Early in August he decided that the just-received offer of a teaching job in a secondary school in Pottstown, Pennsylvania, at a salary of "$35.00 [for] 100 [days' work]" was unacceptable. At the same time he received a letter from Frederick H. Stauffer, owner of the Mount Pleasant Seminary building in Boyertown, Pennsylvania, suggesting that he rent the building and open a private school. Just as he committed himself to the new enterprise, however, Yoder discovered that Isaac B. Hankey, who had been associated with Mount Pleasant Seminary until 1866, was opening a new school nearby that would compete with Yoder's for students. In fact, Hankey remained at his Kallynean Academy for almost twenty years.[19]

Though apprehensive that the competition would cause both him and Hankey to fail, Yoder carried on and began the first school day with ten pupils to Hankey's five. Yoder's total grew to thirty-two students, but over the course of the next several months the number dwindled, and by early in December he was beginning to question the wisdom of continuing the school. Three months later Yoder decided that he was not suited to educational entrepreneurship and that his debts were overwhelming him. On 3 March he noted in his diary, "Have no inclination to do constant manual labor and no aptitude for shrewd business. Stop school as a *failure* when this fact is in its most obvious stage to every observer." Despite Stauffer's request that Yoder complete the term and stay on as the school's principal, Yoder could not be persuaded. On 14 March he wrote, "This evening I have closed school without notice and contrary to Mr. Stauffers wishes." Although he had lost more than one hundred dollars on the venture, Yoder concluded that other than the monetary loss "I have nothing to complain. My students have done well."[20] Two weeks later, Yoder noted in his diary that he was in Philadelphia to study elocution and penmanship with his former classmate and Lynchburg's PFRA superintendent Jacob W. Shoemaker. On 8 April 1867 his diary came to an abrupt end and did not resume until 15 November 1869.

III. Freedmen Education, 1868–1871

Yoder kept abreast of events in Virginia at large and in Lynchburg in particular. He corresponded with former Millersville classmates Frank Forrest, Mark Lloyd, and James Stradling,[21] all of whom had returned to Lynchburg to resume teaching for the PFRA. He also exchanged letters with Samuel Kelso,[22] an African American teacher in Lynchburg, whom Yoder knew from his previous sojourn there. By 1867 Kelso had also assumed a role as a politician with a commitment to universal public education.

The growing political battle over Reconstruction at the national level claimed Yoder's attention as well. In his diary, Yoder expressed his concerns about United States president Andrew Johnson's commitment to civil rights for the freedmen: "The rebels are bolder at this time in their opposition to the U.S. Government than they ever were. The cause can not be accounted for in any other way except we attribute it to President Johnson. He ought to know at this time that this down-trodden people has about suffered long enough. It is doubly his duty to give them impartial protection and impartial justice. First, because it is right to do so, and secondly, because the intelligent loyal Masses, whose servant he is, call for the administration of justice to all white or black. It is certainly the height of folly to depart from the path of virtue and uprightness when it has become fashionable to walk therein."[23]

As events would prove, Yoder clearly gauged northern public opinion far better than Johnson. The latter's vetoes of a bill to extend the life of the Freedmen's Bureau and of the Civil Rights Bill early in 1866 were overridden by Radical Republicans in Congress. The nation's voters delivered a strong rebuke to Johnson in the autumn 1866 congressional elections by increasing the Republicans' majority. To ensure a complete reconstruction of the South and to forestall a return of former Confederates to power, Congress went even further and in the spring of 1867 enacted the first of a series of Reconstruction acts that placed the South under military rule.

The advent of the period of Radical Reconstruction under congressional control had far-reaching effects in Virginia. Under the military Reconstruction acts, the commonwealth of Virginia became Military District Number One, commanded by Major General John M. Schofield. Yoder's friend and colleague Samuel Kelso served as a delegate to the 1867–1868 constitutional convention held in compliance with federal Reconstruction legislation and took a leadership role in proposing a state-financed system of public schools for everyone, black and white. In the autumn of 1867, General Schofield called for the election of delegates to the constitutional convention that met in Richmond from 3 December

Yoder assisted the black Educational Association of Lynchburg in establishing the Polk Street School, seen here ca.1871, which operated after Reconstruction as one of Lynchburg's black public schools. (Courtesy of the editor)

1867 to 16 April 1868. Campbell County's delegate Samuel Kelso introduced a resolution on 28 January 1868 to ensure that the emerging state constitution would "guarantee for the future, a system of common school education, to be supported by the State, which shall give to all classes a free and equal participation in all its benefits." This resolution was then referred to the Committee on Education, which later presented its public school measure to the convention body. After four and a half months of work, the convention delegates completed a document, commonly known as the Underwood Constitution, that for the first time established a statewide system of publicly supported schools and provided for universal manhood suffrage. Virginia's commitment to public education would have a profound effect on Yoder's future career.[24]

While Samuel Kelso and the others were working to ensure the Virginia freedmen's future, Yoder kept his attention focused on Lynchburg and sometime in the autumn of 1868 he returned, this time as the new PFRA superintendent for the region. Before Yoder's arrival, the Lynchburg region's Freedmen's Bureau superintendent, Captain Robert S. Lacey, had succeeded in moving the freedmen's school away from Camp Davis to the African Methodist Episcopal church on Jackson Street. The new location was more convenient for the students and enabled the school to avoid some of the problems that had been caused by its proximity to the Union soldiers at Camp Davis.[25]

As PFRA superintendent for the Lynchburg region, Yoder administered twenty-four schools in six counties. Blacks supported twelve of the schools while the PFRA financed another eight. The rest were either privately operated or were supported by other freedmen aid societies. The Lynchburg school in the AME church was the largest, with three teachers, all single women, who taught an average of two hundred and twenty students. Among Yoder's activities during this period was his assistance to leaders in the black Educational Association of Lynchburg with the construction of their Polk Street School.[26]

The PFRA regional superintendency required considerable travel, taking Yoder to schools in Amherst, Appomattox, Bedford, Botetourt, Campbell, and Nelson Counties. He was both resourceful and enterprising enough to get where he needed to go whether by foot, horseback, rail, stage, or packet boat. Some freedmen's schools in his district closed for lack of local support, but others opened elsewhere that for the most part were not supported by northern associations. Yoder, as a diligent proponent of black education, sought to visit freedmen's schools wherever they were.[27]

Meanwhile, the Underwood Constitution, with its promise of free public schools, languished unratified for more than a year. General Schofield, who did not agree with several of the constitution's provisions, refused to permit the required public referendum on the new constitution to take place. Because Schofield's successor General George Stoneman also postponed elections, a year of political drift in Virginia followed. Finally, in 1869, a nine-member committee broke the impasse and negotiated a compromise among the state's Conservative white leaders, key members of Congress, and President Ulysses S. Grant. As a result, Virginians overwhelmingly approved the Underwood Constitution on 6 July 1869 but rejected two provisions that disfranchised former Confederates and reformed local government. After autumn elections and the General Assembly's ratification of the Fourteenth and Fifteenth Amendments, Congress accepted the election results and on 26 January 1870 President Grant signed the act readmitting Virginia's representatives to the national legislature. "Virginia is once more admitted into the family of states," Yoder noted in his diary for that date. Reconstruction in Virginia was over.[28]

With the ratification of the new state constitution and the end of military reconstruction in Virginia early in 1870, the General Assembly turned its attention to the establishment of a statewide public school system. On 2 March the members chose William Henry Ruffner to be the state superintendent of public instruction, and on 28 March Ruffner presented his plan for establishing free public schools. The General Assembly adopted many of the plan's provisions in the school law passed early in July. In mid-April, Yoder had called on members of the Lynchburg City Council and "prominent citizens of Lynchburg to ascertain the public sentiment in regard to public schools. All reports are favorable. But no one wished to act." On the state level, however, efforts to organize the public school system progressed. For the proposed Lynchburg city and Campbell County public schools, the State Board of Education appointed Abram F. Biggers as superintendent effective 22 September 1870. Lynchburg's first public schools opened on 5 April 1871.[29]

Yoder found himself in a delicate situation during the transition to a public school system. He worried about funding to continue those schools for which he was responsible before public financing of education became available. The Freedmen's Bureau by 1869 had begun rapidly withdrawing from its involvement with black education. At the same time the appropriations of the PFRA were dwindling. While much attention focused on the imminent emergence of public schools for all of Virginia's youth, Yoder and the PFRA busily engaged themselves in encouraging and giving supervisory direction to opening additional freedmen schools in rural black communities. When the PFRA planned to close its schools as usual for the summer of 1870, Yoder was particularly concerned about those infant-but-flourishing schools. He believed that another month of operation was important to the parents of the children in those communities who were willing to continue to support the schools if only a little aid would be forthcoming.[30]

In his first-quarter report for 1870 to the Freedmen's Bureau Virginia schools' superintendent, Yoder listed thirty schools, forty-nine teachers and superintendents, and an average of one thousand five hundred and thirty students. Yoder and the other teachers proceeded to educate as well as they could with limited means. Rather than hindering plans for local public schools, the PFRA schools were an important source of support for public schools that would educate all of Virginia's youth, black and white. Only a minority of black children in the larger region could attend PFRA schools, however, and thus it is no wonder the freedmen's aid societies pressed hard in support of public education for all children.[31]

During this period, Yoder was truly a busy man, visiting his six-county school district, holding teachers' institutes, and even writing an article on education for the *Lynchburg Press*. He was vulnerable to discouragement at times but consistently blamed himself for such feelings. Yoder did not become defensive when criticized by his superiors nor did he rationalize his performance by blaming others.[32]

Throughout these difficult times Yoder received commendations for his work as PFRA administrator. One of Yoder's primary responsibilities was to raise

Sisters Anna (left) and Adaline Whitaker joined many other idealistic New Englanders as teachers in Freedmen's schools. In 1871 Anna married fellow educator Jacob Yoder. (Courtesy of the editor)

money to help support the schools, and while he was not greatly successful, at least Secretary-Treasurer Robert Corson acknowledged that Yoder had raised more funds than others could have done. Corson wanted Yoder to remain as superintendent if the PFRA decided to continue the freedmen schools into the 1870–1871 school term. Worried about the PFRA's continued funding for the freedmen's schools, in April 1870 Yoder wrote to Freedmen's Bureau Education Superintendent for Virginia Ralza Manly, to ask whether moneys from the Peabody Education Fund would be available for Lynchburg's public schools. The issue was resolved happily for Yoder and his students when the PFRA did fund the schools for another year until Virginia's state-financed public education began.[33]

IV. Home and Family

Sometime before Yoder went to Lynchburg early in 1866, he developed a romantic relationship with a young woman named Mary. A cryptic reference to Mary's residence in the home of William Stauffer was the only clue to her identity left by Yoder. Only when he returned to Pennsylvania in July 1866 did the intensity of their relationship become evident. His association with Mary continued at least into 1867. If there were objections from Mary's parents, as his diary seems to suggest, there was also hesitation on his part to marry because of concerns for his financial situation and his professional future in freedmen's education. Eventually the attachment with Mary ended, although the gaps in Yoder's diary leave the precise cause of their estrangement unknown.[34]

Among the teachers who went to Lynchburg in 1866 at about the same time as Jacob Yoder were Anna Whitaker and her sister Sarah, who stayed only a short while. By 1869, a third sister Adaline (Ada) had arrived as well. The three Whitakers were members of a large family in Ashford, Connecticut, and were sent by the Baptist Home Mission Society to teach freedmen in Lynchburg. Yoder, as principal of the Camp Davis School and as a resident at the teachers' quarters, had ample opportunity to become acquainted with the Whitakers. When he returned to Lynchburg late in 1868, he was once more in close proximity to Anna and later to her sister Ada. This time he developed a warm attachment for Anna Whitaker. As with Mary earlier, Yoder hesitated to pursue Anna due to the uncertainty of his financial and professional future. In surviving letters to Anna during the summer of 1870, Yoder's cool professional tone reflected his ambivalence about making a lifelong commitment. Writing to Anna late in August, Yoder explained that although he and the teachers expected to resume their positions in Lynchburg, PFRA Secretary-Treasurer Corson doubted that funding for the PFRA schools could continue into the 1870–1871 school year. If the funding became available, Yoder wrote, he would accept a desirable position in Lynchburg "and gladly meet all the old teachers" there, but whether that happened depended on "Providence." He revealed his love for her, however, by telling Anna that he should not have shown her his special affection and thereby raised her hopes for a mutual future until he could attain a stable means of supporting a family.[35]

When the PFRA decided to fund the Lynchburg operation for the 1870–1871 school year, Jacob Yoder returned from his summer vacation at home in Pennsylvania and opened the freedmen's schools on schedule. Following this last year of PFRA involvement in Lynchburg's African American educational system, the question of Yoder's future career was resolved when the city opened its new public schools on 5 April 1871 and Yoder became first assistant to Principal Amos

Annie Yoder, daughter of Jacob and Anna Yoder. (Courtesy of the editor)

Jacob and Anna Yoder and their five sons, probably from the mid-1890s. (Courtesy of Patricia Yoder Garrity)

Botsford at the old Polk Street School, now Public School No. 7. The security of his public school appointment freed Yoder to take on the added responsibilities of a wife and family. He married Anna Whitaker on 28 June, two days before the end of the short school session. They then traveled to Connecticut and Pennsylvania to visit their respective families and to begin their life together.[36]

Over the next fourteen years Jacob and Anna Yoder became the parents of seven children, two daughters and five sons, all of whom lived to adulthood. The state's futile attempts to repay its prewar debt caused a shortage of state funding for the public schools during the 1870s. Jacob Yoder scraped by, as did school-teachers elsewhere. Always underpaid, he took on other work besides his teaching to supplement the family income, in 1880, for example, helping to compile the decennial United States census.[37]

Yoder attended the churches of several denominations during his early years in Lynchburg, seeking a faith that met his spiritual needs. At one point, he seemed destined to become a Methodist, "the church which I have always loved above all other modern churches." His feelings had not changed two months later after returning to Pennsylvania for the summer when he "spoke with Mother on the subject of religion according to the Methodist faith. We had of course to disagree." Yoder remained inclined toward its beliefs the next year in Pennsylvania, writing in his diary that Methodism had "shown its admirable practicability over any of the other churches here." In November 1869, when his diary resumed, Yoder was still tending toward Methodism, noting that he had attended the Protestant Methodist Conference that began its session in Lynchburg on 12 November. In fact, he

The city of Lynchburg honored Jacob Yoder by naming a new elementary school for African American children the Yoder School, completed in 1912. (Courtesy of the Lynchburg School Board)

seemed to consider one of the Methodist churches "his" church, although he also went to services at Presbyterian and Baptist churches as well.[38]

Yoder ultimately settled on the Baptist faith. His decision may have been influenced by his friendship with a fellow Pennsylvanian who was serving as minister of the First Baptist Church late in 1868 when Yoder finally returned to Lynchburg's freedmen's schools. Charles C. Bitting and Yoder discovered a common interest in public education. Yoder's diary contains many references to Bitting and to Yoder's attendance at the church before Bitting left Lynchburg for Richmond in 1871 to become secretary of the American Baptist Publication Society for the Southern States. Yoder was probably also influenced by his marriage to a Freedmen's Bureau teacher who had been sponsored by the American Baptist Home Mission Society. On 3 September 1878, Yoder became a member of the new College Hill Baptist Church and soon thereafter a member of the church council as well.[39]

V. Administrator of Lynchburg's Black Schools

When Lynchburg's public schools first opened on 5 April 1871, the new principal for the black schools was Amos Botsford, a seventy-year-old New York native and a graduate of Princeton College (now University). Botsford moved to Virginia by 1839 and taught in Lexington until he and his family moved to Lynchburg in 1844. He taught in Lynchburg until 1877. Jacob Yoder became Botsford's first assistant, a position that placed him in charge of the Polk Street School, the main black school in Lynchburg.[40]

The decade of the 1870s was critical for public education in Virginia and in Lynchburg. The state faced a financial crisis brought on by the attempt to fund fully the antebellum debt. State revenues fell to half the amount needed to maintain services, including the new public school system. Even with modest grants from the Peabody Education Fund, the situation was difficult. In Lynchburg, the city council after 1875 was "avowedly hostile to the public high school, and, their opponents charged, inimical to the whole public-school system." In the spring of 1876, the city council appropriated about 25 percent less than the schools had requested and reduced the school superintendent's salary, despite pleas from the school board. The schools ran out of money before the 1876–1877 school year ended and closed before the end of the regular term.[41]

The situation worsened during the next school year when the city council determined to close the high school. The lower schools were overcrowded and mostly located in "unsuitable houses." Despite strong protests from Lynchburg citizens, the city council eliminated the high school from its budget and refused to increase city appropriations to the rest of the school system. There was no high school for the 1878–1879 school year. Such highhandedness reaped its own reward during local elections in 1879 when candidates favoring public education won the majority of council seats. Not only was the high school reinstated, but also "the whole system was rejuvenated and strengthened and restored to the confidence of the community."[42]

Throughout these critical years, Jacob Yoder remained in charge of the Polk Street School. Despite the financial crisis, the school board raised the salary of the seventy-six-year-old Amos Botsford, while it reduced Yoder's salary. In July 1877, however, a mass meeting of Lynchburg's African American community petitioned the board to appoint Jacob Yoder to "the position of Principal of the Consolidated Public Schools of Colored Children in the place of Mr. Amos Botsford recently assigned to the said position." The petitioners believed "that Mr. Yoder from his past record is fully competent and well qualified to perform the duties" of the position, that "he has the confidence of both parents and children," and that "his appointment would be highly esteemed and gratifying to us." The board tabled the petition. For all practical purposes, then, Yoder supervised the black schools for the aged Botsford, but without the latter's authority and salary. On 25 January 1878, the school board finally appointed Yoder as acting supervising principal of all of Lynchburg's black schools.[43]

The financial imbroglio climaxed in May 1878, when the Lynchburg School Board decided to close the schools before the end of the school term. Many teachers in the city school system offered to continue teaching if the board would only pay what it could and give vouchers for the deficiency. All the principals including Yoder signed a resolution to this effect. In addition, the ever-concerned Yoder asked the board for the use of a room in the Jackson school building for private school purposes for his black students during the summer, which was also approved.[44]

On 1 February 1881, the Lynchburg School Board at last removed the "acting" from Yoder's title as supervisor of Lynchburg's black schools, the position he had held since 1878, in fact, if not in name. He lost little time in requesting a modest salary increase because of his added responsibilities. It took another seven months, however, for Yoder's request to be fulfilled. In August the board recommended that Yoder organize and teach a black high school class "in addition to the lower grades which he now teaches" and increased his salary. For several years it had been true that "if any child who finished Polk Street desired to

The Yoder family lived in this house on Monroe Street during much of Jacob's tenure as superintendent of Lynchburg's African American schools after Reconstruction. (Courtesy of the editor)

be taught a higher course, Mr. Yoder, since he was a highly educated man, would teach the child the branches in secondary education. At first there were only two or three students who wished to pursue higher subjects but soon so many began to have the desire that another school was needed and Jackson Street High School was erected" in 1882.[45]

In March 1885 Lynchburg's school superintendent, Edward C. Glass, appointed Frank Trigg the principal of the black high school, but Yoder continued his duties as supervising principal of the black public schools. Yoder also became principal of the recently completed Payne School, named for longtime school board member Robert S. Payne. Yoder stayed at the Payne School until 1895 when he once more became the high school principal, now at Jackson Street High School, a position he held until his death.[46]

During the summers in the 1890s Yoder participated in several teacher institutes as a lecturer. In 1896 he spoke to the institute in Petersburg on "Trees" and at the Midway Public School on "Botany" as part of the Charlottesville School of Methods. Yoder lectured in Charlottesville again in 1897, and in his annual report Lynchburg's school superintendent Edward C. Glass noted that Jacob Yoder gave "five very interesting and instructive lessons on the trees of Virginia." Between 1889 and 1904, Glass conducted "his far-famed 'School of Methods'" during the summers under the auspices of the University of Virginia. Jacob Yoder, who had become "an expert on trees and nature," taught field botany in Charlottesville not only in 1896 and 1897, but in 1898 as well. In 1898 and 1899, he also lectured at a Roanoke "School of Methods."[47]

Jacob Yoder was circumspect as the leading white educator of blacks in Lynchburg. As local leaders and the state government pursued a policy of black subordination, he sought to preserve the gains made in earlier years. He died on 15 April 1905, after several weeks of illness. The *Lynchburg News*'s obituary noted that Yoder "may not have been very widely known" and "was too modest to push himself into public notice," but "those who knew him entertained a high regard and affection for him" because of his character, conscientiousness in his work, and the extent of his knowledge. A memorial service was held at the Eighth Street African Baptist Church at two o'clock on Tuesday, 19 April, and the funeral service two hours later at the College Hill Baptist Church attracted both black and white mourners. Some attendees were turned away because of insufficient room in the church.[48]

Jacob Yoder's death brought forth a resolution of praise for his years of service from Lynchburg's school superintendent, school trustees, and schoolteachers. Meeting two days after he died, the group of educators agreed on a "tribute of respect" to Yoder, saying that his demise "in the 68th year of his age, after more than 35 years of faithful efficient services in our schools, is a most serious loss to the educational interest of this city." In "respect for his memory," the educators declared their high esteem "for his many excellent traits of character, for his intellectual attainments, and for his unremitting efforts in the training of his pupils." Six years later the Lynchburg School Board named a newly constructed school for blacks the Yoder School "after this dedicated teacher."[49]

Lynchburg's African American community also expressed its deep appreciation for Yoder's service. The teachers of the Payne School, the Polk Street School, and the Moorman School published their memorial in the *Lynchburg News* four days after Yoder's death. Declaring that "greater love hath no man than this, that a man lay down his life for his friend," the teachers lamented the loss of just such a man: "Such was the love that characterized the friend whose loss we now so deeply mourn, such his devotion to duty, such his labors in the schools of our city." The teachers "realize[d] that his life was laid upon the altar of devotion to the elevation of our race by that most potent of all means—education." Therefore, they acknowledged their "deep sense of obligation for the service rendered" them, their "high appreciation of a life of earnest, conscientious, untiring and unfailing toil in our behalf," and their "sense of irreparable loss in his demise." Yoder, they declared, had "devoted his life unselfishly, and unstintingly to our race, and wore himself out in service to us."[50]

NOTES TO INTRODUCTION

1. Pennsylvania Census Schedules, List of Inhabitants, 1840, Montgomery County, Douglass Township, 113; Pennsylvania Census, 1850, Montgomery County, Douglass Township, 199; Abraham James Fretz, *A Genealogical Record of the Descendants of Christian and Hans Meyer* (Harleysville, Pa., 1896), 522, 524–527.

2. Yoder's immigrant paternal forebear was Hans Joder (1672–1742). (Miscellaneous Notes and Family Data in possession of Harry Kollatz, Jr., Richmond, Va.) In his 1864 diary entries, Yoder mentioned attending a funeral where the sermon was preached by the Reverend John Bechtel, who was pastor at the Hereford Mennonite Church from 1848 until his death in 1889. Yoder also attended services at the Falkner Swamp Reformed Church and in his 1864 diary referred to reading "a plain practicle [*sic*] sermon" by the Reverend Robert A. Vancourt, who in 1858 had become the first native-born pastor at Falkner Swamp. In addition, Yoder's summer 1866 diary entries contain several references to attending services at the Swamp. His 1864 diary also mentions his walk to Hill Church (another Reformed Church) to hear the Reverend Croll. Hill Church (later Saint Joseph's), in Pike township, was a Reformed Church that had been Lutheran for a while in the 1700s. It was not far from Boyertown in neighboring Colebrookdale township. Morton L. Montgomery, comp., *Historical and Biographical Annals of Berks County, Pennsylvania* (Chicago, 1909), 1:49; Jacob E. Yoder Diaries, Jan.–Feb. 1864, Acc. 27680, the Library of Virginia, Richmond (hereafter cited as LVA); Amy Histand Gehman and Mary Latshaw Bower, *History of the Hereford Mennonite Congregation at Bally, Pennsylvania* (Boyertown, Pa., 1936), [9–10, 14–15]; information from Robert A. Yoder, Schenectady, N.Y.; Lois Ann Mast, "European Yoder Research," *Pennsylvania Mennonite Heritage* 4, no. 2 (Apr. 1981): 18–19; Fretz, *Genealogical Record of the Descendants of Christian and Hans Meyer*, 520–524; Gary C. Hauze, *Ist dieses nicht das gelobte Land?: A History of America's Oldest German Reformed Church* (Gilbertsville, Pa., 1975), 43–44; *The Brethren Encyclopedia* (Philadelphia, 1983–1984), 2:1237.

3. George Landis, Tannery Ledgers, Boyertown Historical Society, Boyertown, Pa.; *Boyertown Battallya, Centennial '66* (Boyertown, Pa., 1966); Gehman and Bower, *History of Hereford*, [7, 9–10]; *Catalogue of the Officers and Students of Mount Pleasant Seminary at Boyertown, Berks County, Pa., 1851–2* (Reading, Pa. 1852), Schwenkfelder Library, Pennsburg, Pa. Yoder taught in Boyertown in 1863–1864, probably at the Mount Pleasant Seminary.

4. Physician's Return of Jacob Yoder Sr., Death Certificate, 1 Aug. 1854; Jacob Yoder Sr., Will and Settlement Papers, all at Montgomery County Courthouse, Norristown, Pa.

5. *Dictionary of American Biography*, s.v. "James Pyle Wickersham"; Lee Graver, *A History of the First Pennsylvania State Normal School, Now the State Teachers' College at Millersville* (Millersville, Pa., 1955), 28.

6. Lawrence Emerson Bair, "The Life and Labors of James Pyle Wickersham" (Ph.D. diss., University of Pittsburgh, 1939), 29–31; *Catalogue and Circular of the Pennsylvania State Normal School of the Second District, Millersville, Lancaster County, Pa., for the Academic Year, 1860–61; 1861–62; 1864–65; 1865–66* (hereafter cited as *Millersville Normal School Catalogue*);

Samuel P. Bates, *History of the Pennsylvania Volunteers, 1861–5*, vol. 5 (Harrisburg, Pa., 1871), 1287–1288. The U.S. Enrollment Act of 3 March 1863, the first national conscription act adopted by the federal government, had no specific exemptions by occupation, but men willing to pay a $300 commutation fee could avoid military service. John Whiteclay Chambers II, *To Raise an Army: The Draft Comes to Modern America* (New York and London, 1987), 51–53. Some states allowed religious and occupational exemptions. See James W. Geary, *We Need Men: The Union Draft in the Civil War* (DeKalb, Ill., 1991), 32–38.

7. *Millersville Normal School Catalogue, 1865–66;* "Proceedings of the Seventh Session or Sixth Annual Meeting [of the National Teachers' Association], held at Harrisburg, Penn., August 16, 17, and 18, 1865," *American Journal of Education* 15 (1865): 807–810; James P. Wickersham, "Education as an Element of Reconstruction," *Journal of Education* 16 (1866): 283–297.

8. Bertha Adams Jordan, "Public Schools of Lynchburg—1871–1881," *Lynchburg Historical Society Historical Papers* 8, no. 1 (1971), 5; American Baptist Home Mission Society, *Baptist Home Missions in America: Including a Full Report of the Proceedings of the Jubilee Meeting and an Historical Sketch of the American Baptist Home Mission Society, 1832–1882* (New York, 1883), 407; Julius H. Parmelee, "Freedmen's Aid Societies, 1861–1871," in *Negro Education: A Study of the Private and Higher Schools for the Colored People of the United States,* Department of the Interior, Bureau of Education Bulletin, 1916, No. 38 (Washington, D.C., 1917), 1:277; Pennsylvania Freedmen's Relief Association, *Report of the Proceedings of a Meeting Held at Concert Hall, Philadelphia, on Tuesday Evening, November 3, 1863, to Take into Consideration the Condition of the Freed People of the South* (Philadelphia, 1863); Philip C. Garrett, Philadephia, to Col. Orlando Brown, 17 July 1865; Yardley Warner to Col. Orlando Brown, 26 July 1865; James E. Rhoads to W. W. Woodbury, 1 Aug. 1865, Unregistered Letters Received, June 1865–Mar. 1867, Roll 6, Records of the Superintendent of Education for the State of Virginia, Bureau of Refugees, Freedmen, and Abandoned Lands, 1865–1870, Record Group 105, National Archives and Records Administration, Washington, D.C. (Bureau of Refugees, Freedmen, and Abandoned Lands, 1865–1870, Record Group 105, National Archives and Records Administration, Washington, D.C., hereafter cited as BRFAL).

9. Parmelee, "Freedmen's Aid Societies, 1861–1871," 1:270; Report of Freedmen's Schools for 7th District of Virginia, by Capt. R. S. Lacey, District Superintendent, May 1866, Monthly Statistical School Reports of District Superintendents, July 1865–Apr. 1869 and Jan. 1870, Roll 12, Supt. of Ed., Va., BRFAL; *Tidings* (Philadelphia), Feb. 1866, p. 20 (published by the Women's Central Branch of the Pennsylvania Freedmen's Relief Association early in 1866, subsumed by the *Pennsylvania Freedmen's Bulletin*); Jordan, "Public Schools of Lynchburg—1871–1881," 5.

10. David R. Goldfield, *Urban Growth in the Age of Sectionalism: Virginia, 1847–1861* (Baton Rouge and London, 1977), 189–190; The Lynchburg Sesqui-Centennial Association, Inc., *The Saga of a City, Lynchburg, Virginia, 1786–1936* (Lynchburg, 1936), 125. The white population in 1850 was 4,102, falling in 1860 to 3,802; the slave population fell from 3,424 to 2,694; and the free black population from 545 to 357, for a total drop of 13.8 percent. J. D. B. DeBow, *The Seventh Census of the United States: 1850. Embracing a Statistical View of Each of the States and Territories . . .* (Washington, D.C., 1853), 1:258; Joseph C. G. Kennedy, *Population of the United States in 1860; Compiled from the Original Returns of the Eighth Census* (Washington, D.C., 1864), 1:519. In 1870, Lynchburg's population had declined by 28 people since 1860 to 6,825. Francis A. Walker, *The Statistics of the Population of the United States . . . Compiled from the Original Returns of the Ninth Census (June 1, 1870)* (Washington, D.C., 1872), 1:279.

11. George S. Morris and Susan L. Foutz, *Lynchburg in the Civil War: The City—The People—The Battle*, 2d ed. (Lynchburg, 1984), 1–3, 38–49; E. B. Long, *The Civil War Day by Day: An Almanac, 1861–1865* (Garden City, N.Y., 1971), 511, 515, 519, 521, 523–525.

12. Frances Adams Deyerle, "Public Education and Public Schools of Lynchburg," manuscript draft of *A Legacy of Learning*, 12 vols., MS1096, Jones Memorial Library, Lynchburg; Benjamin Guy Childs, *The Negroes of Lynchburg, Virginia*, Publication No. 5 of the University of Virginia Phelps-Stokes Papers (Charlottesville, 1923), 15–16; *Lynchburg Virginian*, 2 June 1865, 28 Apr. 1869.

13. The poet Anne Spencer lived in a house built in 1903 on the site of Camp Davis, at 1313 Pierce Street. By 1981 none of the original camp buildings remained. S. Allen Chambers, Jr., *Lynchburg: An Architectural History* (Charlottesville, 1981), 201, 406; W. Asbury Christian, *Lynchburg and Its People* (Lynchburg, 1900), 198–199; "Dedication of a Bronze Tablet in Honor of Botetourt Battery," *Southern Historical Papers* 35 (1907): 33.

14. Report of Freedmen's Schools for 7th District of Virginia, May 1866, Monthly Statistical School Reports of District Superintendents, July 1865–Apr. 1869 and Jan. 1870, Roll 12, Supt. of Ed., Va., BRFAL; Jordan, "Public Schools of Lynchburg—1871–1881," 5; Orra Langhorne described Camp Davis, saying in 1879 that the camp was a "suburb" of the city, "quite a village in itself" with "a pretty little white church" and "laid off in squares and streets." "Homes of Our Colored People," dated at Lynchburg 26 Nov. 1879, *Southern Workman* 9 (Jan. 1880): 2.

15. Diary entry, 20 May 1866. On 19 Sept. 1865, the major freedmen's aid societies met in New York City and formed an umbrella organization, the American Freedmen's Aid Commission. A month later the group assembled in Philadelphia for its first regular meeting. Among the speakers was Henry Ward Beecher, who likened the freedmen's aid societies' mission to that of the Good Samaritan, in this case by "going where the sufferer is, to extend to him a helping hand, to rescue him from darkness, and take him to the school-house and the church." He further enjoined his fellow ministers that "no minister is of the Church of God who does not take part" in the "great work . . . to educate the colored people." Such sentiments no doubt had a profound effect on Jacob Yoder. "American Freedmen's Aid Commission," *Freedmen's Record* 1, no. 2 (Nov. 1865): 175. The *Independent* had been established in 1848 by a group of New York clergymen as a Congregationalist magazine. It also espoused various reforms including antislavery, woman suffrage, and theological liberty. Henry Ward Beecher soon began writing a column for the *Independent* and in 1861 became its editor (1861–1863). Thereafter, the magazine became a general progressive serial and ceased to be denominational. Ada Tyng Griswold, *Annotated Catalogue of Newspaper Files in the Library of The State Historical Society of Wisconsin*, 2d ed. (Madison, Wis., 1911), 179; Clifford E. Clark, Jr., *Henry Ward Beecher: Spokesman for a Middle-Class America* (Urbana, Ill., 1978), 87.

16. Diary entry, 28 Apr. 1866.

17. Diary entry, 3 May 1866; Wickersham, "Education," 294–295; *American Freedman* 1 (Apr. 1866): 3, quoted in George Frederickson, *The Black Image in the White Mind: The Debate on Afro-American Character and Destiny, 1817–1914* (New York, 1971), 180–181. Writing in 1988, Frederickson reiterated the same theme that Radical Republicans (with whom Yoder identified) did not think "that blacks were biologically equal to whites," but supported political and civil equality as they did not believe that genetics should determine citizenship and opportunity rights. Frederickson, *"The Black Image in the White Mind*: A New Perspective," in *Historical Judgments Reconsidered: Selected Howard University Lectures in Honor of Rayford W. Logan*, ed. Genna Rae McNeil and Michael R. Winston (Washington, D.C., 1988), 104–105.

18. Yoder styled himself as assistant superintendent in correspondence for Shoemaker. Diary entry, 3 May 1866.

19. Yoder wrote that if the salary at the school in Pottstown had been forty-five dollars he would have accepted the position. Diary entry, 2 Aug. 1866; the Mount Pleasant Seminary building could accommodate fifty students. Montgomery, *Historical and Biographical Annals of Berks County*, 1:257.

20. Diary entry, 16 Mar. 1867.

21. Frank Forrest was a PFRA teacher at New London, Bedford County, who had been to Millersville Normal School (diary entry, 2 June 1866); Mark Lloyd, also a PFRA teacher, at Buchanan (diary entry, 12 May 1866); and James Stradling, a PFRA teacher. Report of Freedmen's Schools for 7th District of Virginia, by Capt. R. S. Lacey, District Superintendent, Mar. 1866, Monthly Statistical School Reports of District Superintendents, July 1865–Apr. 1869 and Jan. 1870, Roll 12; James H. Stradling to Ralza M. Manly, 18 June 1867, Unregistered Letter Received, Apr. 1867–July 1868, Roll 7, Supt. of Ed., Va., BRFAL.

22. See especially diary entries of 13 and 17 July 1866 for mention of Samuel Kelso (sometimes spelled Kelsoe). Kelso, who had been a free man before the war, ran a transfer agency for the U.S. post office and took possession of his home at Eighth and Taylor Streets by a homestead exemption on 8 Oct. 1872. Although his parents had been slaves, he had been able to acquire enough education to become one of Lynchburg's first African American teachers after the war. In 1870 he taught in the Twelfth Street School. Betty Mansfield, "That Fateful Class: Black Teachers of Virginia's Freedmen, 1861–1882" (Ph.D. diss., Catholic University, 1980), 298; Virginia Census Schedules, List of Inhabitants, 1870, Campbell County, Lynchburg, Samuel F. Kelsoe, page 533A, line 35; Lynchburg Deed Book AA, p. 96. Yoder "conversed with . . . Mr. Kelsoe" on 10 Jan. 1870 and visited Kelso's school on 21 Apr., diary entries; R. A. Smith, comp., *J. P. Bell & Co.'s City Directory of Lynchburg , Virginia, 1879–'80* ([Lynchburg, 1880]), 119, S. F. Kelso, transfer agent for the U.S. mail; S. F. Kelsoe to R. M. Manly, 30 Apr. 1870, Unregistered Letters Received, Dec. 1869–Aug. 1870, Roll 10, Supt. of Ed., Va., BRFAL.

23. Diary entry, 3 May 1866.

24. Richard L. Hume, "The Membership of the Virginia Constitutional Convention of 1867–1868," *Virginia Magazine of History and Biography* 86 (1978): 468–469, 481; Harry S. Ferguson, "The Participation of the Lynchburg, Virginia, Virginia Negro in Politics, 1865–1900" (master's thesis, Virginia State College, 1950), 9–19; William T. Alderson, "The Influence of Military Rule and the Freedmen's Bureau on Reconstruction in Virginia, 1865–1870" (Ph.D. diss., Vanderbilt University, 1952), 191–192; *Journal of the Constitutional Convention of the State of Virginia* (Richmond, 1868), 96, 134; *Debates and Proceedings of the Constitutional Convention of the State of Virginia, Assembled at the City of Richmond, Tuesday, December 3, 1867 . . .* (Richmond, 1868), 1:704–705; *Lynchburg News*, 6 Apr. 1867, quoted in *Twenty-Fourth Annual Report of the Philadelphia Female Antislavery Society*, Feb. 1868; *Lynchburg Virginian*, 9 Sept. 1868.

25. Yoder's name was included in a Nov. list of personnel. District Superintendent's Monthly School Report, Nov. 1868, Monthly Statistical School Reports of District Superintendents, July 1865–Apr. 1869 and Jan. 1870, Roll 12, Supt. of Ed., Va., BRFAL. PFRA Secretary-Treasurer Robert Corson requested that Yoder provide him with a complete list of all teachers, teacher assistants, their specific locations, and other details. Corson to Yoder, 25 Nov. 1868, Private Collection; Capt. Lacey to O. Brown, 5 Sept. 1868, Unregistered Letters Received, Aug. 1868–Apr. 1869, Roll 8, Supt. of Ed., Va., BRFAL.

26. Yoder noted in his 20 Nov. 1869 diary entry that he had made out seven subscription lists for the "new school-house." On 10 Jan. 1870, he recorded that he had "Visited the New School House." John H. Burton, secretary of mass meeting of blacks, to Gen. O. Brown, 2 Mar. 1869; Samuel F. Kelso to Capt. Lacey, 23 Mar. 1869, Unregistered Letters Received, Aug. 1868–Apr. 1869, Roll 8; Z. A. Cozzens to Manly, 20 and 25 May 1869; R. J. Morgan to Manly, 19 Oct. 1869; R. A. Perkins to Manly, 14 Nov. 1869; Royal J. Morgan and Nelson James to Manly, 6 Dec. 1869, including "Bill of Materials for the Erection of a School," Letters Received, A–V, 22 Apr.–31 Dec. l869, Roll 4; Educational Association of Lynchburg, Board of Trustees, 1 Jan. 1870; Morgan to Manly, 1 and 6 Jan. 1870; Perkins to Manly, 13 Jan. 1870; Morgan to Manly, 19 Feb. 1870, Unregistered Letters Received, Dec. 1869–Aug. 1870, Roll 10; Manly to Lacey, 5 and 26 May 1869; Manly to Cozzens, 26 and 28 May 1869; Manly to Lacey, 9 June 1869, Letters Sent, Vol. 2, 8 Oct. 1868 (pt.)–12 June 1869 (pt.), Roll 1; Manly to the Trustees of the Howard Educational Association, 6 Oct. 1869; Manly to Yoder, 7 and 11 Oct. 1869, 4 Nov. 1869; Manly to Morgan, 20 Oct. 1869; Manly to R. J. Morgan and Nelson James, 10 Oct. 1869; Manly to Bvt. Maj. Gen. O. O. Howard, 9 Nov. 1869, Letters Sent, Vol. 3 (53), 12 June (pt.)–10 Nov. 1869 (pt.), Roll 2; Manly to R. J. Morgan and Nelson James, 9 and 10 Dec. 1869, 4 and 21 Jan., 9 Mar. 1870, Letters Sent, Vol. 4 (54), 10 Nov. 1869 (pt.)–28 Mar. 1870 (pt.), Roll 3, Supt. of Ed., Va., BRFAL.

The African American Lynchburg citizens who applied for the new school originally asked in Dec.1868 that the federal authorities give them one of the barracks buildings at Camp Davis (called Camp Schofield by the Union hierarchy) to be used as a school. When Gen. Oliver O. Howard ruled favorably on their request effective 30 Apr. 1869, Ralza Manly notified Capt. Lacey, the military commander at Lynchburg, to have the group form an educational association and send him a list of the board of trustees. While the organizers styled themselves the Educational Association of Lynchburg, the Freedmen's Bureau recorded the group as the Howard Educational Association, of Lynchburg, in Dec. 1868, when the original petition was received. Isaac Preston, president, 1 Jan. 1870, enclosure with letter of Royal J. Morgan to R. M. Manly, 1 Jan. 1870, Unregistered Letters Received, Dec. 1869–Aug. 1870, Roll 10, Supt. of Ed., Va., BRFAL; Register of Letters and Telegrams Received, Vol. 9, p. 276, 1 Jan. 1868–5 May 1869, Roll 9, Records of the Assistant Commissioner for the State of Virginia, 1865–1869, BRFAL.

27. District Superintendent's Monthly School Report, Dec. 1868, Monthly Statistical School Reports of District Superintendents, July 1865–Apr. 1869 and Jan. 1870, Roll 12; Subassistant Commissioner's Monthly Reports, Dec. 1868, Feb. 1869, Monthly School Reports of Assistant Subassistant Commissioners and Agents, Jan. 1868–Jan. 1869, Roll 13, Supt. of Ed., Va., BRFAL; a survey of Yoder's diary entries for 15 Nov. 1869–29 Apr. 1870 reveals his continuous travel to visit schools throughout his district. In Feb. 1870, a seventh county was added to Yoder's district with the opening of the Mountcastle School at Retreat in Franklin County. Robert Hayden, Mountcastle School, Franklin County, Report of Feb. 1870, in Teachers' Monthly School Reports, Feb.-Mar. 1870, Roll 19, Supt. of Ed., Va., BRFAL.

28. Emily J. Salmon and Edward D. C. Campbell, Jr., eds., *The Hornbook of Virginia History: A Ready-Reference Guide to Virginia's People, Places, and Past*, 4th ed. (Richmond, 1994), 52–53, 98; Hume, "The Membership of the Virginia Constitutional Convention of 1867–1868," 468–469, 481–484; quote from diary entry, 26 Jan. 1870. Yoder wrote in his diary on 18 Nov. 1869, "I am pleased to learn that at an early day, steps will be taken to open free schools."

29. Diary entry, 19 Apr. 1870; Frances Adams Deyerle and Janet Shaffer, *A Legacy of Learning: The Lynchburg Public Schools, 1871–1986* (Lynchburg, Va., 1987), 8–9; Jack P. Maddex, *The Virginia Conservatives, 1867–1879: A Study in Reconstruction Politics* (Chapel Hill, 1970), 207–211; *Lynchburg News*, 21 Sept., 8 Oct. 1870.

30. Yoder to Manly, 19 Apr. and 22 May 1870; John Boisseau to Manly, 25 Apr. 1870, Unregistered Letters Received, Dec. 1869–Aug. 1870, Roll 10, Supt. of Ed., Va., BRFAL. Manly wrote to Yoder late in May 1870 to say that Yoder should close the schools in June as the Bureau's aid to the schools would end at that time. Manly to Yoder, 27 May 1870, Letters Sent, Vol. 5 (55), 28 Mar.–31 Aug. 1870, Supt. of Ed., Va., BRFAL.

31. Manly to J. W. Alvord, 16 Mar. 1870, Letters Sent, Vol. 4 (54), 10 Nov. 1869–28 Mar. 1870, Roll 3; Corson to Manly, 6 and 11 Apr. 1870, Letters Received, A–Y, 1 Jan.–24 Aug. 1870, Roll 5; Corson to Manly, 16 Apr. 1870; Yoder to Manly, 22 May 1870; Thomas J. Lythgoe to Manly, 30 May 1870, Unregistered Letters Received, Dec. 1869–Aug. 1870, Roll 10, Supt. of Ed., Va., BRFAL.

32. Yoder to M. E. Shaddock, 25 May 1870; Charles C. Bitting to Yoder, undated, Private Collection. Yoder decided in mid-May 1870 to resign his post, however, as he believed he was not as effective as someone with a more-outgoing personality might be. Writing to PFRA Secretary-Treasurer Corson, Yoder confessed that he had "made a great mistake in my early experience in being too rigidly democratic," and Corson should find a person "of more show" who "can command more influence and hence can be more useful." Yoder admitted that he had made enemies while exposing "the plottings of proud ignorant demagogues," and although he expected time to vindicate him, he knew it would take a while for the "enmity thus created [to] be erased from the hearts of those that were wounded." The resignation clearly was not accepted as on 29 Oct. 1870 Yoder resumed writing in his letterpress book to his PFRA teachers. Yoder to Corson, 16 May 1870, Jacob Yoder Letter Book, 3 Mar. 1870–1 Dec. 1870, pp. 146–147, 156, Acc. 35108, LVA.

33. Corson to Yoder, 18, 24, and 27 May 1869, Private Collection. Yoder recorded one of his fund-raising letters in a letterpress book he kept in 1870, wherein he gave the statistics for the number of schools, teachers, and expenses thereof, underwritten by the PFRA. He also enumerated the race and education of the teachers, described the work they were doing, and stressed how important it was that concerned citizens render monetary assistance. "A nobler work than this of educating the late slaves was never undertaken by any people. . . . It is a success as far as it goes. But it is not yet complete." Yoder to Miss S. F. Corlies, Germantown, Pa., 5 Apr. 1870, Yoder Letter Book, 3 Mar. 1870–1 Dec. 1870, pp. 74–77, Acc. 35108, LVA. Financier and philanthropist George Peabody, of Baltimore, Md., made a succession of "munificent gifts" including $3.5 million for his Peabody Education Fund to promote education in the South. Between 1868 and 30 Sept. 1897, Virginia received $305,949.41. *DAB*, s.v. "George Peabody." Yoder notified three of the PFRA teachers that "the Society expects to keep up some schools or expects to help some schools next year. But they will not be able to help as many schools as they did this year." Yoder to Timothy Smith, 10 May 1870; Yoder to Miss Martha Brent, 10 May 1870; Yoder to Miss. F. A. Couch, 11 May 1870, Yoder Letter Book, 3 Mar. 1870–1 Dec. 1870, pp. 125, 128, 138, Acc. 35108, LVA.

34. Yoder first mentioned Mary in his 7 May 1866 diary entry, but never revealed her surname anywhere in the diary. In his 9 July 1866 diary entry, he indicated that Mary's home was at William Stauffer's, but Yoder was careful never to give any real indication about her identity.

35. American Baptist Home Mission Society, *Baptist Home Missions*, 69–72, 401–409, 411–422, 609–611; Robert Andrew Baker, "The American Baptist Home Mission Society and the South, 1832–1894" (Ph.D. diss., Yale University, 1947), 147–182; Whitaker family gravestone at the Ashford Cemetery in Connecticut. Anna Frances Whitaker was born in May 1844 and thus at age twenty-six was six years younger than Jacob Yoder. Virginia Census, 1900, Lynchburg, E.D. 85, sheet 5, line 88; Philip A. Bruce et al., *History of Virginia, Volume IV,*

Virginia Biography (Chicago and New York, 1924), 398; Reports of Freedmen's Schools for 7th District of Virginia, by Capt. R. S. Lacey, Superintendent, May 1866, Oct. 1868–June 1869, Monthly Statistical School Reports of District Superintendents, July 1865–Apr. 1869 and Jan. 1870, Roll 12; Subassistant Commissioner's Monthly Report, Jan.–Nov. 1868, Monthly School Reports of Assistant Subassistant Commissioners and Agents, Jan. 1868–Jan. 1869, Roll 13, Supt. of Ed., Va., BRFAL; Anna Whitaker to Jacob Yoder, 11 Aug. 1870, and Yoder to Anna Whitaker, 21 Aug. 1870, Private Collection.

36. "Jacob Yoder, Lest We Forget (By One Who Remembers)," ms., 3 pages, given to editor by Yoder's granddaughter Helen Yoder; Jacob Yoder to Anna Whitaker Yoder, 17, 19, and 23 July 1871, Private Collection; *Lynchburg News*, 1 Apr. 1871, p. 3, c. 1. For his work at Public School No. 7 (Polk Street between Ninth and Tenth) Yoder received a salary of $50 per month, while Botsford as principal was paid $75 per month and the second assistant, Miss Esther A. Stevens, $40. Their salaries compare favorably with those of principals and assistants in the white schools. As a male, Yoder, in fact, received $5 more per month than his female counterpart at the white girls' school. At the second black school (Franklin Hill) to open on 5 Apr., however, there were listed no principal or assistants, only Miss Fanny (Fannie) Harvey, who was paid $40 a month. African American children attended either the Polk Street or Franklin Hill school "until No. 9 can be located" (*Lynchburg News*, 4 Apr. 1871, p. 2, c. 3). In his history of the early years of Lynchburg's public schools, Edward C. Glass reported that the second, third, and fourth assistants at the Polk Street School all received $40 per month apiece. In Glass's report, Miss Stevens (Stephens) had dropped to fourth assistant. Miss Fanny Harvey, called *principal* by Glass, conducted the school in her home on Franklin Hill, and a third black school, with Sue M. Bolling as principal at the same $40 per month salary, was also located on Franklin Hill. E. C. Glass, "History of Lynchburg Public Schools," in *Virginia School Report, 1885. Fifteenth Annual Report of the Superintendent of Public Instruction for the Year Ending July 31, 1885* (Richmond, 1885), pt. 3, pp. 102–103; Virginia Bureau of Vital Statistics, Marriages, Lynchburg City, 1859–1901, Jacob E. Yoder to Anna F. Whittaker, 28 June 1871, p. 13, LVA.

37. Superintendent of Schools Abram Biggers engaged Anna Whitaker Yoder to teach in one of the white schools for the 1871–1872 school year. Biggers hired her for five months beginning after 1 Sept. 1871 at a salary of $40 per month. Anna Yoder ended her teaching career that year, however, as she gave birth to her first child, Eva, on 6 May 1872. A second daughter, Annie, was born 13 Oct. 1873, followed by five sons, Wayland Whitaker, 17 Aug. 1875; Adon Allen, 14 Aug. 1877; Edward Eschbach, 16 May 1879; Claude Colegrove, 3 May 1881; and Rozell Roland, 11 Oct. 1886. Jacob Yoder to "Dear Anna," 20 Apr. 1880; Annie to "Dear Papa," 16 July 1893; Adaline to "Dear Sister," 16 Aug. 1894, Private Collection; Miscellaneous Notes and Family Data in possession of Harry Kollatz, Jr., Richmond, Va.

38. First quote from diary entry, 29 Apr. 1866; second quote from diary entry, 2 July 1866; third quote from diary entry, 17 Mar. 1867; diary entry, 15 Nov. 1869.

39. [Mary Sue Davis], *Centennial Celebration, First Baptist Church, Lynchburg, Virginia, 1815–1915* ([Lynchburg, 1915]), 15–16; George Braxton Taylor, *Virginia Baptist Ministers, Fourth Series* (Lynchburg, Va., 1913), 335–337; Adon A. Yoder et al., *View Book, College Hill Baptist Sunday School, Lynchburg, Virginia: A Pictorial Journey Down the Years 1875 to 1915* ([Lynchburg, 1915]), [5, 7]. Bitting served as a trustee from the Second Ward on Lynchburg's first school board in 1871. Deyerle and Shaffer, *Legacy of Learning*, 157; College Hill Baptist Church Minutes, June 1881–2 Mar. 1885, in manuscript minutes, vol. 1, 1876–1887, Virginia Baptist Historical Society, University of Richmond, Richmond, Va.

40. Jordan, "Public Schools of Lynchburg—1871–1881," 5; *Lynchburg News*, 11 Oct. 1870, 12 Jan., 4 and 6 Apr. 1871; *Virginia School Report, 1871. First Annual Report of the Superintendent of Public Instruction for the Year Ending August 31, 1871* (Richmond, 1871), 115–117; Amos Botsford died 20 Jan. 1879 (*News*, 21 Jan. 1879, p. 3, c.1); in the *News* article (23 Jan. 1879, p. 3, c. 1) on Amos Botsford's funeral, the writer noted that the mourners at the First Presbyterian Church included both white and African American citizens. The minister, Dr. Hall, discussed Botsford's life as a ruling elder of the church, as a member of society, and in his family and concluded that "a good man had ceased to rule in the Church, to teach the youth of our schools, and to adorn the family circle." His wife, Juliet, who had been described in the 1850 and 1860 censuses as a schoolteacher as well, died two months later on 20 Mar. 1879. Virginia Bureau of Vital Statistics, Deaths, Lynchburg, 1879, for Amos (a native of Cooperstown, N.Y., and Juliet (a native of Princeton, N.J.) Botsford, LVA; Virginia Census Schedules, List of Inhabitants, Rockbridge County, 1840, and Campbell County, 1850–1870, for Amos Botsford; Rockbridge County Personal Property Taxes, 1839–1842, Samuel Walkup's district, and Lynchburg Personal Property Taxes, 1845–1846, LVA.

41. Salmon and Campbell, *Hornbook*, 56–57; Glass, "History of Lynchburg Public Schools," 106–107.

42. Glass, "History of Lynchburg Public Schools," 107.

43. Lynchburg School Board Minutes, 23 Jan., 10 July, 2 Aug. 1875, 20 Jan. 1876, 1:152–154, 202–203, 208, 244; 1 Apr. 1876, 1:253–254; 2 July 1877, 1:22; 1 Aug. 1877, 2:31; 12 Sept. 1877, 2:120; 25 Jan. 1878, 2:51, Lynchburg School Board, Lynchburg, Va.; *Virginia School Report. 1878. Eighth Annual Report of the Superintendent of Public Instruction* (Richmond, 1878), 91.

44. School Board Minutes, 4 and 6 May and 1 July 1878, 2:64–66, 69–70; 1 Oct. 1879, 2:124; *Virginia School Report. 1879. Ninth Annual Report of the Superintendent of Public Instruction* (Richmond, 1879), "Table No. 3, Graded Schools," XXIV.

45. Charles Euclid Pythagoras Minor, "Brief History of Negro Schools," in Jordan, "Public Schools of Lynchburg—1871–1881," 5–6; Deyerle, "Public Education and Public Schools of Lynchburg," 1:167–168. At its 1 Aug. 1881 meeting, the school board raised Yoder's salary to $85 per month. School Board Minutes, 1 Feb., 1 Mar., 1 July, and 1 Aug. 1881, 2:186, 191–192, 203, 205, 208–210; Glass, "History of Lynchburg Public Schools," 112. At the same time, in response to a desire expressed by the black community, the school board finally began to staff the black schools with qualified black teachers. By the 1884–1885 school year, School Superintendent Edward C. Glass could report that of nineteen teachers in those schools, fourteen were African American. Glass, 112.

46. School Board Minutes, 2 Mar., 1 Apr. 1885, 4:116, 119; 1 July, 1 Sept. 1895, 4:147–148; Lynchburg City Directories, 1887/88, 1891, 1894 (Yoder was listed in 1891 and 1894 as principal at the Payne School), and 1896–1905 (principal at the Jackson Street High School); Deyerle and Shaffer, *Legacy of Learning*, 236.

47. M. Lizzie Harvey, "Biographical Sketch," in Glass's Speller, . . . *A Review in Sixteen Episodes*, by the Teachers' Club ([Lynchburg, 1929]), 7; Deyerle and Shaffer, *A Legacy of Learning*, 17; *Biennial Report of the Superintendent (1896–1898)*, 29, 40, 145; *Biennial Report . . . 1898–1899*, xlix–l, 29–30, 148–150; Joseph W. Southall, superintendent of public instruction, to Jacob Yoder, principal, 6 Apr. 1900, Private Collection.

48. *Lynchburg News*, 16, 18, and 19 Apr. 1905.

49. Ibid., 18 Apr. 1905, p. 4; Jordan, "Public Schools of Lynchburg—1871–1881," 5; Lynchburg City Directory, 1912, p. 23; Deyerle and Shaffer, *Legacy of Learning,* 28; *Annual Report of the Superintendent of Public Instruction . . . School Year 1911–1912* (Richmond, 1914), 59. Of the four new school buildings completed that year, three were for white students, while the Yoder School was for African Americans. Situated on a one-fourth-acre lot, the black school cost $29,962.18 to build and consisted of eight rooms like two of the white schools. The second eight-room school (Miller Park) was also on a one-quarter-acre lot, but cost $36,370.56 to construct, while the third eight-room school (White Rock) cost $20,700 and occupied one and one-quarter acres. All four schools were financed by loans on bond issues.

50. *Lynchburg News,* 19 Apr. 1905, p. 4.

never saw laurel before. At the
foot of the hill we saw a Green
snake. It was about two feet and
a half, long and half an inch in diam
eter. After planning for some time
how we could manage to capture
him alive we agreed to entice
him into a glove. Tied the glove
fast to a cane. So I carried
the animal home.

Sam was at once dispatched
for alcohol. Till his return I
guarded the beast and Mr. Shoemaker waited on the miss Willets
company. Her father arrived in the
evening train

We had a great time to get
the fellow in the bottle of alcohol.
Did not succeed till we took
out the alcohol. Put the snake
in first. Enjoyed the company
of Mr. Willets very much.

He is a radical after the straitest sect. Retired 12 P.M.

Sun. May 13. 1866.
Rose 6½ which was too early it seems.

ACKNOWLEDGMENTS

It is my priviledge to acknowledge the help of numerous persons and organizations in the preparation of this publication. I am grateful to the National Endowment for the Humanities for the 1979 award of a Summer Fellowship at Indiana University in Bloomington where Walter Nugent, professor of history, led the Seminar in Social Change in the United States, 1865–1915. He encouraged and directed my first efforts in research and writing on Jacob Eschbach Yoder. In 1981 the Association for Documentary Editing awarded me a stipend to participate in the Institute for Documentary Editing at the University of Wisconsin at Madison where Raymond Smock provided editorial suggestions.

The Research Committee of Eastern Mennonite University awarded me two research grants to further this project. The Eastern Mennonite University Library aided me by facilitating important interlibrary loans of books, microfilm, and copies of indispensable materials in my research. The National Archives, the Library of Virginia, the Jones Memorial Library in Lynchburg, the Schwenkfelder Library at Pennsburg, Pennsylvania, and the Menno Simons Historical Library at Eastern Mennonite University all provided indispensable help.

Many individual persons deserve special mention. The late Florence Yoder acquainted me with the diary of her grandfather Jacob Yoder, and Yoder's grandson, Martin Luther Brown, went to considerable lengths to enable me to peruse the Jacob Yoder materials in his possession. Helen Yoder, a granddaughter, was helpful as were other members of the Yoder family. Holly Green, an avid historian of the Boyertown, Pennsylvania, community, was always generous with her local sources and perspectives. Caroline Detweiler, Eastern Mennonite University librarian, never hesitated to do all within her power to secure indispensable materials, and Audrey J. Shenk, another librarian, was a constant and patient computer consultant. It was Professor Joseph Mast who taught me to use the computer, in spite of my ingrained habits, and my computer-wise son Kenneth, who urged me to begin the process. My faithful wife Elizabeth (now deceased) was helpful and encouraging as always. I must also recognize the intense interest, encouragement, and help of local historian Wilmer Reinford, of Creamery, Pennsylvania, for his special interest in Jacob Yoder and his concern that I complete this project.

The suggestions of Assistant Professor Diana Enedy and Professor Hubert Pellman, of Eastern Mennonite University, were helpful with respect to the introduction and any imperfections that appear there are mine in spite of their efforts.

Many people at the Library of Virginia deserve credit for this volume. Jon Kukla, the former director of the Library of Virginia's Publications program, was the institutional godfather of this project. Sandra Gioia Treadway oversaw the early stages of revision and production of the diary. John T. Kneebone gave wonderful assistance to the in-house editor on numerous questions of interpretation. Lyndon H. Hart III, head of the Library of Virginia's Description Branch, helped us understand the Yoder manuscript collection that these pages are drawn from.

The creation of a documentary edition is especially demanding on editorial staff. The Library of Virginia's Emily Jones Salmon served as in-house editor, providing much-needed continuity and devotion to a long and laborious process. Brenda M. White and Patricia A. Kloke reliably entered diary transcription into the computer. Kelly Henderson-Hayes painstakingly checked the transcription against the original diary, and helped refine the footnotes, essential to a useful edition. Daphne Gentry, Donald W. Gunter, and Brent Tarter proofread the galley, and Gentry also assisted with fact-checking for the last year of the diary. With Brent Tarter's guidance, Daphne Gentry ably indexed the book. Gregg Kimball joined the Library in February 1996 and had the enviable task of tying up loose ends on a largely completed project, including writing a foreword.

The images in this volume help us imagine the world of Jacob Yoder and the Lynchburg community. Susan Bracey Sheppard and Stacy Gibbons Moore assembled the illustrations, and Harry Kollatz, Jr. led us to several key images, as well as providing information about the family and the children's names and birth dates. The harmonious integration of image and text happened through the good offices of Paris Ashton-Bressler of the Virginia Office of Graphics Communications. Her design and production know-how brought to fruition many years of dedicated labor.

EDITORIAL METHOD
Editorial Style

Jacob Yoder's diary has been transcribed insofar as possible as he originally wrote it—with his misspellings, inconsistent use of capitalization, inadvertent repetitions, and unintentional omissions of words when his thoughts outraced his pen. Many errors were probably introduced into Yoder's diary accidentally because he was writing in it late at night when he was tired. For the sake of consistency, the beginning letter of each sentence is capitalized whether or not Yoder originally used a capital letter. Yoder sometimes added a missed word with a caret; these words have been silently included in the text. Where Yoder omitted a letter in a word or put in an incorrect letter (**moderd**), the correct letter has generally been supplied in square brackets (**moder[n]**). Where he used letters of the alphabet as letters and not as shorthand for a full name omitted, those letters appear in italic type. When Yoder started a word and then marked through one or two letters and wrote another word, these occurrences have not been entered into the text or footnoted ("Jane ran ~~fr~~ to the store").

Where Yoder omitted a word or began it at the end of a line and forgot to finish it on the next, the word or its remainder has been added in square brackets. Instances in which Yoder's misspelling obscures his meaning or when he marked though words and rewrote them are mentioned in the footnotes. Where the connotation is evident despite the misspelling, Yoder's original words are left. In a few of these cases, however, a possible interpretation is given in square brackets (**cocca not [coconut]**). Where necessary for clarity, punctuation marks (most commonly commas and closing periods) have been added and spaces have been placed between some words where Yoder omitted them. Stray marks Yoder made with his pen have generally been eliminated.

The entry dates have been standardized. Notes follow each day's entry, identifying persons, places, and institutions mentioned, and providing other information as necessary. Subsequent references to previously footnoted subjects are not footnoted; the reader is directed to the first index entry for that person. When an identification could not be made through available sources, the reference was left unfootnoted.

Yoder Collection Description

The Library of Virginia received the Jacob E. Yoder diaries as a gift in 1971, and they are maintained as part of the personal papers portion of the Library's archival holdings. The collection consists of three volumes, covering the years 1861–1864, 1866–1867, and 1869–1870. The first volume, which is not part of the present work, contains journal entries from 25 January to 25 February 1864 and financial accounts from 1862 to 1864. During this period Yoder attended Millersville Normal School in Millersville, Pennsylvania, penning lecture notes in his journal. He then taught school in Boyertown, probably at Mount Pleasant Seminary, and recorded class lists and grades in the volume.

The remaining two volumes contain the diary entries transcribed in this documentary edition, chronicling life among the freedmen in Reconstruction Virginia, broken by an interlude when Yoder returned to the North. Yoder's writings from 28 April 1866 to 17 February 1867 constitute one volume, beginning in Lynchburg, Virginia, and ending with Yoder again in his home state of Pennsylvania. The second volume starts on 15 November 1869, after Yoder returned to Lynchburg, and concludes on 14 November 1870. Martin Luther Brown, the grandson of Jacob Yoder, kindly gave us permission to reproduce the diary entries from 20 February to 8 April 1867 in his possession. In addition, he recently gave the Library Jacob Yoder's letterpress book, 3 March 1870–1 December 1870, which contains copies of letters to his relatives, Freedmen's Bureau and Pennsylvania Freedmen's Relief Association officials and teachers, and others.

Programme of Exhibition

Exhibition
of the

Lynchburg Normal Class.
and

Camp Davis Colored School

Camp Davis Church

Wednesday   June 27th   8 1/2 O.c. P.M.
Doors Open at 7 1/2.

Admission   10 Cts

—

J. W. Shoemaker will read several
Choice Selections during the Evening
(This this the extent of first page)

Order of Exercises.

Music   Smith's band
            Prayer
Music Conducted by Miss Georgiana Willets
Opening Remarks   J. E. Yoder

Wednesday   July 4th 1866

A remarkable day in the history of this. This is
a day of rejoicing not only to the white people
of this vast country but also to the late slaves
of the Southern states. They seem to be generally inclined to select this day as an anniversary
day to celebrate their emancipation. If ever it
was appropriate for any people to rejoice in national changes, it is appropriate for this people
who were oppressed with by a yoke like that which
overwore, and who now are translated into the
regions of civil liberty, with a sure promise
that they shall have soon unlimited American
political liberty of the 19th century.

Now they have only to fulfill one condition in
this national contract, and this boon is theirs
not to be wrested from them by traitors or sympathizers with them. It is simply this; they must
govern themselves; for if they do not somebody else
will

I have, however, no doubt but they will do this.
Their past history in slavery is noble. Why should
they not do equally well in the enjoyment of
partial liberty. No class of people on the face
of the earth would have submitted to the
outrages they have endured. In their present
condition they need more education and independ-

The Fire of Liberty in Their Hearts

Jacob Yoder and an unidentified colleague stood behind their pupils in Lynchburg, sometime in the early 1870s. (Courtesy of the editor)

Saturday, 28 April 1866

Had company last night. Its attention and shopping consumed the day. Enjoyed the company well. Had some little occasion to gather facts touching the general sentiments of the people regarding the war. It is too plain that this people still love Slavery with some blind madness. They have only accepted the result of this war, because they must.

Many hate every measure that is intended to elevate them. Education is their only passport to distinction. Therefore the whites so bitterly oppose it.

A company came at eve to serenade the teachers. Kept a colored boy prisoner for truancy he played last week. Yesterday made two boys fight by urging [them] to do so. While I did not mean that they should fight they became so enraged that I had to separate them by physical force. Mr. Varner,[1] teacher at Liberty, has come this evening on a visit. His stay at Liberty has of late become unpleasant; for his life is sought after. These reconstructed rebels it seems are still thirsting for blood. If [the] President persists in his infamous [conduct] towards them our stay can not long be prolonged.[2] Had occasion to go down town after night. Since I am acquainted with the treacherousness of the people I don't like to go out at night.

This people as well as the President take every occasion to prove to the colored people that they and not the Northern Radicals are the true friends of the the Colored race. Two kinds of arguments come in to decide this question. Actions and words do not correspond. Their words even are often inconsistent. They frequent[ly] say to or of us "Nigger lovers" or "Nigger Friends."

Sin is still master over me.[3] I have revolted against the despot of Tobacco; another lust ruler must be dethroned. God help.

1. Alvin Varner, originally from Berwick, Pa., was a Pennsylvania Freedmen's Relief Association schoolteacher in Liberty, Bedford County, Va., now the city of Bedford. See Henry L. Swint, *The Northern Teacher in the South, 1862–1870* (Nashville, 1941), 198.

2. Andrew Johnson (1808–1875), who became the seventeenth president of the United States following the assassination of Abraham Lincoln on 14 April 1865, initiated a reconstruction plan in May in the hope of restoring the South to full partnership in the Union as

expeditiously as possible. His view that the newly won freedom of blacks did not require special federal protection was bitterly opposed by Radical Republican members of the U.S. Congress. In 1867, Congress abandoned Johnson's milder reconstruction policies in favor of a plan that maintained a military presence in the South until the civil rights of African Americans were protected by state and federal law.

3. JY referred to his tobacco-chewing habit.

Sunday, 29 April 1866

Arose at six. Soon after spent an hour in private meditation: then some time in light conversation. Listened to a sermon read of Beechers[1] on the subject "Whatsoever is honest &c." Weather is not so oppressive as yesterday.

The rebels are so anxious to have representation in Congress for this purpose especially—that all Military be removed and that they may rule their former slaves again with a rod of iron.

If they should [be] successful they [will] pass laws that the Negroes can not be taught. Such sentiments they set forth boastingly. Now if they deprive him of the privilege of educating himself he[2] is as poor as he used to be.

In the afternoon heard a sermon by parson Humphey. He can actually preach, though, as he said he had no instruction before Lee's surrender of any kind. He painted vividly the necessity of having religion.—Read some in Schoenberg Cotto Family.[3] At half past four started out to make a trip to the grove in search of flowers; returned at Seven, conscious of an adequate reward in honey succles, or Columbine, and Pansies. Heard at night a Methodist minister. The audience was large. When I beheld their worship many thoughts crowded themselves into my mind. Is this the methodist church founded by Wesley?[4] Is this the church which I have always loved above all other modern churches. It seems this is the most aristocratic church of this place.—Gen. Curtis[5] is in Lynchburg. Retired at 12 P.M.

1. Henry Ward Beecher (1813–1887) was an influential Congregationalist clergyman and prewar antislavery leader. His sister Harriet Beecher Stowe, also a passionate abolitionist, was the author of the novel *Uncle Tom's Cabin: or Life Among the Lowly* (Boston, 1852). See Clifford E. Clark, Jr., *Henry Ward Beecher: Spokesman for a Middle-Class America* (Urbana, Chicago, and London, 1978).

2. JY originally wrote "they" and then substituted "he."

3. JY was reading *The Chronicles of the Schoenberg-Cotta Family by Two of Themselves*, a novel about Martin Luther and his times by Elizabeth Rundle Charles (New York, 1864).

4. John Wesley (1703–1791), was a theologian, an evangelist, and the founder of Methodism.

5. Union Brig. Gen. Newton Martin Curtis (1835–1910), from New York, commanded the thirty-one-county District of Southwestern Virginia, with headquarters in Lynchburg. Mustered out of the army later in 1866, his future career included service as a congressman

from New York from 1891 to 1897. U.S. Army, Department of Virginia, *General Orders and Circulars, 22 January 1865–15 August 1866* ([Richmond, 1866]), General Orders No. 89; *The Union Army: A History of Military Affairs in the Loyal States 1861–1865: Records of the Regiments in the Union Army, Cyclopedia of Battles, Memoirs of Commanders and Soldiers, Biographical* (Madison, Wis., 1908), 8:67.

Monday, 30 April 1866

Rose at 7½. Fixed up School room before breakfast.[1] Called School in 9¼. Twenty new pupils. Sent home two as being minor.[2] Promoted quite a num[ber] of pupils to higher classes. In the morning one hundred and sixty-seven pupils were in attendanc; in the Afternoon Seventy four. Received a lot of Books from Phila. Association.[3] Made reports. Evening and night schools were small. Some pupils are preparing for the May Queen. The colored people take a delight in doing any[thing] that the white people had denied them in slavery times. Played "April Fool" on the blackboard, as this has been the last day of Apr. Retired 12¼ the Next Day.

1. JY taught at a freedmen's school located at Camp Davis, a former Confederate military camp in Lynchburg, situated in a wooded area on the southern outskirts of town near present-day Miller Park, bordered roughly by what are today Pierce, Kemper, Twelfth, and Sixteenth Streets. After the Civil War, the camp was appropriated by the U.S. government. Both soldiers and freedmen resided there in numerous single-story frame buildings situated in rows. One of these buildings housed JY's freedmen's school. Frances Adams Deyerle, "Public Education and Public Schools of Lynchburg, Virginia," manuscript draft of *A Legacy of Learning*, Vol. 1, 1720–1867, Chapter 1, "Notes from Lynchburg and Its People," 25, 12 vols., MS1096, Jones Memorial Library, Lynchburg; S. Allen Chambers, Jr., *Lynchburg: An Architectural History* (Charlottesville, 1981), 201, 406; W. Asbury Christian, *Lynchburg and Its People* (Lynchburg, 1900), 198–199; Bertha Adams Jordan, "Public Schools of Lynchburg—1871–1881," *Lynchburg Historical Society Historical Papers* 8, no. 1 (1971): 5.

2. JY originally wrote "premature" and then substituted "minor."

3. Pennsylvania Freedmen's Relief Association. JY and most of the freedmen's school personnel in the Lynchburg area were sponsored by this organization. Established in 1862 as the Port Royal Relief Committee of Philadelphia, it became the Pennsylvania Freedmen's Relief Association early in 1864 and by 1866 the Pennsylvania Branch of the American Freedmen's and Union Commission (hereafter cited as PFRA). See Willie Lee Rose, *Rehearsal for Reconstruction: The Port Royal Experiment* (New York, 1964), 42, 75–76, 417.

Tuesday, 1 May 1866

Rose at seven. A cloudy first of May. Very busy at teaching, making out monthly reports, making a monthly roll. Preparing for Queen of may makes the Normal Class very small again, for this day. Wrote a letter. Saw a gold Dollar passed as currency. This is some thing most rare. Had a fine night class of 24 pupils. Had an application to give private instruction. This I have been conscious of: a more firm and steady desire to please God in all my actions. Retired at twelve when in the next ward (used as a hospital) a voice was heard going up in the apparent agony of death, to god for pardon. It came from an old man. Oh! how I was impressed with the need of a blameless [life] always. How dangerous to put off religion to the close of life. That that despairing voice of last night still rings in my ears: "O, Jesus take my heart."

Wednesday, 2 May 1866

Rose at 7½. Still work at reports. Whipped four boys in school; one of them while school assembled. A great deal of quarreling is constantly going on among the children. The number is very great this day—two hundred and thirty five. If each one of them plays a little mischief it makes a great quantity when placed together. One boy came into my room to day. I thought he had come for books. When I finally inquired as to his mission, after hesitating a little he said, "Miss Georgiana[1] said I was a naughty boy." He spoke this with a very hones[t] look in his eye. Did I then punish him?

Called on Mrs. Ellis[2] who lately established a school was not in operation. Obtained all desirable information and saw a part of the performance of the "queen of May." Considering all things concerned the thing was grand. To describe it to any satisfaction would require more time and skill than[3] I now possess.

The performance has connected with it a great [number][4] of literary exercises. The most lasting truth I have learned there is this; What the colored people were prohibited from doing when they were in slavery they *will* do now. There are three coronations of queens in this town during the month.

Called on Mr. Edward Lynch.[5] He and his wife told me their experience in slavery and in getting freedom. The church has had a love feast this Eve. They were happy. Received a letter. Practised penmanship. The gentleman above referred to showed how the master opposed the slaves learning to read or write. He related an incident which took place bet[ween] him and his Master and runs: *Master.* Ned, will you tell me if you know that any of my boys *do write*? *Ned* "Charles, Jack, Thomas, and Richard, each of them spell right smart but if any of them write they do it out of my presence." Of course all did write and they did write in as well as out of his presence. He made the impression on the Master, however, that none of them did write. The master told ned when the Union Army came to L. that Ned should go and hide himself in the woods; but ned replied it would be more suitable for him (Master) to hide himself.

Ned's wife had thought of staying with her master after the Surrender. But when she had worked for him a few weeks she asked on what terms he would employ her, he said he would not have any of his slaves about him that considered themselves free.

1. Georgiana Willets, originally from Jersey City, N.J., was a PFRA teacher at Camp Davis in 1866. Two years earlier she had taught African American students at Camp Barker in Washington, D.C., and had nursed wounded soldiers on the Virginia battlefront. See Samuel L. Horst, *Education for Manhood: The Education of Blacks in Virginia During the Civil War* (Lanham, Md., 1987), 195, 199, 202.

2. Emeline F. Ellis and her husband, Carrington Ellis, ran a private freedmen's school on Thirteenth Street in Lynchburg. Carrington Ellis in Report of Freedmen's Schools for 7th District of Virginia, by Capt. R. S. Lacey, District Superintendent, Mar.–June 1866, Monthly Statistical School Reports of District Superintendents, July 1865–Apr. 1869 and Jan. 1870, Roll 11; Emeline Ellis in Subassistant Commissioner's Monthly Report, Feb. 1868, Monthly School Reports of Assistant Subassistant Commissioners and Agents, Jan. 1868–Jan. 1869, Roll 13; E. F. Ellis in Schedule of Schools under the Pennsylvania Freedmen's Relief Association in the State of Virginia, Together with Rental Account for the Quarter ending 31 Mar. 1870, Letters Received, 1 Jan.–24 Aug. 1870, Roll 5, Records of the Superintendent of Education for the State of Virginia, 1865–1870, Bureau of Refugees, Freedmen and Abandoned Lands, Record Group 105, National Archives and Records Administration, Washington, D.C. (Bureau of Refugees, Freedmen and Abandoned Lands, Record Group 105, National Archives and Records Administration, Washington, D.C., hereafter cited as BRFAL); *Lynchburg Virginian*, 10 Sept. 1868.

3. JY originally wrote "that" and then substituted "than."

4. JY originally wrote "the performance has with it connected with it a great of literary exercises." The first occurrence of "with it" has been deleted and "number" added after "great" to clarify JY's meaning.

5. Edward Lynch, called Ned, was identified by JY as a former slave. The 1870 Campbell County census, Western Division, p. 159, shows an Edward Lynch, age eighty-two, a retired farmhand, living in the household of Archibald Noel, a black farm worker. This is probably the Edward Lynch to whom JY referred, although neither this Edward Lynch nor the only other one in the Campbell County 1870 census (a twenty-five-year-old hack driver in Brookville township) was listed with a wife.

Thursday, 3 May 1866

There is in many respects after all a great difference between freedom and slavery. The slave could not go any where without a pass. Any one person must gradually become a free woman or a free man; yet It is not uncommon to find men and women that have quite exalted ideas of freedom. Their very looks show the fire of liberty in there hearts.

One thing the colored people are to[o] dull to see, that Andrew Johnson is their [enemy?].[1] It is a real pity that they can not see who their true friends are. Papers of L. pronounce Tom Elliott[2] the most respecteable and intelligent man among the colored people for chiming his tone of report to Gen. Steedman[3] to suit that of the white people.

A Letter to Rev. R. A. Vancourt[4]:

Dear Friend

This is not the first time my thoughts have been with you since my arrival. While my labors hardly allow me to correspond with friends their cheering words and sympathetic counsel are no less desirable. When I meditate on the magnitude and responsibility of my labors, this thought comes in my mind: "Who is sufficient for these things?" To effect the popular education of this people is[5] no less difficult than it is desirable. They are immensely poor; profoundly ignorant; remarkably vicious. All these qualities, as a mass, they possess beyond a natural degree; they inherited a large share of each of them from the peculiar institution.

It is not an unimportant reward for us to know that we are laboring in a cause for the accomplishment of which thousands of the North's noblest hearts are praying.

At no future period will education be so much needed as it is at present; nor will they at any other time lay hold of the pearl of great prize in the same good earnest they do now. Of course, the assistance if they are to have any must come from the North; and at this time persons coming from there and showing their friendly feelings for them command a powerful influence among them. Now their enthusiasm is aroused. Let it be suppressed without feeding it, and it will never be so active again. There is another incentive to them for learning that they will not have in the future, though it[6] must be confessed it is not a very laudable one in itself. They delight in doing any thing, that, in ante bellum days they were disallowed, and the white people allowed, to do. So some will *now* learn just for the sake of doing it.

In accordance with this principle they carry on some things to excess that are good in themselves. About one month ago when one morning I met a young man coming from the previous nights prayer meeting and asked him for what purpose they had thus imprudently prolonged their service: he replied, Before Gen Lee's surrender they were not allowed to hold meetings of this sort; so while they have an opertunity they will embrace it.

Our work is most encourageing at this time; but the rebels are bolder at this time in their opposition to the U.S. Government than they ever were. The cause can not be accounted for in any other way except we attribute it to President Johnson. He ought to know at this time that this down-trodden people has about suffered long enough. It is doubly his duty to give them impartial protection and impartial justice. First, because it is right to do so, and secondly, because the intelligent loyal Masses, whose servant he is, call for the administration of justice to all white or black. It is certainly the height of folly to depart from the path of virtue and uprightness when it has become fashionable to walk therein.

That the thickness of the skulls of this people is a hinderance in their acquiring knowledge can only be substantiated by admitting that this want of native capacity is balanced by a superior attention and application.

Business dull; money scarce; prices range with the temperature but [the] temperature is not as steady. Expecting to hear from you soon. I conclude

> Very Respectfully Yours
> J. E. Yoder
> Assist. Supt. F. S.[7]

Not half the evils were told to set forth the evils of slavery. Mr. S[8] had charge of Normal Class. Night had twenty eight in attendance, a pleasant time. This evening two weeks since I have declared war against tobacco. The contest is still successful.

1. Presumably JY meant the president was a foe of the freedmen because of his leniency toward white southerners who had supported the Confederacy.

2. Thomas Elliot was a conservative African American leader, who served as president of the Colored Conservative Club of Lynchburg in 1868. *Lynchburg News*, 12 Mar. 1869.

3. Union generals James B. Steedman and Joseph S. Fullerton, who were sympathetic to President Johnson's reconstruction objectives, were sent into the South by the president in Apr. 1866 to investigate the activities of the Freedmen's Bureau in hopes of preventing the passage of a new law to strengthen the powers of the Bureau. The effort failed. George R. Bentley, *A History of the Freedmen's Bureau* (New York, 1974), 125–133.

4. Robert A. Vancourt was the first American-born pastor of the Falkner Swamp Reformed Church, which JY attended in his Pennsylvania home community near Boyertown. Vancourt was elected as minister on 28 Dec. 1858 and preached his introductory sermon on 13 Feb. 1859. Gary C. Hauze, *Ist dieses nicht das gelobte Land?: A History of America's Oldest German Reformed Church* (Gilbertsville, Pa., 1975), 45–51 (hereafter cited as Hauze, *Falkner Church History*).

5. JY originally wrote "To effect the popular education of this people than it is desirable is no less difficult than it is desirable." He then deleted the first occurrence of "than it is desirable."

6. JY originally wrote "though is must be confessed it is not a very laudable one in itself." The first "is" has been changed to "it."

7. Assistant Superintendent of Freedmen's Schools.

8. Jacob W. Shoemaker, from Westmoreland County, Pa., was the PFRA superintendent of freedmen's schools in the Lynchburg region. James E. Rhoads to Razla M. Manly, 22 Sept. 1865; Rhoads to Manly, 27 Sept. 1865; J. W. Shoemaker to Manly, 6 Oct. 1865, Unregistered Letters Received, June 1865–Mar. 1867, Roll 6, Supt. of Ed., Va., BRFAL.

Friday, 4 May 1866

Work passed off smo[o]thly. After School on the way down town Mr. Shoemaker proposed to hire a carriage and [go] out riding. Paying Eight dollars we obtained a rigging till eleven o'clock. First went a few miles East of Camp; then three south of; saw Gen. Hunters[1] battle ground. Returning and taking supper the whole par[ty?] went to the meeting of the Howard Union where Mr. S. read a lecture on the subject of "Freedmen."

We had a gay time.

1. Union Maj. Gen. David Hunter attacked Confederate Lt. Gen. Jubal Early at Lynchburg on 18 June 1864. After some light fighting, Hunter withdrew from the area as Confederate reinforcements there had proved too strong to defeat. George S. Morris and Susan L. Foutz, *Lynchburg in the Civil War: The City—The People—The Battle*, 2d ed. (Lynchburg, 1984), 1–3, 38–49; E. B. Long, *The Civil War Day by Day: An Almanac, 1861–1865* (Garden City, N.Y., 1971), 511, 515, 519, 521, 523–525.

Saturday, 5 May 1866

Had a sound sleep on my ride last night. Read as has been usual of late a portion from the bible. Wrote a letter. Miss C. Read the American Freedman,[1] conversed on the subject of religion. Worked at the monthly consolidated.[2]

At 9½ o'clock P.M. a little Colored boy by the name of Robert Edgar was found under our stair case. Took him in and gave him lodging for the night. For an excuse for his being out late he says his mother Send him for chips[3] and not being able to find any, he was afraid to go home where punishment awaited him for his none performance.

Mr. McMahon the teacher at Appomattox[4] arrived this evening. His difficulties at home with the reconstructed rebels are removed for the present. Ate a philopena[5] with Miss Willets. Mr. Shoemaker took [ill] suddenly after supper. A soldier colored that came to this hospital a few days since died and was burried in the Morning. Another one was burried yesterday. He came here a day and a half previous and [was] well. Some believe that he was poisoned.

Corporal Homes[6] called to see us. He was black drunk. O what a pity that such a good young man should give himself up to Bacchanalian service. He is drunk all the time not minding his business any more.

Oh how many of the worlds best men give themselves [as] a living sacrifice upon the [altar] of Bacchus. God deliver me and all men from this dreadful curse. Felt a great hankering for tobacco. Tobacco and liquor are brother: acquaintance is apt to give you an introduction to the other. I despise the society of both. But for all this I know that I am in danger to be taken captive by tobacco when I get toothache.

1. The *American Freedman* was published by the American Freedmen's and Union Commission in New York from 1866 to 1869. The cover title on vol. 1, no. 1, reads: "The American freedman. A monthly journal devoted to the promotion of freedom, industry, education, and Christian morality in the South."

2. Monthly Consolidated School Report.

3. Probably wood chips used as kindling to make a fire.

4. Charles W. McMahon was a PFRA teacher from Plymouth, Mass., who taught in a freedmen's school at Appomattox, Va. Report of Freedmen's Schools for 7th District of Virginia, Jan.–June 1866, Roll 12, Supt. of Ed., Va., BRFAL.

5. A game played by two persons who try to draw each other into paying a forfeit, or the forfeit itself. Generally the players shared the twin kernels of a nut and paid the forfeit when some condition was met, such as being the first to say "yes" or "no" or the last to say "philopena."

6. JY misidentified "Corporal Homes" who was in fact Sgt. John W. Holmes, Co. A, 11th Regt. U.S. Army, assigned to duty in the 7th District in Lynchburg and in charge of the barracks. His name does not appear on the May 1866 roster. Roster of Officers and Men on Duty in Bureau of R.F.&A.L., 7th District of Va., Apr.–May 1866, Capt. R. S. Lacey, A.Q.M., Personnel Records, Unbound Returns, Rosters, and Reports of Changes of Officers, Enlisted Men, and Civilians, July 1865–Sept. 1866, Roll 63, Records of the Assistant Commissioner for the State of Virginia, 1865–1869, BRFAL.

Sunday, 6 May 1866

The boy got up before I did. Sam[1] says "Robert is the Freedmen's Bureau's[2] boy." I had a restless night. I offered my services to take Robert home to his mother. He, taking me through a large portion of the town, then said he did not know where his mother was living. Then I took him home designing that Sam should take him home but before Sam started with him, he skedaddled. Saergent Homes[3] is under arrest. After dinner with Mr. McMahon made a call at Miss Fannie Harvey['s].[4] There met Mr. Spooner one[5] of the printers of the daily Virginian.[6]

I suppose he heard a great many things that he did not like to hear. Mr. Mac and Miss Fannie were freely conversing on Politics and Rebels. On return took a little nap. The people in the church had a very lively time. Never saw the like in dancing. It was similar in the evening. Read Harpers Magazine.

Had company to Tea, Mr. Work.[7] After tea, Capt. Lacy.[8]

The day is gone. I am not pleased with the manner I have spent it; Not once attended preaching. I know I care little to hear the white people. But afterall do they not preach like the people of the North Generally?

A Freedman came to quarters at [the] Bureau: being sent to Lieutenant Wodell[9] for a recognition, said "Are you Luturner?" "I want something to eat."

Capt. Lacy says Jef. Davis[10] will be pardoned. I thirst not for blood, yet, if Davis is not to be executed no other murderer—wholesale or retail—should be executed. Sin of indifference.

1. This was probably Samuel F. Kelso (ca. 1825–1880), a self-supporting black teacher who was born in Virginia and taught at a private freedmen's school on Twelfth Street. Although his parents had been slaves, he had been able to acquire enough education to become one of Lynchburg's first African American educators after the war. Kelso (sometimes spelled Kelsoe), also served as a delegate to the Virginia Convention of 1867–1868 and took a leadership role in proposing a state-financed system of public schools for both black and white youth. In addition, he became a trustee of the Polk Street School erected in 1870. Thereafter, Kelso, who had been a free man before the war, ran a transfer agency for the U.S. post office. He also owned his home at Eighth and Taylor Streets. Report of Freedmen's Schools for 7th District of Virginia, Jan.–June 1866, Monthly Statistical School Reports of District Superintendents, July 1865–Apr. 1869 and Jan. 1870, Roll 12; S. F. Kelsoe to R. M. Manly, 30 Apr. 1870, Unregistered Letters Received, Dec. 1869–Aug. 1870, Roll 10, Supt. of Ed., Va., BRFAL; Betty Mansfield, "That Fateful Class: Black Teachers of Virginia's Freedmen, 1861–1882" (Ph.D. diss., Catholic University, 1980), 298; Virginia Census Schedules, List of Inhabitants, 1870, Campbell County, Lynchburg, Samuel F. Kelsoe, page 533A, line 35.

Kelso received a homestead exemption for a house at Eighth and Taylor Streets, 8 Oct. 1872. Lynchburg Deed Book AA, p. 96; Virginia Bureau of Vital Statistics, Deaths, Lynchburg, 1880 (Kelso died 4 Dec. 1880, age fifty-five), LVA; *Debates and Proceedings of the Constitutional Convention of the State of Virginia* (Richmond, 1867), 1:60; Jordan, "Public Schools of Lynchburg—1871–1881," 6.

2. Congress created the Bureau of Refugees, Freedmen and Abandoned Lands on 3 Mar. 1865 to provide relief for refugees of both races, enforce labor contracts between planters and freedmen, and cooperate with freedmen aid associations in the operation of freedmen's schools.

3. Holmes's place in the roster was taken by Sgt. William Andre, Co. A, 11th Regt., U.S. Army, who assumed charge of the barracks later in May. Roster of Officers and Enlisted Men on Duty, 7th District of Va., May–June 1866, Capt. R. S. Lacey, A.Q.M., Roll 63, Records of the Assistant Commissioner, Va., BRFAL.

4. E. Fannie Harvey was born in Lynchburg and raised in a slaveholding family. She was a freedmen's teacher in early 1868 at the African Methodist Church on Jackson Street and was partially supported by the PFRA. After public schools were established in Lynchburg, she became principal of Public School No. 8, located in her house on Franklin Hill, for young black men and women. Orra Langhorne, "Visit to Colored Schools," *Southern Workman* 9 (July 1880): 77–78; Jordan, "Public Schools of Lynchburg—1871–1881," 6.

5. JY originally wrote "it" and then substituted "one."

6. The *Lynchburg Daily Virginian* was edited and published from 1857 to 1885 by Charles W. Button, an ardent prewar Whig and pro-Unionist. After the war, he supported the Democratic Party.

7. The 1870 census for Lynchburg, Va., lists a J. B. Work, age twenty-six, a post office clerk who was born in Ohio. Virginia Census, 1870, Campbell County, Lynchburg, 71.

8. Captain Robert S. Lacey, assistant quartermaster, 7th Military District of Virginia. R. S. Lacey to R. M. Manly, 3 Nov. 1865, Unregistered Letters Received, June 1865–Mar. 1867, Roll 6, Supt. of Ed., Va., BRFAL.

9. Isaac P. Wodell, 1st lt., 12th Regt., Veteran's Reserve Corps, Company K, 94th New York Infantry, assistant superintendent, 7th District of Virginia, Dec. 1865–Jan. 1867. Roster of Officers and Enlisted Men on Duty, 7th District of Virginia, May–June 1866, Capt. R. S. Lacey, A.Q.M., Roll 63, Records of the Assistant Commissioner, Va., BRFAL.

10. In May 1865 Jefferson Davis (1808–1889), president of the Confederate States of America, had been arrested in Georgia, incarcerated at Fort Monroe, Va., and indicted for treason in a federal court in Virginia. The indictment was lost, however, and Davis was reindicted in May 1866 and thereafter awaited trial. After spending two years at Fort Monroe, he was released on bond in May 1867. Salmon P. Chase, chief justice of the Supreme Court, finally dismissed the case in Dec. 1868, ruling that the Fourteenth Amendment, which deprived Davis of his citizenship rights, had already punished him. William C. Davis, *Jefferson Davis: The Man and His Hour* (New York, 1991), 634–638, 642–644, 652–657, 663. Davis was never pardoned.

Monday, 7 May 1866

Rose at 6 with some sort of consciousness that I have not done my duty in full last week. The resolution in my mind come[s] forward and asserts I will try this week. With my laying aside the tobacco I must lay aside other sins. God free my soul of every stain of sin. Do it in thy own way. The birds have a concert. All around is beauty, in sound and sight, and sweet.

My desire is if God sees fit to prolong my life this week that at the end of it I may be able to say I have not committed any palpable sin. Every sin is wrong.

[Began] the day with unusual satisfaction. The day school at Camp has been very full. One boy comes five miles from the country. Copied one consiolidated report of schools, and prepared and assisted in another. My observations of to day lead me to conclude that there is a great want of ener[g]y among the people of color. They have not proved very reliable to day.

Received a long looked for letter from Mary.[1] Contents pleasing. Have come to the conclusion it would be better for my health to stop using coffee. The next thing of this sort tea goes overboard.

The rebels no doubt think the Negroes are becoming superior themsel[v]es if they do not burn their school houses and destroy their spelling books. They have commenced the first in memphis[2] on a large scale.

1. JY had developed a romantic relationship with the young woman named Mary, whose surname he does not reveal anywhere in his diary. In his 9 July 1866 diary entry JY indicated

that Mary's home was at William Stauffer's, but JY was careful never to give any real indication about her identity.

2. White mobs in Memphis, Tenn., killed at least forty-six blacks, raped five black women, and plundered or burned hundreds of African American homes, churches, and schools during a rampage that began on 1 May 1866 and lasted three days. Eric Foner, *Reconstruction: America's Unfinished Revolution, 1863–1877* (New York, 1988), 261–262.

Tuesday, 8 May 1866

Early up and doing. Have laid out a plan for to days work. Lucy contemplates to get married soon with Mr. David Murr. Read an account of the Memphis riot. It must have been terrible. From what I have read I am not able to decide who is the most responsible for this demonstration of hostile feelings. It would seem, though what I read was written by a white citizen, that the whites are more responsible than the blacks.

Did some sewing for Mr. S. Reporting. Making an other consolidated report. The criminal statistics of New York show that arrests of Irish people and negroes compare thus: While the population of both is nearly equal in a certain time the negroe arrests were between one and t[w]o thousand, those of the Irish in the same time over thirty two thousand. Mr. S. heard the Normal Class for me. Wrote two letters for the renewal of "S.S. Times" and "Morning Star."[1] Wrote another letter to I. S. Erb.[2]

Had an Oyster supper. Enjoyed it well. The Guests were the Freedmen's Bureau officers.

1. In 1859 the *Sunday School Times* succeeded the *Sunday School Journal*, founded by the American Sunday School Union in 1830 and published in Philadelphia. The *Times* was an evangelical weekly journal. The *Morning Star*, founded in 1826 in Limerick, Maine, and published in Dover, N.H., 1833–1874, was the leading periodical of the Freewill Baptists. *George P. Rowell and Company's American Newspaper Directory* (New York, 1869), 61, 98; *N. W. Ayer & Son's American Newspaper Annual* (Philadelphia, 1880), 79.

2. Isaac S. Erb was an acquaintance of JY who founded the Keystone Cigar Factory in Boyertown, Pa., in 1864. *Boyertown Battallya, Centennial '66* (Boyertown, Pa., 1966), n.p.

Wednesday, 9 May 1866

Wrote to Daniel H. Keck[1] and Geo. W. Sisson.[2] Read another article on the war of races. Made another report. Had a pleasant rain.

1. Daniel H. Keck was JY's brother-in-law. He had married JY's sister Eliza in 1856. Abraham James Fretz, *A Genealogical Record of the Descendants of Christian and Hans Meyer* (Harleysville, Pa., 1896), 525.

2. George W. Sisson, originally from Edinboro, Erie County, Pa., attended Millersville Normal School from 1864 to 1865 and 1865 to 1866. *Catalogue and Circular of the Pennsylvania State Normal School, of the Second District, Millersville, Lancaster County, Pa., for the Academical Year, 1864–65* (Lancaster, Pa., 1865), 14; *1865–6* (Lancaster, Pa., 1866), 18 (hereafter cited as *Catalogue*).

Thursday, 10 May 1866

All the schools small on account of the holiday. The people in Dixie celebrate this day in memory of the Death of Gen. Stonewall Jackson.[1] They honor this christian hero with many honors. Processions formed in the morning and went out [to] the burieal Places. There on the graves of friends and Confederate soldiers they placed their floral wreathes.

First in the morning they went to the cemetery where the soldiers are principally[2] buried. The first wreathes were placed on union grave[s] by mistake. As soon as they discovered the error if such it was, the[y] removed them. After school that part of the Freedmens living in Camp Davis went to see the Union Graves. These are bare. Does nobody honor these graves? Yes, they honor themselves nobody else needs to do it.

All this celebration amounts to is simply this: it shows the feelings towards the United states Government.

Read a N.Y. Baptist Paper. The Reading Matter is good.

Wrote a letter to Brother Nathaniel.[3] I practised penmanship. Discussed the subject of practical phrenology[4] and also womans Rank in society.

1. Confederate general Thomas Jonathan "Stonewall" Jackson (1824–1863), made famous by his brilliant Shenandoah Valley campaign of 1862 and considered to be "Lee's right arm," was fatally wounded by his own troops on 2 May 1863 at the Battle of Chancellorsville.

2. JY originally wrote "where the soldiers are principally are buried." The second "are" has been deleted.

3. Nathaniel E. Yoder was JY's younger brother, born 17 Dec. 1841. Fretz, *Genealogical Record of the Descendants of Christian and Hans Meyer*, 527.

4. The study of the conformation of the skull as indicative of mental faculties and traits of character.

Friday, 11 May 1866

Lived unusually temperate this day used no coffee, no tea, no candy, and no tobacco. Wrote a letter to Mr. W. Eisenberg.[1] Was to Express Office for a package of Goods for Mr. Shoemaker. Could not get it because my order[2] was not dated.

Did some sewing for Mr. Shoemaker. Retired at ten & a half by reason of headache.

1. William Y. Eisenberg, of Pottstown, Pa., attended Millersville Normal School in 1864–1865. *Catalogue*, 11.

2. JY originally wrote "note" and then substituted "order."

Saturday, 12 May 1866

Rose well at 6³/₄. Weather most delightful. Fixed a box [of] books for Lloyd[1] and a package for Varner. Then we took them down to depot. On the way coming home I was invited to Mr. Kelsoe's to give himself and assistant[2] instruction in grammar and arithmetic.

The instruction at all times seems to be appreciated and made use of. Mr. Perrit gave me a kind of an abridged history of his days in slavery.

His Master was very anxious that he should learn. He gave him opportunities to do so. The Master was killed at seven days fight.[3] Perrit speaks very highly of his Master.

After noon Attended to some some weekly business record. At 3 P.M. Mr. Shoemaker proposed to go out and cut some mischief. Then I proposed that the trip be towards the mountains. It met his approval. He got a horse. Off we started for the top of the Chandler mountains.[4] After many wild conjectures on both sides, and taking turn[s] about in riding; for we had only one horse, we reach[ed] the top. A wide and truly grand prospect opens from this point in every direction. Towards the North East and towards the West there extends one boundless plaine. Ranges of hills, sometimes growing into mountains, extend along the North East bounda[r]y towering in the distance above them all are the peaks of otter.[5] There is no end to the Mountains. One ledge rises after [another] out of the hazy sea.

We are perfectly delighted with the scenery. But the sun is fast approaching the horizon so we must bid farewell to this charming place. Gathering flowers we retraced our steps. Among the flowers gathered were laurels. Never saw laurel before. At the foot of the hill we saw a Green snake. It was about two feet and a half long, and half an inch in diameter. After planning for some time how we could manage to capture him alive we agreed to entice him into a glove. Tied the glove fast to a cane. So I carried the animal home.

Sam was at once dispatched for alcohol. Till his return I guarded the beast and Mr. Shoemaker waited on the miss Willets company. Her father[6] arrived in the evening train.

We had a great time to get the fellow in the bottle of Alcohol. Did not succeed till we took out the alcohol. Put the snake in first. Enjoyed the company of Mr. Willets very much.

He is a radical after the straitest sect. Retired 12 P.M.

1. Mark R. Lloyd, of Pottstown, Pa., was a PFRA teacher at Fincastle in Botetourt County, Va. Report of Freedmen's Schools for 7th District of Virginia, Mar.–June 1866, Roll 12, Supt. of Ed., Va., BRFAL. Lloyd continued to teach in Botetourt County through the 1868–1869 school year but not in 1869–1870.

2. George W. Perrit was a self-supporting black teacher who assisted Samuel Kelso at the Twelfth Street School. Ibid., May 1866.

3. The Seven Days' campaign (25 June–1 July 1862) was a series of battles fought near Richmond by the Army of Northern Virginia and the Army of the Potomac. The Confederate and Federal casualties for the week totaled more than 35,000.

4. Candler Mountain in Campbell County is named for Daniel Candler, a Quaker pioneer who in 1779 received a land grant of 370 acres encompassing the mountain.

5. The Peaks of Otter in Bedford County, approximately twenty-five miles west of Lynchburg, are two distinct peaks in the Blue Ridge Mountains rising to approximately 4,000 feet.

6. Mr. Willets, probably of New Jersey, is identified by JY as the father of Georgiana Willets and a former conductor of the Underground Railroad.

Sunday, 13 May 1866

Rose 6½ which was too early it seems. The day commenced very warm. Read Sunday School Times. Atended S.S. at Camp D. hearing a large class of female pupils. Before completing the lesson, however, at the request of Mr. S. I resigned my duty leaving it to a colored teacher to continue to work. The company was to proceed forthwith to Baptist C.S.S. The company consisted of Georgy Willets, her father, Shoemaker & I. Arrived there only a little before the close. The attendance very large. From this place passed the court House to see capt. Lacy. The interview was a pleasant one. The topic of conversation, of course, was the Freedmen and their relations to the White People.

Returned home to dinner. Read paper after dinner. We have no lack of papers: five weeklies, one daily, three or four monthly magazines besides occasional and Lynchburg papers. The political sentiments of Mr. Willets ar radical all through. He is not ashamed of it. He is one of the conductors of the ante bellum underground Rail Road.

Attended worship at colored Methodist church. the text was "All ye that labor and are heavy laden and I will give you rest." The sermon in itself nothing rare. About a dozen "mourners" came forward. This afternoon a gentleman from Boston called to see us. His name is Pierce.[1] He is connected with the Boston Freedmen Society.[2] The day ended not as it began—cold.—Read a Story in the Greensburg Pa Paper about how the kind lady teacher governed and [made][3] a man out of Tom.

    1. Edward L. Pierce was a Massachusetts abolitionist who began working with freedmen during the war, first at Fort Monroe in 1861 and later at Port Royal, S.C. See Horst, *Education for Manhood*, 6–8.

    2. New England Freedmen's Aid Society.

    3. JY originally wrote "and and a man out of Tom." The second "and" has been changed to "made."

Monday, 14 May 1866

Did not have sleep enough, felt it all day. The schools prospered as usual. Got a letter from brother Jonathan.[1]

    1. Jonathan E. Yoder, born 22 Oct. 1845, was one of JY's younger brothers. Fretz, *Genealogical Record of the Descendants of Christian and Hans Meyer*, 527.

Tuesday, 15 May 1866

Wrote Mary and J.L. Douglass.[1] The s[c]hools were well attended and worked satisfactory.

    1. J. L. Douglas, of Bald Eagle, York County, Pa., attended Millersville Normal School in 1864–1865. *Catalogue*, 11.

Wednesday, 16 May 1866

Wrote and read before breakfast. Now the people of the south begin to talk about educating the Negro. They say as "he is a freeman he *must* be educated." That is just right. "In slavery his ignorance was harmles and perhaps beneficial when he was under the control of superior intellect. *Now* education makes him a beter workman for us, and more useful to the state and his family. The necessity of his education can not be questions any more. The question now who shall do it? The Yankees necessarily mix with their instruction their foolish and pernicious ideas of equality. They also awaken an improper ambition[1] to ascend above his sphere and consequently be discontented. We know him better in all his peculiarities. It is our duty to educate him. We do not mean at this time to tax our impoverished people at least not to any great degree. He should pay for his own education *under our supervisory* control." This last clause shows that they are at [it] again.[2]

The Freedmens Bureau's boy has come to school again this after an absence of more than two weeks.

This place will not flourish before it shall have received large accessions of Yankees. Wrote a letter to Moses Stauffer[3] and one to Elder Coulter.[4]

Attended a May Party. this was indeed and grand display. Was highly pleased with the whole performance[5] except the extravagance did not meet my approval.

1. JY originally wrote "idea of" and then substituted "ambition."

2. JY is quoting loosely from an editorial that appeared in the *Lynchburg Virginian* on 18 May 1866, which quoted from an editorial in the *South Carolina Carolinian*.

3. Moses Stauffer was an acquaintance of JY from Douglass township, Pa. Richard E. Stauffer, *Stauffer-Stouffer-Stover and Related Families* (Old Zionsville, Pa., 1977), 135.

4. Elder or the Reverend James Coulter (Colder). JY mentioned writing to Elder Colder on 31 Jan. 1864 to express his views on and experience with theology. Jacob E. Yoder Diaries, 1861–1864, Acc. 27680, the Library of Virginia, Richmond (hereafter cited as LVA).

5. JY originally wrote "all" and then substituted "the whole performance."

Thursday, 17 May 1866

Attended three schools to day. Wrote a letter for Sarah English.[1] Attended to shopping. Read three papers. Received a letter from I. S. Erb. The Normal Class was very incouraging. Attendance above average and attention unusual. Papers are big for Jef Davis.

1. This may have been the Sarah English listed in the 1870 census for Lynchburg who was a twenty-one-year-old cook working in the household of Jacob Franklin, a retail grocer. Virginia Census, 1870, Campbell County, Lynchburg, 492.

Friday, 18 May 1866

Visited Mr. Kelsoe's school. Heard a number of his classes.

Had speeches for the first time in Camps Davis Union School. Some were real good.

The whole family visited at Uncle John Kinkle's.[1] Had the most stylish enter-tainment. There are two considerations which render the preperations extrava-gant among colored people when we[2] visit them.

Received a letter from Mary.

Night school larger than usually.

1. John H. Kinkle, age fifty-six, and his wife Rachel, age twenty-nine, were mulattoes who had been born slaves in Virginia. Sold by their original master to pay debts, they were purchased by an Episcopalian minister who married them and baptized their children. The minister freed the entire family and allowed Kinkle to repay him gradually. Kinkle worked as a baggageman and was well-respected in Lynchburg. In the 1870 census, Kinkle was listed as a wagon driver. Virginia Census, 1870, Campbell County, Lynchburg, 491; "A Wedding at the African Church," *Southern Workman* 11 (Sept. 1882): 90.

2. JY originally wrote "when they" and then substituted "when we."

Saturday, 19 May 1866

Heat unusual. Heard a private Recitation. Received a letter from Varner, on[e] from Henry Fegley,[1] one from Geo. W. Sisson, and one written by myself on 28 of March [to] John H. Martin,[2] Phila.

Wrote a letter to Mr. A. Stauffer,[3] one to brother Jonathan.

Besides talking nonesense, attended to various little chores. Copied a plan of Appomattox Court House Freedmen school. Visited Freedmen's Hospital. Gen. Ewel[4] was here at camp to inspect the freedmen department.

1. Henry S. Fegley, one of JY's acquaintances from Boyertown. He may have been the son of John and Maria Fegley, of Colebrookdale township, Berks County. In 1860 John Fegley was a forty-two-year-old shoemaker there, and his son Henry was sixteen years old. Pennsylvania Census Schedules, List of Inhabitants, 1860, Berks County, Colebrookdale Township, 169.

2. John H. Martin, of Mount Joy, Pa., attended Millersville Normal School from 1860 to 1862. *Catalogue, 1860–61*, 13; *1861–62*, 11.

3. Albert Stauffer, son of Moses Stauffer, was a close associate of JY. Stauffer, *Stauffer-Stouffer-Stover and Related Families*, 135.

4. This may have been former Confederate general Richard Stoddert Ewell (1817–1872), although it seems unlikely. Otherwise, Ewel cannot be identified from standard military regis-ters.

Sunday, 20 May 1866

Read the Sunday S.T. It contains a good selection of matter.

Attended S.S. a Short time. Heard a class. Before it was closed I left. Went with Ladies & Shoemaker to Dr. Mitchels Church.[1] He had an unusual[ly] large audience. But at that it was but small. He read a good discourse on the words of christ,—"Peter, lovest thou me." Was for the first time inspired with[2] a holy feeling,—in a confederate Church.

Heat is great. The Dr. prayed so long that I got tired standing till he got through. God[3] let this be a specially holy day. Always better, let be my motto.

To the refecting mind it must be evident that we live in a time of great past progress and full of [occasion][4] for future improvement. The civil rights bill speaks for itself. But the last step to glory has not yet been taken. This nation must give impartial liberty to *all* her citizens. Ere that is accomplished, Our system is imperfect. Its accomplishment is a very important step just at this time.

Instead of deploring the state of the colored people, give them just a chance to take care of himself and they will do it. If the christian Religion becomes so corrupt as to recognize American Chattel Slavery consistent with its precepts, that religion should at once assume another title; for Christ cannot own it.

The work of reconstruction & Reformation is gloriously progressing. Hope God will manage it wisely.

Read the Independent[5] that always noble sheet, but surpassingly so last week. Its dignified dress is in keeping with the noble sentiments it contains.

Must again revert to our civil strife. If Andrew Johnson was reconstructed, then the reconstruction of the states would go on uninterruptedly.

We have fought the Rebels in the field but now we have to fight them morally.

Attended colored Methodist meeting in the evening. Dozens of the women were shouting and dancing. I suppose they thought the meeting was a great success. I should think and do think so. A great many "mourners" were out to the anxious seat.[6] I do not enjoy the noise in the church.

Read with interest a large portion of the Schoenberg Cotta Family. Miss Willets is not sociable to day. Yesterday we "agreed to disagree." This has been a pleasant Whitsuntide.[7]

O what a different time we live in from that Dr. Luther lived in. No, I verily believe that this time is similar here in the South to Luther's times. This people hate us for the truth's sake. Lately in Mississippi [?][8] was publicly beaten for the simple reason that he taught the gospel to the colored people. God let a light shine from around this people that they may see with their eyes.

Lucy has a beau this eve.

1. There were two pastors named Mitchell in Lynchburg at this time: H. P. Mitchell of Centenary Methodist Church and Jacob D. Mitchell of Second Presbyterian Church. Christian, *Lynchburg and Its People*, 204.

2. JY originally wrote "to" and then substituted "with."

3. JY originally wrote "Good let this be a specially holy day," but clearly meant "God let this be a specially holy day."

4. JY originally wrote "accation." Within the context of the sentence, this seemed to be a phonetic spelling of occasion.

5. The *Independent* had been established in 1848 by a group of New York clergymen as a Congregationalist magazine. It also espoused various reforms including antislavery, woman suffrage, and theological liberty. The famous Congregationalist minister Henry Ward Beecher soon began writing a column for the *Independent* and in 1861 assumed the magazine's editorship (1861–1863). Thereafter, the *Independent* became a general progressive serial and ceased to be denominational. Ada Tyng Griswold, *Annotated Catalogue of Newspaper Files in the Library of The State Historical Society of Wisconsin*, 2d ed. (Madison, Wis., 1911), 179; Clark, *Henry Ward Beecher: Spokesman for a Middle-Class America*, 87.

6. The anxious seat, also known as the mourner's bench, is a seat near the front of the meeting reserved for mourners to confess their sins.

7. Whitsuntide is the week beginning with Whitsunday, the seventh Sunday and fiftieth day after Easter, celebrating Pentecost.

8. JY did not indicate who was beaten.

Monday, 21 May 1866

Rose at 5 o'clo[c]k to start for Liber[t]y at seven. The whole family joined in the journey. Arrived at L. in due time. As soon as Mr. Varner was found we took a survey of the lately built school house for freedmen Children. Thence proceeded to the Piedmont Institute.[1]

Here it was agreed to visit the Peaks of Otter before going. In a short time a conveyance, consisting of a farmer's wagon, two mules, one horse and a colored driver, was engaged to take us that afternoon to the place of destination and return next day [be]for[e] twelve.

At 2¾ P.M. set out [to] the mountains. To our great suprise there were no seat[s] on the wagon.

We hunted up some planks first for seats. Then also two colored folks were to go along with our special train.

We passed through a level country for about seven miles, the land being for the most part poor. Some spots indicate very great richness of soil. Passed one good wheat field and one of grass.

We surely had the jolliest time imaginable. We were near the mountains when at Liberty and apparently approach it very slowly.

Reached the Mountain House at sunset located half the distance to the top.

Apparently we were still at the foot of this cloud capped tower, but when looking down upon the exp[a]nse below one would almost come to the conclusion that [we] were already at the top. After all had taken their cup of coffee among such other indispensable ritual as they had (I had none for the reason that the establishment could not furnish more than five cups) we retired at 9 oclock to set out for the top at 3½ the Next Morning.

At Liberty our party attracted considerable attention. Every body must have a glance at the nigger teachers, for I suppose soon after our arrival the village was informed of it.

1. The Piedmont Institute was founded in Liberty in 1847 as a school for boys. During the Civil War, it was used as a Confederate hospital and afterward reopened as a boarding school for girls. The school lasted just a few years and was then converted into an apartment house. It next became a public school for black children in 1883. Lula Jeter Parker, *The History of Bedford County, Virginia: The Colorful 200-Year Record of One of Virginia's Oldest and Proudest Communities, Bicentennial Edition, 1754–1954* (Bedford, Va., 1954), 44, 78–79.

Tuesday, 22 May 1866

Rose at 3 to reach the summit till sunrise. Two of the party were not quite able to attain it till the time appointed. I, the first of the party, reached it at 20 minutes of five. Just as I arrived there a forrest songster raised his *sweetest* voice of praise. Oh! how appropriate! Who should not magnify the Lord for his wonderful works! Uncovered my head and bowed to God in adoration. How prominent the thought of God's infinity and man's insignificance! The feeling awakened was truly sublime.

The sight of the sun rising was truly aweful.

The haze prevented the eye in following the distant objects with accuracy. To give a picture of scenery I decline. Towards the North one range of mountains rises after another. Two valleys are distinctly visible and not less than four ledges of mountains. East and west nothing but mountain meet[s] the eye. Towards south, a Boundless plain is spread before you. One or two mountains are seen in Tennessee, at least a distance of 140 Miles. I think a hundred miles can be seen any direction. If this is correct nearly 40,000 square miles of land can be viewed. The peak we ascended is 5,150 feet high, the other a little distance to the Northeast is 150 miles [feet] higher. But the sides are not so distinct. It appears lower. It has trees on top which the other has not. The smaller one has a flat top of about one fifth of an acre. From this plain rises five granite pillars to heaven of unequal hights and irregular shapes.

These rocks can be asscended from only one place without.

Before the war there was a house within the pillars. It is now destroyed.

There is a good carriage [trail] to within about half a mile from the top. The vegetation consists of a great variety: the Principal heavy wood is Chestnut, shrubbery, laurel, honeysuckle, and wortleberry. At the Top, vegetation is at le[a]st three weeks later than it is at the foot.

Is considerable difference in temperature between foot & summit. After a stay of two and a quarter hours we began to retrace our step. Hands full of flowers we arrived at [the] hotel at nine. At ten departed for liberty with a little better accomodations than we had coming. The driver had only two ani[m]als and sat on the wagon instead [of] on the horse as the previous day. This road to Liberty is the road on which Sheridan[’s] Cavelry[1] traveled. Mr. Varner, one of the company, was with that raid and recognized many of the places. It was amusing to him to hear the Landlord tell how the Yankees had destroyed and plundered his property—, for he was one of them. Came to Liberty cafe at 1 o’clock. The expense for each to Mountains was $5.00. Took dinner. Arrived at Lynchburg 6 o’clock.

A letter apprising me of the death of Samuel Boyer[2] awaited me. The colored people were glad at our return: the white, or at least some of them, were displeased, as it appeared from the remarks of some as we came through town.

Had twenty pupils in night school. The whole trip to and fro is seventy miles.

1. From 27 Feb. to 24 Mar. 1865, Maj. Gen. Philip Henry Sheridan (1831–1888), and 10,000 cavalrymen destroyed Confederate railroads, canals, mills, barns, and supplies from Winchester to Petersburg.

2. The 1860 Pennsylvania census lists six Samuel Boyers living in Berks or Montgomery Counties.

Wednesday, 23 May 1866

Made trip to town. Visited Mr. Kelsoe’s School. Had a letter from my good old friend Robert Turner.[1] Gave private instruction to Mr. Perrit and Mr. Kelsoe. Used a little tobacco to cure toothacke. Saw nearly ripe cherries.

Retired very early.

1. Robert Turner, of Millersville, Pa., attended Millersville Normal School from 1860 to 1862. *Catalogue, 1860–61*, 13; *1861–62*, 13.

Thursday, 24 May 1866

Wrote a letter [to] John Stauffer[1]: Received one from Mary. Filled a requisition of Books for James Bradley (colored) to start a school in Appomattox

County. Used tobacco to cure toothache. Night school very well attended. Others only tolerably.

1. John Stauffer founded Mount Pleasant Seminary, a private school in Boyertown, Pa., in 1842. In 1849, he erected a new school building and the seminary reopened in 1850. It was enlarged again in 1855. "Boyertown Seminary," undated clipping in possession of Holly K. Green, Boyertown, Pa.; *Boyertown Battallya*, n.p.

Friday, 25 May 1866

Rose late. Started school with a large number. Attended market. Partook again of the "filthy weed." Visited First Court Street School[1]; addressed it on the subject of the thoroughness of studying. Found in it a prosperous condition.

Visited Robert Perkins School.[2] Came home in time to dismiss school.

Had a private interview with Robert Perkins, a most intelligent colored man, concerning the state of the country. He is a teacher, a white lady not long since told him if he would only teach white children, she would send her children to him. Gave some private instruction. Attended Night School which was attended as usual.

Wrote Mary.

1. In May 1866, Court Street School Number One had four teachers sponsored by the American Baptist Home Missionary Society of the Northern Baptist Church: Charles E. Brown, Clara Gowing, Anna Frances Whitaker, who would become Jacob Yoder's wife, and her sister Sarah Whitaker, who stayed only a short time. The Lynchburg Freedmen's Board of Education sponsored a fifth teacher there, Jesse Owings, an African American. Report of Freedmen's Schools for 7th District of Virginia, May 1866, Roll 12, Supt. of Ed., Va., BRFAL; Jordan, "Public Schools of Lynchburg—1871–1881," 5.

2. Robert A. Perkins was a self-supporting teacher at a freedmen's school on Federal Street. He would later become the first black teacher in the Lynchburg Public School system. Report of Freedmen's Schools for the 7th District of Virginia, May 1866, Roll 12, Supt. of Ed., Va., BRFAL; Jordan, "Public Schools of Lynchburg—1871–1881," 6.

Saturday, 26 May 1866

Had school to day to make up for the day lost last Tuesday. Some of the primary scholars said speeches. They showed the interest they take in declaiming by their actions.

Waged a successful war with appetite till three o'clock when tobacco once more ruled me.

Was out shopping for myself.

Fixed a coat, which would have cost me two dollars and a half at least. Read the News.[1]

Stopped at Shoemaker shop. While waiting for the yet unfinished boots, the conversation turned on the condition of the Freedmen. The Shoemaker is a freedmen. Upon my inquiry he gave me a brief history of his life. On one occasion he received thirty nine lashes on his naked back for having an incidental prayer meeting. In addition he was confined in jail for six more weeks. A newspaper which was found in his house sent him seven weeks to jail.

One of his Grand children in Richmond immediately after Lincoln's election was named Abraham Lincoln Jackson. They threatened to kill the child and punish his grand father. All his persecutors are brought to nought. None survive:— even the very prison is burned to the ground in which he was confined. I saw its ruins some time before.

He spoke highly of his master. He was in the habit of hiring himself and his two sons from his master. Last year he paid for his two sons $4500. He likes it better since Gen. Lee gave up the Ghost.

1. The *Lynchburg News* was established in Jan. 1866 by Edward D. Christian, a prominent local attorney, and edited by Colonel Robert E. Withers, afterward a U.S. senator. Lester J. Cappon, *Virginia Newspapers, 1821–1935: A Bibliography with Historical Introduction and Notes* (New York and London, 1936), 120.

Sunday, 27 May 1866

Read a speech by Beecher on Woman's rights. Attended colored Sunday school. Heard a class of six boys. Attended for the first time an Episcopal church. Was rather agreeably surprised by the performance. The services were more agreeably than I had anticipated with the exception of the ministers surplice.[1] His text was Judes Epistle 3 verse.

Afternoon[2] attended colored methodist. Peck[3] preached powerfully to a large audience from the words "Call the laborer to give them their hire"—Read a large portion of the Schoenberg Cotta family. Wrote a letter to James Dotterer.[4] Used Tobacco again. Gave a lesson to a boy in the hospital in Reading. There is a young man in hospital from Alabama whose language is different from the language spoken here. Has the appearance of a man that is of the original African.

Drunk tea and coffee.

1. A surplice is an outer vestment of white linen worn usually over the cassock.

2. JY originally wrote "affernoir."

3. Jesse Truesdall Peck (1811–1883) was a Methodist minister from New York who was active in the Freedman's Society of the Methodist Episcopal Church. James P. Brawley, *Two Centuries of Methodist Concern: Bondage, Freedom, and Education of Black People* (New York, 1974), 540–541.

4. James Dotterer was from Trappe, Pa., a small town adjoining Collegeville in Montgomery County about twenty-seven miles southeast of Boyertown.

Monday, 28 May 1866

Felt some what sick last night. Can a healthy person always prevent sickness? I know I am accountable for my indisposition. Gave a private lesson to a boy in the hospital. He does improve very well. Heard two classes in Mr. Kelsoe's school which I have visited.

The day school had 252 pupils to day—a larger number [than?] that was in before. The normal class had as large a number, if not larger, than ever before. There were thirty three. The night school was unusually large. The number was twenty five. Some of them rehearsed speeches for the first time.

Used Tobacco nearly all day. At three o'clock the news reached us that there had been a riot in Gordonsville[1] last night and to day. But this evenings train from that place knows nothing of[2] it.

Filled a requisition of books for Mr. Owings.

Mr. Shoemaker has returned from a one weeks trip into the country. We were of course all glad to see him. He saw the Natural Bridge.[3]

Made some selections for the exhibition at the close of the present school term.

1. Gordonsville, in Orange County, Va.

2. JY originally wrote "from" and then deleted "rom" and added an "o."

3. Natural Bridge is a rock formation located in Rockbridge County. The county was named for the rock formation.

Tuesday, 29 May 1866

Schools very full and interesting. One of the girls stole a book evidently but could not make her acknowledge it. Made selections for the Normal class. Mr. S. gave me lecture on the use of Tobacco. Not time to write.

Wednesday, 30 May 1866

The busiest day I have lived for a long time. Making reports and roll for all my classes, besides giving public and private instructions, engaged every moment to this time (Sundown). Gen. Scott[1] is no more. News received this eve. Mr. Jones, the colored teacher of Lexington, called to see us this evening. Went down town after ten o'clock. On the way home I [saw] a police man standing. The idea of having watch men to watch men called[2] forth a little reflection on the depravity of human nature. Going a little further on I met a crowd of drunken soldiers who gave a practical illustration.

1. Virginia-born Union general Winfield Scott (1786–1866) became chief of staff of the U.S. Army in 1841 and occupied that post until his resignation in Nov. 1861. He developed the war strategy, known as the Anaconda Plan, to split, blockade, and then strangle the Confederacy that ultimately led to Union victory. He died at West Point, N.Y., on 29 May 1866.

2. JY originally wrote "seemed" and then substituted "called forth."

Thursday, 31 May 1866[1]

Am astir at 5 this morning. Other people generally go to bed when they are sick. I do the opposite. I need not guess long for the cause of my indisposition. Yesterday my conduct was any thing but temperate.[2] My mental and bodily constitution requires that I should be eminently temperate. O God be gracious! heal my body and soul.

Tried repeatedly to be up and doing. Every attempt proved fruitless. Took nothing as food till noon when I tried it but soon after I had to part with more than I took to myself. At two took purgative medicine. At four drank Lemonade.

All disorder seems to be in the stomach. The use of tobacco if not the direct cause of this indisposition is at least the occasion for it.

No desire for the weed which I had yesterday.

If I fail in this attempt to quit the use of tobacco my character is gone. The free use of tobacco for which I am responsible is a great stimulant. By unduly exciting my passions an occasion is given for innumerable sins. At tea began to recover. Mr. Varner arrived from Liberty this eve. He and Miss Willets assisted me in my night school which has been larger by seven than at any previous time.

This has been Friday and not Thursday as the heading indicates.

1. JY indicated at the end of this diary entry that the date was actually Friday, 1 June 1866, rather than Thursday, 31 May 1866.

2. JY originally wrote "intemperate" and then deleted the "in."

Saturday, 2 June 1866

Rested well last night. Heavy rain. Mr. Frank Forrest[1] called. Heard the Normal scholars perform some of their dialogues for the exhibition. Wrote Mary and also Jerrie Swinehart.[2] Fetched tobacco. Used a little. What does it mean? Mr. Shoemaker read the Maniac and Pernassus the Painter.[3] Exceeding[ly] heavy rains. Passed the evening in social enjoyment.

1. Frank R. Forrest, of Brandywine Manor, Chester County, Pa., was a PFRA teacher at New London, Campbell County, Va. He attended Millersville Normal School in 1864–1865 and 1865–1866. *Catalogue, 1864–65,* 11; *1865–66,* 13.

2. Jeremiah Swinehart appears in the 1850 Berks County census, in Colebrookdale township, as a twenty-five-year-old wheelwright (p. 320A). In the 1860 census, his last name was spelled Schweinhart (the German spelling) and he was now a thirty-seven-year-old wheelwright master (Berks County, Colebrookdale Township, 168).

3. Shoemaker could have read at least two poems titled "The Maniac,"one by Thomas Russell (1762–1788), and the other by Matthew Gregory Lewis (1775–1818). *The Oxford Book of Eighteenth Century Verse* (London, 1926), 610–612; William Cullen Bryant, *Library of Poetry and Song,* vol. 1, rev. and enl. (Garden City, N.Y., 1935). Pernassus the Painter has not been identified. Perhaps the work could have been either *Parnassus Biceps: Or, Several Choice Pieces of Poetry* (1656; London, 1927) by Abraham Wright (1611–1690); or a play titled *The Retvrne from Pernassvs: Or The Scourge of Simony* (London, 1606).

Sunday, 3 June 1866

Rose late. Weather cloudy and hot. Attended Sabbath school. Took charge of an infant class. Hope time was passed pleasantly. Asked the class to promise to pray [to] God daily for a new heart. They comeplied with the request. After School the pastor insisted on the children to stay and hear his sermon which usually closes at some tome past one. Sunday school commences at nine. This is evidently to[o] long for children. One cannot fail being impressed with the necessity of a knowledge of human nature if he wishes to have the care of children, and so much more if he wishes to supply them with either mental or spiritual food. Who is sufficient for the training [of] the young and tender mind for celestial society. After dinner Mr. Shoemaker read a christmas Sermon by Beecher also Tilton's editorial,[1]—a splendid article on the current events at Washington especially on Seward[2] and Staunton.[3] Then in company of Miss Willets and Mr. Varner, visited Miss Fannie Harvey. Enjoyed the society as usual when there. Weather sultry. Returned at four.

Engaged in a great variety of conversation. Read a capital article in the New York Baptist[4] on the now-in-Progress Temperance Reformation.[5]

1. Theodore Tilton (1835–1907), a New York journalist and an advocate of social reform, was editor in chief of JY's favorite newspaper, the *Independent*.

2. William Henry Seward (1801–1872), was secretary of state under Presidents Abraham Lincoln and Andrew Johnson. After the war, he supported President Johnson and urged conciliation toward the South. He retired in 1869. See Glyndon G. Van Deusen, "Seward and Johnson," chap. 30 in *William Henry Seward* (New York, 1967).

3. Edwin McMasters Stanton (1814–1869) was appointed secretary of war by President Lincoln in 1862 and retained by President Johnson. He was an ardent radical reconstructionist and resigned his cabinet post in 1868 after a struggle between the president and Congress over his tenure forced him out of office.

4. The *New York Baptist Register* was founded in 1823 in Utica, N.Y., as the publication of the New-York Baptist State Convention. The *New York Recorder* began publication in 1845 and joined with the *Register* for the first six months of 1855 as the *Recorder and Register*. The Reverend Edward Bright bought the paper later that year and renamed it the *Examiner*. Griswold, *Annotated Catalogue of Newspaper Files in the Library of The State Historical Society of Wisconsin*, 173, 209; *Dictionary of American Biography*, s.v. "Edward Bright" (hereafter cited as *DAB*).

5. Although temperance had been a subject of interest since the early days of English settlement in the New World, the temperance movement did not begin on a national scale until 1826 with the establishment of the American Temperance Society. By 1832 Temperance Reformation had become an accepted description for the movement. See Joseph Mosby, *An Address on the Temperance Reformation* (Richmond, 1833); Lebbeus Armstrong, *The Temperance Reformation: Its History, From the Organization of the First Temperance Society to the Adoption of the Liquor Law of Maine, 1851* (New York and Boston, 1853). For a discussion of the temperance movement, see Ian R. Tyrrell, *Sobering Up: From Temperance to Prohibition in Antebellum America, 1800–1860* (Westport, Conn., 1979).

Monday, 4 June 1866

Rose at six: brakfasted [at] seven. Opened school, attended to the monthly promotions, changes, and admissions.

Used and abused tobacco again not however [with][1] a peaceful conscience. Resolved repeatedly not to yield to the sensual appetite. Thought considerable of the subject. Surely I must confess, on this point appetite is stronger than Reason.

Entered a Tobacco Factory where I saw the process of making tobacco.[2] Heard a grammar class for Mr. Kelsoe. After my arrival home heard some of the morning scholars. Wrote a letter to Mr. W. C. Barr for Mr. Shoemaker.

Received a letter of James Dotterer at Trappe.

Looked for pieces for children to deliver at the exhibition.

Worked all evening for the getting up of bannars for tomorrow. The principal one our party made has Lincoln's picture in the center; above the picture, "With malice to none;" and below "Wish[3] charity to all." Two small union flags are perched on top of it.

It looks quite imposing.

In times past the flag was a protector. Now, at least in these parts, it needs itself to be protected. We sent it down town covered over.

1. JY wrote "not however is a peaceful conscience." The "is" has been changed to "with."

2. Processing tobacco was Lynchburg's chief industry. In 1859, there were forty-seven tobacco factories in Campbell County, most of them in Lynchburg. J. Alexander Patten, who visited Lynchburg in 1859, noted that "you could hardly turn into a street without seeing tobacco factories, . . . often old tottering buildings, but sometimes substantial structures of brick." "Scenes in the Old Dominion, Number Two—A Tobacco Market," *New York Mercury*, 21 Nov. 1859, p. 8, in Eugene L. Schwaab, ed., *Travels in the Old South* (Lexington, Ky., 1973), 2:535–543. The best overview of the antebellum tobacco industry is still Joseph C. Robert, *The Tobacco Kingdom: Plantation, Market, and Factory in Virginia and North Carolina, 1800–1860* (Durham, N.C., 1938).

3. JY wrote "Wish charity to all," but he most likely meant "with charity to all," quoting from Abraham Lincoln's Second Inaugural Address, 4 Mar. 1865: "With malice toward none; with charity for all."

Tuesday, 5 June 1866

Cloudy morning. Its a question whether we can have our anniversary. Against all odds the celebration must go on.[1] When we came down town to Mr. Brown,[2] we learned that he has issued an order that the meeting must be postponed to the first fair day. But the sun is now coming out and the children are gathering from all parts of the town. Mr. Brown at once revoked[3] his order. When we came to church, church yard and street were full of children. Efforts we made for there leaving. An hour afterwards they were ready to leave. Marching forward and backward through town the procession made for Camp Davis, where they arrived at half past eleven. After they had all settled down, addresses were delivered by Rev. White[4] (colored), Mr. J. W. Shoemaker, Mr. Warwick,[5] (colored). There followed refreshments which were of the most dainty character, which, however, were not sufficient to satisfy the hunger of the great multitude. Then the appearance of a shower made the party disperse at 3½.

Nearby all the whites that participated in the exercises except soldiers, repair to our residence for a social chat, among whom was Mr. Lidig,[6] a union man through the war, and Miss Sarah Harvey,[7] a union woman during the same time.

Captain Williams, reporter for the Republican,[8] gave us a call, to get all information concerning the demonstration he could. It seems he was well pleased with the exercises. So was an editor of one of the other papers, who expressed that it was the grandest procession that ever was witnessed in Lynchburg.

Mr. Williams was not very well pleased with the motto, We are Free, on a banner. The thing was simply a grand success. The weather was the most pleasant on the whole that we could have had.

The interference by the rowdies was feared by some of the people; but to their most pleasant disappointment good feeling was manifested with some slight exceptions for which the mass is not responsible. At the request of Captain Lacy, the police force was out to guard all places in town where the procession marched. One colored man told me that on their return at many houses in town the ladies waved their handkerchiefs to manifest their feelings of approbation.

They were well pleased with the banners of which there were about ten. One contained Lincoln's Photograph mounted on it two small union flags, with the quotation, "With malice toward none and Charity to all." Others had "Faith Hope Charity"; "Do Right," "Love the Truth"; "Do not despise these little ones"; "Jesus loves little children"; "In God is our trust:" "Lynchburg Sabbath Schools founded June 5th 1865"; & c.

A whole society whose name is the Dawning Star of Liberty was out en masse with an appropriate banner. These were all in the same dress. This was the first exhibition it ever had. The society called the "Sons of ham" were afraid to come out.[9]

The whole procession counted almost fifteen hundred hundred. In all there were about twenty four hundred persons out.

They had fixed up a table expressly for the white teachers. It was rather extravagant. The people is remarkable for their love of fine dress and good appearance in general. They were nearly all tasefully attired, few of the girls not having on white dresses. The expense of such a[10] getting up is not small. It is to be hoped that they will however find ample reward in giving and additional impetus to make them ambitious. They are not to be found behind time when they have money: and they manage to have some always too.

The object of the demonstration was of course in honor of the establishment of their first Sunday Schools a year ago. Some of course thought it was political, for they never had any thing of this kind before. They rejoiced, the old and the young that they are permitted to do as they have done. One old man told me: "This looks like the better day coming of which I had heard when I was a boy but were not permitted to see till now." They gave hurrahs for various purposes, but not for Andrew Johnson.

I can not at all express my feelings at the sight of the procession. Never saw any thing prettier in my life. The order was excellent. So short time ago a people pressed down by a proud aristocracy now rejoices in their freedom for which, as an old man tremblingly said today "I have prayed sixty years." They naturally love freedom. Many of them have a more proper appreciation of the boon of liberety than tens of thousands of Pennsylvanians have.

Suffrage is due to many of them for their own sakes and for the government's sake.

Vocal music formed a part of the o[r]dder of the day.

Have seen decidedly the most magnificent sunset ever seen before. The yellow c[l]ouds on which played the last lingering rays of sun were spread out far around resting upon the heavy one pressed down so that the peaks of otter[11] pierced through them their towering heads.

Attended to night school which numbered forty. Good success to it.

1. This anniversary celebrated the establishment of the Lynchburg Sabbath Schools, the first black Sunday schools in the city, on 5 June 1865.

2. Charles E. Brown was a teacher at the Court Street freedmen's school, which was sponsored by the Baptist Home Mission Society. Report of Freedmen's Schools for 7th District of Virginia, May 1866, Roll 12, Supt. of Ed., Va., BRFAL.

3. JY originally wrote "ordered his" and then substituted "revoked his."

4. Sampson White was the sixty-five-year-old black pastor of the Court Street African Baptist Church. He died on 20 Nov. 1870. Virginia Census, 1870, Campbell County, Lynchburg, 75; *Lynchburg News*, 22 Nov. 1870.

5. William Warwick's name was included on the *Lynchburg Virginian* editor's Role of Honor of blacks who had voted for the Conservative Party in the 6 July 1869 election. He was a fifty-six-year-old carpenter who resided on Fifth Street near Taylor. *Lynchburg Virginian,* 19 July 1869; Virginia Census, 1870, Campbell County, Lynchburg, 42; Benjamin R. Sheriff, comp., *Sheriffs Lynchburg City Directory, Containing a General Directory of the Citizens; Together with a Complete Business Directory of the Cities of Lynchburg and Danville; Also a List of Post-Offices in Virginia, West Virginia, and North Carolina* (Lynchburg, 1876–1877), 106.

6. William H. Lydick was a local, politically active Radical Republican. *Lynchburg News,* 9, 19 May 1871. He also served as a delegate to the Virginia Convention of 1867–1868 (the Underwood Convention), representing Campbell and Pittsylvania Counties. Cynthia Miller Leonard, *The General Assembly of Virginia, July 30, 1619–January 11, 1978: A Bicentennial Register of Members* (Richmond, 1978), 504.

7. Sarah Harvey and her sister Fannie (see diary entry for 6 May 1866) resided on Gum Street near Union. Ross A. Smith, comp., *Lynchburg City Directory, 1881–82* (Lynchburg, 1881), 87.

8. The *Lynchburg Daily Republican* was founded in 1840 by Robert Cawthon and Bennett DeWitt to counteract the influence of the *Lynchburg Virginian* whose parent newspaper, the first *Lynchburg Press*, had been established in 1809. The *Republican* merged with the *Virginian* in 1875. In 1893, the *Virginian* itself merged with the *News*, which had been founded in 1866 by Edward D. Christian and A. Waddill and taken over by Carter Glass in 1886. John V. Horner and P. B. Winfree Jr., eds., *The Saga of a City, Lynchburg, Virginia* (Lynchburg, 1936), 95, 98; Cappon, *Virginia Newspapers, 1821–1935,* 121–124.

9. In the antebellum period, free blacks and slaves formed illegal, and therefore, secret societies to further their interests. In the postwar period, those societies and many newly

formed ones became public including the Dawning Star of Liberty and the Sons of Ham in Lynchburg. See John Thomas O'Brien, Jr., *From Bondage to Citizenship: The Richmond Black Community, 1865–1867*, Studies in Nineteenth-Century American Political and Social History (New York and London, 1990), 328–334, 493.

10. JY originally wrote "an" and then substituted "a."

11. JY originally wrote "pointy" and then substituted "peaks."

Wednesday, 6 June 1866

Was caught in a shower before breakfast when marketing. Fixed up the school room which was disarranged yesterday by the picknick. Started school. Visited Mr. Kelsoe's school to give instruction in Grammar. Engaged a carpenter to repair yesterday's broken tables. Read Morning Star. In the afternoon finished reports and ruled paper for consolidated reports. To my inexpressible joy as well as surprise my chum and very dear friend Mr. Sisson called to see us this evening. What a pleasant chat we had: He is employed by the association[1] to teach the Freedmen. Mr. S. does not yet know where to send him. Used again tobacco. Last night I had most solemnly reresolved to abstain from its use. But I dont give up the ship yet. Have had to do double work to day, as our colored servant is sick. Have not heard from him today. Made a call at Mr. John Kinkle's. Had a pleasant social chat.

Read with much pleasure the accounts in the city papers of yesterday's proceeding regarding the picnic. They all speak very favorable of it.[2] Wrote a note to Mr. McMahon from Mr. Shoemaker.

Mr. Sisson brought with him the good wishes for Mr. Shoemaker and me from old Normal[3] Friends. They are kindly received.

One thing seems not to suit Mr. Sisson; he thought he was to labor in Lynchburg, instead of going into the country as he has to.

Received a welcome letter from brother William[4] and wife.

1. Pennsylvania Freedman's Relief Association.

2. The *Lynchburg News* of 6 June 1866 (p. 3) described the celebration as a "creditable affair" that was conducted with "propriety and decorum" and commended the remarks of speaker J. W. Shoemaker, the PFRA school superintendent.

3. JY enrolled at Millersville Normal School on 1 Apr. 1860 to pursue a teaching degree. The principal, James Pyle Wickersham, had started the school as a teachers' institute in 1855. Following passage of the Normal School Act of 1857, it became the first state normal school in Pennsylvania. It is located in Millersville, Lancaster County, about forty-five miles southwest of Boyertown. Lee Graver, *A History of the First Pennsylvania State Normal School, Now the State Teachers' College at Millersville* (Millersville, Pa., 1955), 16–23, 29–35; *DAB*, s.v. "James Pyle Wickersham."

4. William Yoder, born 19 Jan. 1837, was a year older than JY. Fretz, *Genealogical Record of the Descendants of Christian and Hans Meyer*, 526.

Thursday, 7 June 1866

This day has been one of the most crowded in all my life. Whipped two boys before commencing school. The schools were very full. Taking the three s[c]hools together—the num[ber] has bee[n] three hundred.

Saw the first ground hog I have seen. It was much prettier than I thought it would be.

One of my night scholar[s] brought me some new apples.

Received a letter of Mr. Cook. Made a proof sheet report. Used tobacco. Saw the new apples of this season. Could not attend to our visitor.

Friday, 8 June 1866

Wether very hot. Instruction to Kelsoe's school in Grammar. Was most unpleasantly perplexed with the footing [?] up of the numbers of the consolidated reports for May. Calling roll of morning school is almost impossible to be done without getting angry.

Wrote a long letter to brother William.

Practised for the exhibition. Sisson and I attended to nightschool which was made interesting by the speeches the scholars had. Did some sewing for Mr. Sisson afterwards. Then practised penmanship until 1½ hours after midnight. Weather hot.

Saturday, 9 June 1866

Breedlove[1] the post master has died this morning at four o'clock.

Robert Edgar has his lodging place last night in the little ho[u]se in the grove. Sisson left for Lovingston this morning. Weather is most delightful in the early part of the day.

The near mountains are of inestimable value for the cool vigorous breezes they afford to the dwellers of the valley.

Heard the rehearsing of a dialogue for coming exhibition.

Gave private instruction to Mr. Kelsoe.

Then had a long conversation with him on the topics of politics and religion. It was of the most interesting character. I do love to hear some of these colored people talk.

Mr. Kelsoe proposes to raise an additional salary for me if I should return next session. Of course they can not induce me a motive of that kind. Still I can not yet decide not to return.

Made some efforts to collect money for books sold. Only partially succeeded. If I die a bad man, it is not because I never made an effort to d[o] right. At this time three o'clock, I solemnly resolve to abstain from the use Tobacco which has for so many years been the efficient means of destroying my happiness and preventing my usefulness and the sure and fruitful source of a thousand evils.

God, I feel more than possitive that the further indulgenc in fostering an appetite that has so few and insignificant redeeming qualities, is highly sinful, I call upon thee to help me to conquer this habit. I can not do it unless thou help. I have failed so often, times without number. Help me to pray without ceasing that I may not fall into temptation. O make it at all times as odious to me as it now is.

The children are gathering now to devour lemonade and cakes which was left over at the picnic.

Oh, how much grace it takes to abstain!

1. Breedlove's name is not found in Record of Appointment of Postmasters, 1832–September 30, 1971, Virginia, Cabell–Floyd Counties, Roll 131, National Archives and Records Administration, Washington, D.C. (hereafter cited as NARA), and the 1860 Virginia census index, nor is there an obituary for a Breedlove in the *Lynchburg Virginian*, 9–13 June 1866. Lynchburg's postmaster in 1866 was John B. Walthall. A check of the 1865–1866 Lynchburg personal property taxes showed a J.W. Breedlove listed in 1865 but not in Nov. 1866 when that year's tax list was compiled. He may thus have been the post office employee of whom JY wrote.

Sunday, 10 June 1866

The day commenced fair. Attended the burial [of] Breedlove, one of the post office clerks. He was a native of this state, yet he was Yankee in sentiment. The methodist minister Judkins[1] officiated. Mr. Breedlove was not a church member.

Real or imaginary toothacke gave me an excuse to use some tobacco, I cannot interpret God's ways, nor my own. I wish that the day might speedily come when I shall be enabled to be free from every sin. At three o'clock I witnessed the baptizing of eight persons (colored) in the James River. There was an innumerab[l]e crowd of spectators present.

Read The Morningstar and Independent.

Attended worship at the Court St. Methodist Church.[2]

The performance seems to me more adapted to draw out the fash[ion]able folks than the spirit of God.

To day's conduct though it is to almost unavoidable, yet it pains me. Wrote a letter to Mary; also one to Mr. I. S. Erb, but have not dispatched.

The colored Methodists have had a very lively and as they suppose a very good meeting. I cannot appreciate such [a] service. It may however be the best that there is for those that prefer such a mode of worship.

1. William Elliott Judkins served as the pastor for the Centenary Methodist Church, 1866–1868. He was transferred to Petersburg, Va., in July 1869, returning to the Court Street Methodist Church in 1873 for a further stay. John J. Lafferty, *Sketches and Portraits of the Virginia Conference, Methodist Episcopal Church, South* (Richmond, 1890), 52–55; Christian, *Lynchburg and Its People*, 249; *Lynchburg News*, 28 July 1869.

2. In 1850, six members of the First Methodist Church in Lynchburg withdrew and established the Court Street Methodist Church at Seventh and Court Streets. The new church building was dedicated on 29 June 1851. Chambers, *Lynchburg: An Architectural History*, 158–159.

Monday, 11 June 1866

Received last month's salary. This is not an unimportant item when expenses are so high as they are in our family. If the management was what it ought to be they would not be so high. Received a letter from Mary. Wrote one to Mr. I. S. Erb but never dispatched it. Attending to three schools left me little time for meditation, amusement or observation. Nearly the whole of the afternoon school recited short speeches. Rehearsing performances for the coming exhibition was witnessed though not assisted.

At present the feelings between the two races of this place are very amicable. To day at Campbell C. H. some arrangements for erecting some fifteen houses for poor blacks have been commenced. If the colored people have energy and perseveranc to continue faithful as they have been, that war of races which is now predicted by some and prayed for by others will be one of the evils that never shall happen.

The better portion portion of this community seems not to be unfavorably disposed towards the colored schools but even seem to secretly delight in them.

There are many people in this this town that would be friendly to us if nobody would find it out.

The business portion or some of them makes themselves rather hateful as by being sociabble and friendly when nobody sees such intimacy but when in public hardly look at us.

It is of course easily accounted for such conduct. Family relations are very amicable to day.

Tuesday, 12 June 1866

A pleasant morning. The sweet music of birds is heard. The children are early here at school. Heat is oppressively hot. Wrote a long letter I. S. Erb. Rev. Gladwin[1] from Richmond called to see our school which he addressed. Mr. Brown also was with him and also addressed the school.

After Normal class had a conversation with Dr. Kemper[2] on the subject of the Negroes' capacities for education. He sees little that is commendable in him, but *much* that is blamable.

Took Rev. Gladwin to[3] see the hospital. The inmates seem to to be made as comfortable as possible. No cases of great suffering now. Mr. Gladwin inquired concerning the religious status.

Some old men profess faith in Christ. One old uncle said in reference to faith. "I have a great big hope in Jesus."

To day I have again been reminded of the corruption of human[s]. It manifested itself "on this wise." I saw one man glory in another onse's misfortune. Although this is not of rare occurrence, still it is little and betrays a bad heart.— Night school was not quite full. Mr Shoemaker practised several classes for exhibition till after midnight. Let us be [. . .][4]

1. Albert Gladwin, a Baptist minister from Connecticut, was superintendent of contrabands in Northern Virginia during the war, a position in which he won little respect. See Horst, *Education for Manhood*, 190.

2. Dr. Kemper has not been identified. It seems unlikely that JY was talking to James Lawson Kemper, a native of Madison County and a former Confederate general, who had served five terms (1853–1862) in the House of Delegates and was Speaker from Dec. 1861 until Oct. 1862. After the war, Kemper returned to his law practice, supported Virginia's Conservative Party, and served as governor of the state from 1874 to 1877. The Lynchburg personal property taxes show that a Hugh T. Kemper was living in the city at the time, however, and he may be the one to whom JY referred.

3. JY originally wrote "called to see" and then deleted "called."

4. JY did not finish this thought, perhaps inadvertently starting the sentence at the wrong place as he seems to have tried to erase it.

Wednesday, 13 June 1866

Could not finish my dreams till half past seven—and terrible ones they were. I had fallen into the hands of a murderous party. I, however, manage to escape with my life. Morning. The weather is sultry. Following the regular routine of business I came to the days end at twelve o'clock when I retired.[1] Wrote a letter to H. S. Fegley.

1. JY originally wrote "when I retired at twelv" and then deleted "at twelv."

Thursday, 14 June 1866

This day has [been] more active, though if possible hotter. Mr. Shoemaker is sick. I fear he will have to leave, or at least [leave] his labors to me before we all[1] leave. Made three trips down town. Shipped Mr. Sisson's trunk to him. Visited Sam's mother. She is poor in this world's goods; yet I do believe she is rich in heavenly treasures. In speaking of her blindness she said, I cannot see with my natural eyes but I am not blind spiritually. My vision of faith is bright and clear. I have nothing in this life but I trust I have a house in heaven. I have children and friends there now.

I made her a little present. She was very profuse expressing her appreciation. She *is* happy. She rejoicing that she has such a kind son as her Sam is to her. May many blessings be his for this truly noble conduct in him. O, what a comfort a child can be to a parent in old age.

The property owners are too hard on the poor. This poor woman must pay three dollars a month for a small room nearly in the ground and nothing inside only the roughest kind of wall. The house stands out of town almost inapproachable on a piece of ground valueless for anything except for poverty people that prefer it to living out of doors.

The extreme poverty of this people is indicated in many ways. In refreshment halls generally a[2] wooden bucket filled with [water] and a tin dipper graces the counter. Some times the order is varied by having a cocca not [coconut] or calabash[3] dippers.

My attention has been again called to the mode of worship of the colored people. All of them are quite unanimous in their noisy worship. If no expression is given to their feelings[4] by dancing or vocal expression they think their worship is not acceptable.

One of their peculiar notions of sin is "Singing Songs."

I have heard of a case to day in which a colored lady felt insulted by receiving a love letter from a white teacher formerly employed by our association.

Had a pleasant time in Normal class. A great interest was manifested in spelling. They spelled on sides.

Met Mr. Young[5] from Lehigh county Pa. He was a soldier hear. After his discharge he returned with his family. He is tailor by trade. I was perfectly delighted with his company.

Had a conversation with another U. State sold[i]er, living in Main Str.

Conversed also with a Confederate. This meeting was the happiest if possible. Though Southerner in Sentiments generally he is liberal and reasonable. He is a native of Germany. He said "I believe that the slaves will in ten years be better off than they ever were before. But he believes the "radicals are too radical."

Mr. Shoemaker has had another attack of sickness. Sat up with him till three o'clock.

Wrote three letters for Mr. S. Gave instruction in grammar to Mr. Kelsoe's School.

Weather exceeding[ly] warm. My health has been very good.

1. JY originally wrote "before we all we leave." The second "we" has been deleted.

2. JY originally wrote "the" and then substituted "a."

3. A calabash is a gourd.

4. JY originally wrote "If no expression is given to their feelings is given by dancing." The second "is given" has been deleted.

5. JY refers to Mr. Young frequently but does not ever reveal his first name in the diary. Young was from Lehigh County, Pa., but living in Lynchburg. A check of the 1870 Virginia census index, however, reveals no one named Young in Lynchburg who had been born in Pennsylvania. There are many Youngs in the 1860 Pennsylvania census index for Lehigh County.

Friday, 15 June 1866

Fixed up Mr. Shoemaker for leaving tomorrow morning. Send Dr. Hinkle a dispach informing him of his coming. Closed my night school which was now more prosperous than ever. Mr. Holt has commenced cutting[1] his wheat to day.

1. JY originally wrote "commenced his cutting his wheat" and then deleted the first "his."

Saturday, 16 June 1866

According to yesterdays arrangeme[n]t, at seven o'clock Mr. Shoemaker, who is better to day, and I are at the depot. I am to accompany him at least [to] Washington. Having bought a through ticket and trunk packed in the car, he finds that his health has so much improved. He thinks he can stay here now. After due preperation, we rode back. Well the whole thing was an agreeable disappointment. Send a dispatch to Philadelphia.

Gave instruction in Grammar to Mr. Kelsoe. Visted different members of exhibition class, on business concerning their performances.

Met with several disappointments. Classes were expected to rehears pieces. None turned out in full. If these children could realize how I look upon such conduct they would in some instances change their conduct. I am not at all pleased with our boarding concern. Our boarding must cost the association at least thirty five dollars a month. I cant alter it unless I make myself unpleasant to the family and as we have agreed to live to gether for the time, peace, every one knows, is not an unimportant item in a family. I hope this will be of some value to me in some way. It is a good *"lehr gelt."*[1]

Wrote a letter to brother William and one to Mary. Mr. Frank Forrest is with us.

1. *Lehr gelt* (today Lehrgeld) can be translated as "a good investment."

Sunday, 17 June 1866

A rainy day—eminently so. Read a sermon in the Independent by Beecher, on the subject of conscience. It is good—instructive—besides read morning Star. Mr. Young, formerly of Lehigh Co. Penna. called to see. Had a pleasant interview. But I am not spiritual enough on this Sabbath.

Two of my pupils in night school came to day to bid me good bye and thank me for my services. God bless them that they may still pursues the path of learning and by all their getting knowledge may they get wisdom.

Oh! how much I feel for the temporal and spiritual welfare of this people: They are in danger on every hand. Poor and ignorant.

I have not enjoyed this day as I should. I dont like company on Sundays especially, if by this means a servant or any person is kept all day at work.

Attended Dr. Mitchel's Church. Came too late to to here the text. He has a large church but a small congregation. All his powerful preaching does not seem to take a hold on the hearts of this people.

The the congregation in our church have a lively time this evening. Every time they have church I think less of such a mode of worship. Perhaps it is the best that they can have but it dont suit me.

Shoemaker is improving rapidly. By his sickness I hope I have learned to prize health more highly. How foolish man is that he is not contented when he has health, food and raiment! Our lives—our all is in the hands of God who giveth and taketh life.

Yesterday I had a letter from Mr. Sisson. The people in his vicinity seem not to differ from other parts of Virginia. Cursing and swearing seems in that place fashionable. One thing I have now noticed several times. If any one should molest a nigger teacher at his boarding house the man of the house will take sides with the teacher and will fight for him if necessary.

Lucy said to day that she could not go to church for the last four months. I will not be responsible for such conduct.

Read considerable in papers. A little sketch about Gen. Scott's dying moment. In life many wish to be partakers in the laurels he has gathered in life time. But I should think many an obscure and poor man would not have willing to exchange his crown of glory which begins to shine after death with the laurel crown of Gen. Scott's which begins to fade when life is ended.

He lived as if *this* life were all of life.

Monday, 18 June 1866

This has been one of the busy days. I know hardly what I have done when you except practising for Normal Exhibition. There were forty three in class. While spelling some members of the class became displeased and I was provoked if any thing in the world could provoke me. They spelled remarkably well so they practised their pieces. Some did admirably well.

Gave instruction in grammar at Mr. Kelsoe's S[c]hool, and taught promiscuous[1] class at Camp School.

Made a part of a box for Miss Howard[2] to send home some of her housekeeping apparatus.

Received a letter from Mary and one from W. Y. Eisenberg. He gives good news. He has made a start to follow the Savior. Another young friend of mine has also lately made a profession of Religion.

Last week I send a note to Mr. Corson, Cor. Sec.,[3] that Shoemaker would come on if not too ill; this evening I have sent him another telegraphic dispatch informing him that he will not come now unless he will be more ill. Heard a class practising between tweve and one oclock at night.

1. Consisting of a heterogeneous or haphazard mixture of persons.

2. Elizabeth and Jane Howard both taught at the Camp Davis School. Report of Freedmen's Schools for 7th District of Virginia, Jan.–June 1866, Roll 12, Supt. of Ed., Va., BRFAL.

3. Robert R. Corson was the corresponding secretary for the PFRA.

Tuesday, 19 June 1866

Weather has been very fair. Took a box to depot [to] send to New York by express to New York. Visited Mr. Edmonds[1] school, the only white native teacher of colored schools in this district. This is decidedly the most aristocratic colored school of this place. The pupils have an appearance that would do credit to many of Penna. schools. Sold books; heard promiscuous scholars; heard recitations for exhibition; made new selections for the same; attended to Normal. It was full and prosperous. Wrote four business letter[s] for Mr. Shoemaker. His health, though rapidly improving is not yet recovered.[2]

This has been a great day for company. Mr. John Echols[3] of New London dined with us. He is the first rebel that took meal with us. He is quite free to converse with. I am sure I can not have such a free conversation with a man in the North, who is of opposite political sentiments, as I have had with him.

Some Ladies of town called to see Shoemaker. Capt. Lacy and his clerk took supper with us. It seems the feelings between the two races are gradually becoming more amicable.

There are now quite a number of citizens here whose eyes are beginning to open. Our late Anniversary made as very favorabl impression upon the public mind. I have not heard anything medling with our work for some time, except the papers lately found fault with Mr. Brown schools alleging that his children are not orderly on the street. Had made a mistake I presume by telling his children not to give more than half the sidewak[4] which is quite narrow in this town. All this trouble I believe arose from consideration. He frequently takes a lady friend of his out on the street. They are in the habit of walking with linked arms.

Some white children practised the rule he gave to his children. Practised penmanship.

1. George Edmunds established a self-supporting school for freedmen in Sept. 1865 on Main Street. In May 1866 he reported an enrollment of twenty-five students. Report of Freedmen's Schools for 7th District of Virginia, 9 May 1866, Roll 12, Supt. of Ed., Va., BRFAL.

2. JY originally wrote "improving" and then substituted "recovered."

3. The best-known "rebel" of this name was John Echols (1823–1896), lawyer, Confederate army officer, and railroad president, who was born in Lynchburg, but left there long before the war and was living in Staunton at this time, not in New London. *DAB*, s.v. "John Echols." JY probably was referring to John Minor Botts Echols, son of Peregrine Echols, who had owned land at New London in Campbell County that became the site of Bedford Alum Springs, established in 1852 as one of Virginia's many mineral water health spas. John M. Echols was still living in Campbell County in 1866. Later in the century when the spa ceased operation as a health resort, John M. Echols became associated with a short-lived company formed there to manufacture salts from the mineral waters. R. H. Early, *Campbell Chronicles and Family Sketches Embracing the History of Campbell County, Virginia, 1782–1926* (Lynchburg, Va., 1927), 40–41; *A Representative Record of Results Attending the Use of the Bedford Alum & Iron Springs Water* . . . (Lynchburg, Va., [1878]); Stan Cohen, *Historic Springs of the Virginias: A Pictorial History* (Charleston, W.Va., 1981), 11–12; Virginia Census, 1850, Campbell County, 133; Campbell County Personal Property Taxes, 1865–1866, LVA.

4. JY originally wrote "pave" and then substituted "sidewak."

Wednesday, 20 June 1866

Practised penmanship some. Wrote more neatly than I have ever done before. Wrote and copied a requisition for June expenses. Attended to the regular duties of the day. Was again worried by the house keeping arrangement. Well, its no wonder. I could get boarding for myself for little more[1] than half of what our boarding costs. I only console myself by the thought that I can not alter it and so am not responsible for it. I look upon it in this way. These enormous costs are at the direct expense of the poor colored people. Who is to be blamed for this? Who chances to peruse these lines may guess it. I need not guess.

I have this day resolved to practise penmanship and elocution during July and perhaps August. Practising for the exhibition gives me about as much improvement in elocution as it does to any one concerned in this affair.

Judgeing from present appearance the performers will do very well. Heard several pieces rehearsed today. Gave instruction to Mr. Kelsoe. He is very anxious that the old teachers should return.

Wrote a letter to my good old friend I. A. McCrum.[2]

Read a portion of Sunday School Times. Made additional selections for exhibition.

1. JY originally wrote "less" and then substituted "more."

2. I. A. McCrum was from Lucesco, Westmoreland County, Pa., and attended Millersville Normal School in 1861–1862. *Catalogue, 1861–62*, 12.

Thursday, 21 June 1866[1]

I feel as if I had not done my duty to this people in every respect. I have attended but few of their religious meetings. My example in this respect is not good. Always excused myself by not having time. Well would it not have been better to have *taken* the time when I did not have it? I do not know but what I should have been more influential among them in every respect by being more religious.—Our district has lately been enlarged by adding three more counties to it. One after another of the Bureau officers is removed and the territories of those remaining increased. I think next captain Lacy has to have his discharge. At the beginning of this week he has had his discharge. But his commission or this order has been recalled. The Freedmen of this district should lament his removal at this time, and the whites should heartily rejoice in such a measure. Those disposed to accord any kind of justice to to the Freedmen could not gain any thing by such action, but would stand a good chance of wishing him back whose good judgement has managed the affairs of the freedmen so successfully in the past.

But colored people would be the real sufferers in the case. There were many cases that the Bureau has impartially adjusted that would otherwise have resulted in the deprivation of simple common sense justice to the negro.

Ask brother Lewis[2] for the chu[r]ch to hold the exhibition. He gave his consent. O[h]! This oh has no signification.

Assisted Mr. Shoemaker in preparing the programe for the coming exhibition. Read the constitutional amendment. It is not what it ought to be. It is covering up the truth. There is no occasion for it. Truth should have its free course.[3]

Had an interview this morning with an old gentlemen by the name of Alic Nash, who related his history in old times. His treatment reminded me of that of the apostles and early christians. He told me how he was imprisoned for his holding meeting. How [he] fought the city government of this place. He was in a great measure victorious. For finally he was allowed to hold whenever he chose. This gentlemans history is real interesting.

Had a letter from Varner. All the colored people take every occasion to express their feeling of regret at our leaving soon.

Called to see Mr. Young. He is going to become wealthy in a short time if he keeps on working as he now does. He earns about twenty five dollars as week. His trade is tailoring.

I heard a number of small classes to day in schools. I was really provoked at their dullness. They ought surely go through a course of instruction of at least three months before they should be set to study letters. If teaching is properly understood children will not begin thier learning with the alphabet.

One week from now we will be ready for leaving. Then in two days we'll be at our dear homes. How many pleasant pictures of the past come up in the mind at the mere thought of home.

Programme of Exhibition
Exhibition
of the
Lynchburg Normal Class
and
Camp Davis Colored School
Camp Davis Church

Wednesday	June 27th	8½ O'c. P.M.
	Doors Open at 7½.	
Admission		10 Cts

—————————

J. W. Shoemaker will read several
Choice Selections during the Evening.
(This this the extent of first page)

Order of Exercises

Music   Smith's band

Prayer.

Music   Conducted by Miss Georgiana Willets

Opening Remarks   J. E. Yoder

Music   Kelsoe's band

Select Reading   Miss Rachel Kinkle   — My Mothers Bible

Dialogue   Questions and Answers.

Recitation —   Miss Ellen Wills[4] — The world is growing old

Dialogue   Doctor and Patient

Tableau—   Arranged by Miss E. Howard   Ancient and Moder[n] Belle

Dialogue   Never Seem to be What You are not

Select Reading —   Miss Elmirra Curle —   forty Years Ago

Tableau — Arranged by J. Howard—Family Flour and the flour of the family

Dialogue   The Spelling Clues

Music   Samul Kelsoe

Address to the Exhibition

Music   Camp Davis Minstrels

Select Reading —   Mrs. Mary E. Higgumbottom —   We'll all meet Again
                                                              in the morning

Charade   No Rose without a thorn

Select Reading —   Miss Emma George —   Paddle Your Own Canoe

Dialogue   Choise of Occupations

Pantomime —   Arranged by Miss G. Willets —   "A Big thing"

Select Reading —   Miss Anna Warwick[5] —   A Psalm of Life

Select Oration —   Geo. W. Perrit — Liberty and Union (Webster)

Tableau —   Arranged by Miss E. Howard —   Emancipation

Dialogue   Robert Perkins Wesley Rose —   Rival Orators

Music   Conducted by Miss J. Howard

Closing Remarks   J. W. Shoemaker

Music   Smith's band

Benediction

Music   Kelsoe's band

1. JY wrote 20 June's date two days in a row.

2. George W. Lewis was pastor of the African Methodist Episcopal Church on Jackson Street between Fifth and Sixth. He resided on Harrison Street near Eighth. *Chataigne's Lynchburg City Directory, 1875–76* (Lynchburg, [1876]), 80.

3. As part of the process for readmitting the former Confederate states to the Union, Congress decided that the states must pass the Fourteenth Amendment to the Constitution.

The amendment, however, was not without controversy. In an effort to protect the rights of the freedmen, the amendment prohibited the states from abridging equality before the law and from depriving their citizens of life, liberty, and property without due process of law. In addition, the amendment reduced the voting population in each state proportionally by the number of adult males who were denied the franchise except for those guilty of "rebellion, or other crime." It also disallowed election to any state or federal office of anyone guilty of having supported rebellion after having taken an oath of allegiance to the United States. And it prohibited the payment by any former Confederate state of its wartime debts or for the loss or emancipation of slaves. By simply reducing the proportion of eligible voters by the number of those who might be denied their voting rights, the amendment left open the possibility that inimical southern whites could effectively disfranchise the freedmen by simply accepting a reduced representation in Congress. The amendment also enraged the leaders of the woman suffrage movement because it used the word *male* for the first time in the Constitution, thus omitting a large segment of the population from the possibility of gaining the vote. And many were troubled by the loss of the provision in an earlier draft that had prohibited those who had voluntarily supported the Confederacy from voting in national elections until 1870. Simply barring them from state and national office seemed too lenient. The amendment was first submitted to the states in June 1866 and became law on 28 July 1868. Foner, *Reconstruction: America's Unfinished Revolution*, 254–261; James M. McPherson, *Ordeal By Fire: The Civil War and Reconstruction* (New York, 1982), 517–518.

4. Ellen Wills was a Camp Davis Normal Class student who later taught a rural freedmen's school at Allen's Creek in Amherst County. Program of the Exhibition of the Lynchburg Normal Class, Camp Davis School, Camp Davis Church, 27 June 1866, Private Collection; Schedule of Schools under the Pennsylvania Freedmen's Relief Association in the State of Virginia, Together with Rental Account for the Quarters ending 31 Mar. 1870 and 30 June 1870, Letters Received, 1 Jan.–24 Aug. 1870, Roll 5, Supt. of Ed., Va., BRFAL.

5. Anna Warwick was probably the Ann Warwick listed in the 1870 census as a forty-five-year-old music teacher living in the household of Charles W. Price, general merchant. Virginia Census, 1870, Campbell County, Lynchburg, 534.

Friday, 22 June 1866

Mr. Perrit called early this morning to have Mr. Shoemaker extricate him (Perrit) as he has got into difficulties with the Society by which he is employed as a teacher.

The colored people must learn a great many things before they are what the country wants them to be.

They are not reliable enough. They lack independence and energy. They would eagerly grasp for the blessings that freedom gives; but the responsibilities which freedoms brings are a different question with many of them. While they are making a start at governing themselves, and all eyes, north and south, are fixed upon them to see the result, the result of their trial is all important. Nothing is more obvious in governmenttal economy than that they must be governed. If they fail to do it themselves others must do do it. Who will be a freeman must be a governor in the empire of reason.

Rose at 5½ this morning. Mr. Shoemaker left by South side Train[1] for Appomattox County to secure a deed for a lot that has been purchased on which a freedmen School House is to be erected. On account of this fact it is difficult to get a deed for it.

Two of the [s]chool boys have been "rocking" each other this morning on their way to school. I caught them at it. On examination it was found that Wm. Davis, the one that made the start is now on probation for his good conduct. I gave him an ellaborate lecture on the subject. At first I thought I would severely "whoop" him, but on close examination I discoverd that he gets a good share of this punishment at home, so I gave it all to him in talk. I made him promise that he will tell me two years hence by letter if living then how he is getting along then. If he then still "rocks" the boys. Taking my address with him he faithfully promised to do so. God bless him wonderfully.

Wrote a little essay for exhibition. Wrote a letter to Brother William. Received a letter from brother William. Also one from Mary. Heard several dialogue classes. Was called on by a colored delegation for information. Rose Warden one of my pupils told me that she must work a great deal harder since she has been free. Her master tried to have her learn but she would not do it. Now she learns well.

Essay—Education

Centuries ago Galileo declared that the world moves. A superstitious and tyrannical government compelled him to retract his heresy. When he was dismissed by his persecutors, he said, Well, it *does* move. He was right. The world moves through boundless space around the sun; so the human family moves. This progression is in every way similar to the motion of the earth. The course of both is tending ever onward and never reaching the end of their course.

To the scientific observer scaling the hill of science, and looking back [over] the course of history through all its windings it is evident that human progress marks every period through which the the human family has moved. Thus from history alone, without mentioning the hosts of proof which would fain lend their assistance, if it were required that it is Gods design that the human family must progress; and that your and my whole and sole business in life is to improve myself and fellow man physically, morally and intellectually. The the three duties ar in many respects so closely allied that none of them can be performed perfectly without making considerable progress in the others also. The occasion leads us to consider the intellectual to night.—Let us look a moment at the inducements held out to incite us to intellectual improvement.

Education enables a man better to provide for his bodily wants and comforts. This is surely not an unimportant item in any ones domestic economy. No one can be indifferent as to what he shall eat or what he shall drink or where withal he shall be clothed. Without the modern intelligence under ordinary circumstances the present population could not live one year. If the soil were to be tilled according to the ancient fashion the earth would not yield enough to satisfy their hunger to say nothing of the comforts of life.

Education gives the mind employment. The human soul is so constituted that it can not be for any length of [time] without employment. The only question for us to decide, is "What employment is the mind to have?" If we do not direct and control our thoughts—if we do not give the mind useful thoughts, our passions and the Devil will control them. Of the passions of the human soul it may with equal propriety be said, as it is said of Satan himself, they always find some work for idle hands to do. The *least* advantage the studious mind possesses over the idle one, may finally result in inestimable good. Education, if it had no higher end than merely steal[ing] away the leisure hours which the passions would employ in [a] thousand ways, if *you* do do not, would be of sufficient importance that every state should provide for the education of her citizens; and it would be of sufficient importance to enlist a a large share of the attention of every man that has the welfare of the community at heart. If the youth and the aged would apply their minds to study instead of going out and seeking the society of the idle, what a different world we would have in a short time! Thus by giving less occasion for mischievous and sinful employment, education is valuable.

But Education can do more for us than merely keep us out of sinful employment. It can not fail to inspire us with a keener sense of our duties to God by studying his wonderful works all around us. Not only our mind[s] but also our hearts are expanded, the truths of God every where displayed if we but open our senses to receive them. The earth, the air, and the clouds are full of the power [and] wisdom and Goodness of God. Thus education may not only be the means of securing our happiness[2] in time in time but throughout all ages of eternity.

Again: we should strive for knowlege because the very act of acquiring it affords pleasure for the mind. So does the possession. You can not find a man on Gods earth that would sell his education, if [he] has any on any terms.

It is a small consideration that if [it] affords pleasure? No it is the very pearl for which every individual is striving. No human power can divert the soul from the pursuit of enjoyment. It is an identical part of the soul. The world is not to be reformed by destroying its[3] pleasures, but by increasing them.

Again: the rank we occupy in creation and our natural fitness for that rank demand our our intellectual improvement. Man is called the crown of creation. He is called the link between matter and deity. To him i[t] was said every living thing on the land in the sea and in the [air] shall be under thy control. In order that he may answer this purpose he must [be] educated. The ox is wiser than man without education. He knows the grass from the poison; he lets it alone. Man eats it and dies.

There is a special reason why you should be educated at this time. The nation is waiting in suspense, as it were to see what you will do for yourselves [and] to legislate accordingly.

You have made a start to scale[4] the hill of science. To the credit of many of you it may be said you have gained a fair[5] step. But do not faint by the way. Let no obstacles deter you. But cheer up and take courage look not down with contempt on those below. Let your aim be high.

Read the independent. Some good articles too. When I shall have setled down in life I will have this paper. Retired at 12 o'clock P.M.

1. The South Side Railroad, which had been virtually destroyed during the war, ran 123 miles from Lynchburg to Petersburg. Service to Lynchburg was not reestablished until 1 Feb. 1866. *Seventeenth Annual Report of the President and Directors to the Stockholders of the South Side R. R. Company, for the Year 1866* (Petersburg, 1866), 5–6; Henry V. Poor, *Manual of the Railroads of the United States, for 1868–69* (New York, 1868), 92. On 12 Nov. 1870, the South Side Railroad became part of the new Atlantic, Mississippi, and Ohio Railroad Company. Poor, *Manual of the Railroads of the United States, for 1875–76* (New York and London, 1875), 318–319.

2. JY originally wrote "temporal" and then substituted "happiness."

3. JY originally wrote "the" and then substituted "its."

4. JY originally wrote "sclale."

5. JY originally wrote "godd" and then substituted "fair."

Saturday, 23 June 1866

I am compelled to change my hours of retiring.[1] My [————][2] are beginning to hurt me every morning. My bowels are disordered. Used tobacco to free[l]y yesterday. I[t] was the occasion of much dreaming. If next Saturday will be so pleasant a day as this I shall be glad.

Where and whither shall the son of man go to escape temptation to sin? I would not ask to be relieved from this duty;—but I wish that God would give me grace sufficient to overcome all temptations.

Rambled out into the fields this morning, to invigorate my health. Coming to a small stream I took a bathing. I met a "Master" in the performance of office. Three colored men were plowing corn. He looked after them. He soon inquired for the "Fenian" News.[3] This and his general appearance betrayed his Irish descent. He swears without a blush.

Discussed freely with him the state of the country. In his opinion "the country is ruined," yet finally he admitted that it will be more prosperous than before the war. The abolition of slavery is no harm to the country nor to the nigger. On[4] the subject of the negroes capacity for education, he said, "some are smarter than the white man a few seem duller." On suffrage, "I will neve[r] walk with a white [black?] man to the poll. Give him a vote and in ten years [we] will have a nigger president." If their is any danger about that he should have a vote at once.

Among other things, he said, "I am glad that slavery is gone. I believe in treating the nigger right if he behaves himself. If they treat me with proper respect. They do not take care of themselves. If you give them a farm with all its [a]ppurratus they cannot make their bread. I love the stars and stripes. You did not whip us,—you only overpowered us. We have the best fighting men. Buchanan[5] is to be blamed for the war as any man. Lincoln was a good man. Giving every body a vote has ruined this country. The negroes will all steal.

Nearly every white man will associate with negro women. The women seldom refuse." The numerous other things I can not think of all this moment.

This is very lazy weather.

1. JY originally wrote "reqing" and then substituted "retiring."

2. JY failed to disclose the site of his pain.

3. The Fenians were a secret Irish organization that sought to overthrow British rule in Ireland.

4. JY originally wrote out "for" and then substituted "on."

5. James Buchanan (1791–1868), of Pennsylvania, became the fifteenth president of the United States (1857–1861), espousing anti-abolitionist sentiments that garnered him the electoral votes of all of the slaveholding states except Maryland. When the so-called Black Republican candidate, Abraham Lincoln, won the presidential election in 1860, many Southerners decided that the Republican victory justified disunion. During the four-month period between Lincoln's election and his inauguration, Buchanan denounced the idea of secession saying that the Constitution did not convey such a right on the states, but he also claimed that the federal government had no constitutional power to coerce a seceding state into submission. Thus Buchanan did almost nothing to avert the deepening crisis. James M. McPherson, *Battle Cry of Freedom: The Civil War Era* (New York, 1988), 230–235, 246–248; *DAB*, s.v. "James Buchanan."

Sunday, 24 June 1866

Attended colored Sabbath School. Visited Mr. Young's family.

Took supper with Misses Harveys. In the evening attended preaching at the first Presbyterian Church.[1] Retired early.

1. The First Presbyterian Church was located on Main Street between Twelfth and Thirteenth and was built in 1858. Chambers, *Lynchburg: An Architectural History*, 158, 172.

Monday, 25 June 1866

Rose at six. This morning predicts a regular miscellaneous day. The heat is intense. Arranging platform curtains and other requisite arrangement[s] for exhibition are now beginning to crowd themselves upon my attention. Closing up accounts and and making out reports should have a part of the same attention. Had seve[r]al horseback rides to town; made one trip on foot. The Normal Class made a poor rehearsal. They perfectly provoked me by their inattention.

Heat more intense than ever before this season.

Tuesday, 26 June 1866

Spent the morning in distributing complimentary tickets for exhibition, in the afternoon put up a stage for performers. Night had the first rehearsal on the stage.

Wednesday, 27 June 1866

This morning all the picket men came. Not a great deal of any thing was accomplish till noon. In the afternoon the performance was rehearsed before a large audience of children. This rehearsal was for the special benefit of the scholars. Admission was free then for them. Good o[r]der and decorum was manifested in the audience.

The exhibition proper commenced 8½ P.M. with a crowded room, consisting of black, yellow and white populations. The whites consisted of Yankee Teachers, Bureau officers, military officers, Southern Union Citizens, Yankee citizens and and common citizens. Have omitted one important class, namely: news paper editors. All classes were favorably impressed with the excellent entertainment the colored community gave. The whole eminently a success. Capt. Lacy remarked that he had never seen an exh[i]bition that equalled it. The emancipation tableau called forth the most intense feelings of joy, to which they gave mingled expression with their voices and clapping of hands.

The tableau entitled, "Freedmens Bureau" raised the greatest laugh among all classes. The audience dispersed at twelve o'clock well pleased but many of them were wet[t]ed pretty well before they came home. According to previous arrangements, I had to see home some ladies. This was the most unpleasant trip I have made for a long while. On the way home the rain came down in torrents.

Thu[r]sday, 28 June 1866

Late retiring and early rising is the order of the day this week. What a [s]ight of work is to be done this day! It goes rather slow in the start. Took down the platform down in the first place. There are a number of things that have a tendency to make me fret: I commence to be gay and happy. I wont fret. This resolution I have carried out—talked as much nonesense as I possibly could all day.

Clothed a ragged colored boy and made him work for it.

Every thing was upside down. Had to pack trunk, school furniture, housekeeping furniture, and freedmens clothing.

Afternoon made a trip through town to see some of my old scholars for their photo graphs.

At six sent trunks to Hotel.[1] In company with for teacher went to take tea with Miss Harveys. Arrived at hotel midnight. The colored people do not like to see us leaving.

1. JY originally wrote "tavern" and then substituted "Hotel."

Friday, 29 June 1866

Some of the colored people accompanied us to depot and one of the whites went with us by rail road some distance for our company. Bought a paper for ten cents which was offered for five cents. One of our party had a great trouble to get on the ladies car.[1] Shoemaker succeeded with a great deal of importunity to get him on it but his demijohn of Alum water[2] had to be left off.

The weather for traveling was most delightful. Our party consisted of thirteen teachers and a Mrs. Young and her three children of[3] whom I had to take care.

The trip was decidedly a pleasant one. Wheat crop is very poor where there is any, but from Gordonsville to Washington there is very little out. There is but one field of destruction for this hundred miles. At Washington, having had a few minutes time till train left, a party of us ran up to the Capital. Of course, considering what is to be seen there we saw little. What we *did* see exceeded my expectation very greatly. 6½ P.M. left for Phila. At Baltimore Mr. Varner and the Misses Howards left us. They were not in a pleasant temper when they did so, that is, the ladies.

Now darkness covers the sky. Some of the boys try to sleep and I suppose they succeed too.

At 1 o'clock in the night arrived at the City of brotherly love.

Went to Merchants Hotel in Third Street with Mrs. Young.

Had a short but good sleep.

1. JY originally wrote "train" and then substituted "car."

2. A demijohn is a narrow-necked bottle enclosed in wickerwork and usually holding from one to ten gallons. At Campbell County's Bedford Alum Springs in 1877, for example, alum water was bottled in five-gallon demijohns and sold for three dollars apiece. The company's alum water contained trace elements of various salts including aluminum, zinc, nickel, cobalt, and calcium sulfates, and was taken to counteract a variety of ills, among them indigestion, diphtheria, chronic sore throat, and neuralgia. *Representative Record of Results Attending the Use of the Bedford Alum & Iron Springs Water*, 1–3.

3. JY originally wrote "for" and then substituted "of."

Saturday, 29 [30][1] June 1866

Accompanied Mrs. Young to depot. Called to see Shoemaker. Then made for train in 13th St. which I made only in time at 8 o'clock. With rapid speed came to Pottstown at 10 A.M. Called to see Mr. Jonathan Kehl. Wrote several notes. At eleven left for home where I arrived at 12½ P.M. The distance from Lynchburg is 360 miles. Found friends well. Made many short calls. But was not a little disappointed with a letter informing me that Mary, whom I had expected to meet this eve, will not come to "B" [Boyertown] till Monday Eve.

1. JY misdated this entry 29 instead of 30 June.

Sunday, 1 July 1866

Called at Moses Stauffer's. Went to cherry tree to gratify my long cherished desire for this for this luxury. Attended S. School at Swamp Creek. It was full of children, but parents were few. This is a sad prevalent fault with many of our Sabbath schools. At the request of the supt. addressed it. Had rather more than ordinary success. Returning home to brother Williams we had a prayer mee[t]ing. Albert Stauffer took the lead. Had a good time. Mr. Stauffer made a profession of religion since I saw him last so has my brother Jonathan.

The weather seems cold to me who was used to extremely warm[1] weather.

Retired at 8½ P.M. to make a full night in the land of dreams, which I had not done for nearly a week past. This I have done.

1. JY originally wrote "cold" and then substituted "warm."

Monday, 2 July 1866

Rose at 5½. Not to early. Ground a scythe. They set me to work when I am at home. I do not know how I shall get through this season, for I do not do any heavy work as I will take writing lessons.

Spoke with Mother on the subject of religion according to the Methodist faith.[1] We had of course to disagree.—Did some writing. Here I am at 11 o'clock A.M. in this book and in Mother's little cooking Room.

Called on friends. In the evening called to see Mary after an absence of more than six months. Had a pleasant meeting. Our joy was unspeakable. Slept the remainder of the night in Brother's barn.

1. JY attended the churches of several denominations including the Methodist, Presbyterian, and Baptist, especially while he was in Lynchburg, seeking a faith that met his spiritual needs. Although he seemed inclined toward Methodism, JY finally settled on the Baptist faith, joining Lynchburg's College Hill Baptist Church in 1878.

Tuesday, 3 July 1866

Have regretted that I lost so much sleep last night. I have formed a good resolution in regard to visiting which if carried out as I hope it may, will make it more valuable to all concerned.

Evening called to see Mary. Visited at Mr. H. Keely's. Returned at twelve o'clock. Arrived home at 3 next morning.

Wednesday, 4 July 1866

A remarkable day in the history of this country. This is a day of rejoicing not only to the white people of this vast country but also to the late slaves of the Southern States. They seem to be generally inclined to select this day as an anniversary day to celebrate their emancipation. If ever it was appropriate for any people who were oppressed by[1] a yoke like that which oxen wear, and who now are translated into the regions of civil liberty, with a sure promise that they shall have soon unlimited American political liberty of the 19th century.

Now they have only to fulfill one condition in this national contract, and this boon is theirs not to be wrested from them by traitors or sympathizers with them. It is simply this: they must *govern themselves*: for if they do not, somebody else *will*.

I have, however, no doubt but they will do this. Their past history in slavery is noble. Why should they not do equally well in the enjoyment of partial liberty. No class of people on the face of the earth would have submitted to the outrages *they* have endured. In their present condition they need more education and independence. Ignorance and sin are their dangerous foes. If they are strong enough to conquer these then all will be right. Then the historian can with pleasure, paint a long and glorious existence among the nations of the world for them.

May this Fourth of July remind afresh every citizen of this Land of the value of our free institutions, and more especially of the duties he owes to it.

Practised penmanship. Fetched trunk at Boyertown. Had heavy rain. Albert Stauffer called to see me. Unpacked trunk.

I dont like to live in this place, because the mail arrangement is so poor.

1. JY originally wrote "with" and then substituted "by."

Thursday, 5 July 1866

Visited at brother William's in the morning. Met Rev. Simon Huber.[1] Picked cherries. Practised penmanship a great deal. Wrote three letters to Dan Keck, C. Comly,[2] to Mary. Called to see her a few minutes. Retired early.

1. Simon M. K. Huber served as a Reformed Church minister from Skippack in Montgomery County, Pa., about eleven miles southeast of Boyertown. Hauze, *Falkner Church History*, 58–59, 63. In 1860, Huber had been a twenty-two-year-old stove tender living in the Montgomery County household of Franklin M. Gearhart, merchant. Pennsylvania Census, 1870, Montgomery County, Limerick Township, 176.

2. Clement Comly was from the Gwynedd and North Wales community in Montgomery County, Pa., and attended Millersville Normal School in the school years 1864–1865 and 1865–1866. *Catalogue 1864–65*, 12; *1865–66*, 10.

Friday, 6 July 1866

Sowed a cover for a carriage. Folks are busy at the hay. Weather is good for it. The responsibilities of life are beginning to appear to me more gigantic than ever before. O, that I might be enabled to meet them nobly. "Life is real; life is earnest, and the grave is not its goal," come up in my mind. When I look back and see how useless I have spent my life thus far, I tremble. I am no hero to battle with temptation. He is a cunning foe. He knows how to apply his forces to advantage.

Yet I am not discouraged: still I will fight on.—not with the carnal sword which too often cuts the hands that wields it, but with the spiritual sword which is sharper than any two edged sword. It is strong. It is the instrument with which are constantly battered down the strongholds of Satan.

Read in the bible; cut wood; unloaded a load of hay.—Among my old books I found one entitled the art of speaking. The authors name I do not know. It is ninety one years old. I commenced to read more out of curiosity than an expectation to gain useful information. It, however *does* contain some useful information. It is remarkable to notice how language changes from time to time. To be sure, when a language has attained so nearly what is deemed perfection as our has, changes are slight. The first difference observed is the old fashion S'S. Though this is but a slight difference the change was a decided improvement. In the German language their is room for similar improvement. Some words are used that now have a different signification some that are now obsolete.

The author criticises pulpit oratory most rigidly. No doubt it was in place then in England. I am sure, a great many preachers in America could profit in our own times from it.

Meet an army of haymakers in the field. They were not under proper drill. Their leader lacks energy and skill. On a moments reflection it becomes evident what smartness will do for a man. I feel again, how important it is to succeed in *little things*. Little acts make the sum of life. *Little* done well, makes life successful; done badly, makes it a failure. This is a subject every mortal should meditate on *carefully*.

The heat has been most intense. Mother had been working very hard. Katie[1] has been with brother Abraham.[2]

Since I haved determined to p[r]actise penmanship I have also determined not to do any heavy manual labor. I can not easily carry out this resolution when I am here. It is at least hard work for me to keep *from work*. I have now for several days past more earnestly thought of my future employment. So I ought to under the present circumstances. But have not come to any definite conclusion. I fear I shall not be able to come to any conclusion for the present month. There is a reason for every thing, so there must be one for this. I even try to think there is a wise reason for me not to have decided in the past on any kind of business for life. I have, however, done s[o]me thing at fixing my fate. I have marked out some avocations, which do not suit me. So I have to make the selection from a small list.

1. Katharine E. "Katie" Yoder, born 18 Dec. 1848, was JY's youngest sister and the youngest child in the family. Fretz, *Genealogical Record of the Descendants of Christian and Hans Meyer*, 527.

2. Abraham E. Yoder, born 17 Nov. 1829, was JY's oldest brother. Ibid., 524.

Saturday, 7 July 1866

Commenced the day soberly, diligently, and prayerfully. Hoping that God will give wisdom and zeal to pass the whole day in usefulness for all these are essential to success in this sinful world.

Wrote a long letter to Robert Turner. Weather is sickening hot. I can't hardly breathe. If the heat does not not subside I will have to change programme, namely, staying at Philadelphia. At this rate, terrible destruction of lives in our large cities will soon result. All proper precautions for the prevention of sickness should at once be taken. Every one should make himself sure that he has healthy food and healthy atmosphere.

If the weather will be so hot tomorrow that anticipated trip to Pottstown have to be postpone. Practised penmanship; but fingers are too stiff. Chopping wood and practising penmanship do not correspond together. One or the other may as well be dropped at once.

My health is "only toler[a]ble" as the Virginians would say: besides I am desp[er]ately lazy. This no doubt aggrevates in some degree my illness. One cause of it is the poor tobacco I use, another perhaps the the change of climate and a third imagination and a fourth not to be named.

Sowed on buttons. Fretted a litt[le] because my shirts were not "done up" as I thought they should be. But when I began to reflect all ungratefulness died away, and I thought of other things more pleasing.

To day Sarah Waitman committed Suicide, a respected lady of nineteen summers. Can so young a life have gathered to many burdens to bear down a strong form in its youthful strength to the grave:—the cause is a mystery. A curious public has been busy to find a cause. Though this investigation gave rise to numerous conjectures and guessings, and finally many true, yet conflicting, theories became current setting forth the cause of the troubled mind or conscience or both that would plunge itself into the unknown dark whence no step can be retraced. She alone of mortals seems to know why she sought relief in the jaws of the king [of] terrors. Called to see Mary. Remaind late.

Sunday, 8 July 1866

Rose late. In company with Sister Amanda[1] went to cherry tree to gratify the stomach. Had a very pleasant shower of rain. The heat which was very intense was checked by it. Went to church with Amanda. Had an English sermon by Rev. Groh[2] from the passage—"If any man sin we have an advocate with the father, Jesus Christ the righ[t]eous." If I could speak *good English* I would say the minister spoke bad English.

1. Anna Amanda Yoder, born 21 May 1844, was JY's third youngest sister, six years his junior. Fretz, *Genealogical Record of the Descendants of Christian and Hans Meyer*, 527.

2. The Reverend Leonard Groh was the pastor at Saint John's Lutheran Church in Boyertown, Pa. Information from local historian, Holly K. Green, Boyertown, Pa. See also W. Edmunds Claussen, *The Boyertown of Editor Charles Spatz* (Boyertown, Pa., 1973), 11, 48.

Monday, 9 July 1866

I have been to Philadelphia, to obtain information concerning the decition of the Board of Education. The trip was for naught. Saw J. W. Shoemaker. He is happy. Came to Boyertown at Sunset. Took supper at Mr. John Fegley's.[1] Mary was there saw her home. This home was at Mr. Wm. Stauffer's.[2] Left at one o'clock. Intended to find a place to stay the remainder of the night at Graff's Hotel.[3] Failed to obtain admission. Did not like to go home through rain leaving umbrella behind and carpet bag. Went back to Heller's.[4] Spent three hours uncomfortably till stage left to take me home. Slept, what I did sle[e]p, on chairs.

Received two letters, one from Shoemaker the other from Lloyed containing a photograph of his.

1. JY boarded at John and Maria Fegleys' in 1864 while teaching school in Boyertown. Yoder Diaries, 1861–1864, Acc. 27680, pp. 108–110, LVA. There are two families in the area of Boyertown headed by a John and Maria Fegley. Living in Colebrookdale township, Berks County, were John Fegley, age forty-two, and his wife, Maria, age thirty-nine, with their four children. Pennsylvania Census, 1860, Berks County, Colebrookdale Township, 169. In Douglass township, Montgomery County, where JY and his family lived, was the household of John (age sixty-four) and Maria Fegely (age sixty-one), who may have been the parents of the younger John Fegely. Pennsylvania Census, 1860, Montgomery County, Douglass Township, 8.

2. There were several William Stauffers living in the vicinity of JY. The most likely one with a Mary in the household who was JY's age was William K. Stauffer (a farmer), who lived in Douglass township (where JY lived), Montgomery County, in 1850, with wife, Lydia, and six children; and in 1860 in New Hanover township, Montgomery County (next to Douglass township where JY lived). In 1860 this Stauffer's household also contained a young woman named Mary Young (age eighteen), who was also a cigar maker. Stauffer himself (now listed as a cigar maker), was given with wife, Lydia, and seven children. Pennsylvania Census, 1850, Douglass Township, 192; ibid., 1860, Montgomery County, New Hanover Township, 947.

In addition, the other possibilities, though much less likely, were the two William Stauffer families living in Colebrookdale township, Berks County, in 1860, who would have resided not too far from the Colebrookdale John Fegely family. Both were named William K. Stauffer, one a justice of the peace and the other (listed in 1850 as William K. and in 1860 as William R.) a blacksmith. There was no one in either household named Mary. Pennsylvania Census, 1860, Berks County, Colebrookdale Township, 151A, 169.

Finally, the least likely William Stauffer was the one living in 1860 in Washington township (just north of Colebrookdale township), Berks County, but with no Mary in the household. Pennsylvania Census, 1860, Berks County, Washington Township, 815. For a discussion of the various census records in Berks and Montgomery Counties for the Stauffer family, see Stauffer, *Stauffer-Stouffer-Stover and Related Families*, 18–29, 129–148.

3. Graeff's Hotel was also known as the Old Union House or the Union Hotel. On 2 Nov. 1866, it was the scene of the first town council election, and on 19 Nov. the council of the new Borough of Boyertown held its first meeting there. *Boyertown Battallya*, n.p.

4. Daniel Heller was the proprietor of the Boyertown Hotel, which was sometimes referred to as Heller's. Ibid. The 1860 census for Colebrookdale township lists Daniel Heller as a landlord and Henry Heller as a barkeeper. Pennsylvania Census, 1860, Berks County, Colebrookedale Township, 160. Daniel Heller, a hotelkeeper, was listed in Amity township, which is located a few miles southwest of Boyertown, in 1850 with many of the same children who were given in the 1860 census. Pennsylvania Census, 1850, Berks County, Amity Township, 436; *Boyertown Battallya*, n.p.

Tuesday, 10 July 1866

Rose very late. Wrote Sisson and Mary. Determined to go visiting in day time instead of night. Vancourt is ruined.[1] He can't pay his debts. The prop[h]ecies and prayers of many are at last fulfilled. Strange! one mans destruction is an other man's delight. If any ones character is confided into the hands of ignorance and malice it is not safe.

1. Gary Hauze, author of the history of Falkner Swamp Reformed Church (1975), could not find in the church records any mention of the troubles that ruined Vancourt. Vancourt and the congregration, he says, had been having trouble for some time and the latter were becoming alienated. Between Feb. 1864 and Mar. 1865, in fact, the church grappled with a large debt that each member finally had to help pay off. Twenty-five congregants refused and were dropped from church membership. Vancourt himself had entered the tobacco business on the side and evidently that enterprise had finally failed as well. *Falkner Church History*, 48–49.

Wednesday, 11 July 1866

Called to see Isaac S. Erb. Practised penmanship. Read some in Atlantic Monthly. Attended prayermeeting at Henry Gilberts,[1] New Berlin.[2] I was considerably refreshed. If I did only attend such meeting weekly I would not be so careless [and] unconcerned about my spiritual state. Had again trouble to to get into the house on returning home.

My conduct does not suit me by any means. I would like to be more devoted but it seems I can't. May the time speedily come when a brighter day will dawn.

1. There are two Henry Gilberts listed in the 1860 Pennsylvania census for Colebrookdale township, where New Berlin was located. One was a thirty-nine-year-old horse doctor and the other a sixty-three-year-old farmer. Pennsylvania Census, 1860, Berks County, Colebrookdale Township, 154, 165.

2. New Berlin, now New Berlinville, was two miles northeast of Boyertown.

Thursday, 12 July 1866

Called early in the day to see Mary. She was not at home. I was sorry that she was not. Now I have to call again at night, and I felt then just in the proper mood for talking. Of course I have a great deal to talk to her. Followed the regular routine business of the day. Wrote a letter to Varner.

At night attended teachers meeting at Boyertown. Took Mary Home. Enjoyed the interview though, in a measure, in violation of my late resolve.

Had again trouble in getting home. Was attacked by two large dogs. To escape their wrath I went a way around the fields. At my arrival at home when I had enterred the house, I found somebody in my bed. Being desirous not to make any disturbance in the land of sleep, went again down stairs and slept on the carpeted floor which was not what is generally called comfortable. Aint I becoming fully convinced that I am being chastised by providence for transgressing laws (visiting at night) which I preached up in the past by example and precept.

Friday, 13 July 1866

Have not had sleep enough. Sorrowed over my last nights arrangement. Wrote for practice. Went to store for mother. Wrote a note, not to Amanda, but for her. Wrote a letter Sam Kelsoe, colored, also one to Mr. Young in Lynchburg. Called to see Mary again at night but it would not suit at any other time. When I shall see her again I know not. I called rather late which was the occasion of much anxiety. Though there were many considerations that had a tendency to make our parting a sad one, there was also a great deal to, induce is to incourage. Not a little of the future was spoken. Our enjoyment was great. It was such that only true lovers can have an idea of. After prayer to God who doeth all things and doeth them well too, we left each other to his care and keeping. Came to brother Abrahams at 2 o'clock.

Saturday, 14 July 1866

Rose at six. Conversed an hour on the condition of the South. Came home at 9. Read the Morning Star. In it is an account of a sceptics conversion. Shed tears profusely when reading it. O may it have a lasting impress[ion] on my mind. Mary must meet angry parents this evening. Practised Penmanship a great deal. It was suggested yesterday that I should start a select school at Boyertown. I have to day considered the matter. If I do fail to get the position in Lynchburg, I will still farther examine into it. But for this position I should first pursue my studies still, further.

This past week I have not accomplished as much I should. In this busy life there is no time for play—for indifference. Too much is to be done. No moment is to be lost. But many a one is not only spent in idleness, but some are spent in doing *worse* than nothing. Sin reigneth boldly everywhere. Who can conquer it in his own person? Still fighting the good fight of faith I will.—Weather is very dry and hot. It would be so pleasant to have rain! Sister Amanda is home to day assisting mother. The farmers are all busy taking in their grain.

Was in the water bathing. Got out too soon and got wet. I should have remained in the water to keep dry. The rain has come but it was not enough. It [was] cool immediately after.

Our neighbor Mr. Miller intends to keep a harvest party this evening, or rather a frolic. Have not the youth of this land enough opportunity to sin? Well what['s] the use of such as party then? To enlarge the temptations of the young, to engage in such business as the success of such a party requires, is one of the great crimes of our land. And yet persons that would claim respectability will go there to engage in so low a practice.

The rain happily made it a decent party. Nearly all stayed at home. At this time the rain performed or rather answered a double purpose. How welltimed it was. Vegetation was on the point of death. This gave it a new life.

Sunday, 15 July 1866

Vegetation wears a new Sunday garb this morning. The commotions of the elements are faithful ministers of God to execute his will.

Read the bible and slept in the morning. Afternoon attended Keck's Sabbath school. It is well attended. Industry seems to characterize it. Its greatest want is a set of faithful selfdenying teachers. Spoke to the school in a general way but with only tolerable satisfaction, as I had to speak in "dutch."

Visited at Keck's, conversed with him on the question of the Freedmen. He sees the destruction of the country, if justice will be done. But I do not believe that the path of justice is such a dangerous one. He believes or hopes a great many evils in regard to this policy, but when asked for the grounds of his belief, he *believes*.

Attended English preaching at New Berlin. Mr. Shafer discoursed on the words "Call upon [me] in trouble, I will deliver thee and thou shalt glorify me." The young speaker should do better, if he would first pursue a course of instruction.

Monday, 16 July 1866

Wrote a note for Mary Beitaman.[1] Wrote a letter R. R. Corson Cor. Sec. Penna. F.R.A. In the Afternoon Mr. I. S. Erb called to see me. Went to Post Office.

Penmanship does not flourish well at home.

I engage but little in manuel labor, yet sometimes I do.

The election contest is rapidly coming on.[2] Both parties are preparing for it. There is a singular coincidence in the gubernatorial candidates. The Democratic candidate Mr. Clymer[3] was formerly a republican. The republican Mr. Geary[4] was formerly a Democrat.

"My policy" will be defeated and the policy of the people will be victorious! It is strange. When Andrew Johnson carries out his drunken policy the democrats will praise him. Of late we don't hear any thing of the president carrying out Lincoln's policy. I think he has carried it out and left it out.

I can not forget Wm. H. Seward. What a different man he is from the one that headed that small band of freemen then true to the core.[5]

1. JY may have meant the Mary Beitenman who was twenty-two years old in 1860 and the daughter of Francis Beitenman, a carpenter. Pennsylvania Census, 1860, Berks County, Earl Township, 219. There was also a Mary Beitaman, age twenty-eight, living in the household of Charles Keely in 1850. Pennsylvania Census, 1850, Berks County, Colebrookdale Township, 320.

2. The 1866 Pennsylvania gubernatorial election.

3. Hiester Clymer (1827–1884), of Berks County, Pa., originally had been a Whig, but joined the Democratic Party and served as a delegate to the Democratic National Conventions at Charleston and at Baltimore in 1860. He was also a member of the Pennsylvania State Senate from Oct. 1860 until he resigned in Mar. 1866 to run unsuccessfully as the Democratic candidate for governor. Accused of having wartime dovish views by Pennsylvania's War Democrats and Republican supporters of another candidate, Clymer was offered a diplomatic post in Russia or Spain if he would withdraw his nomination. He irately refused, and, after campaigning as a supporter of President Johnson's lenient prosouthern policy, lost the election by 17,000 votes. His career continued, however, and he served as a member of the U.S. House of Representatives, 1873–1881. Obituary, *New York Times*, 13 June 1884, p. 1, c. 6; *Biographical Directory of the United States Congress, 1774–1989, Bicentennial Edition* (Washington, D.C., 1989), 796–797; Edward L. Gambill, *Conservative Ordeal: Northern Democrats and Reconstruction, 1865–1868* (Ames, Iowa, 1981), 58, 71, 72.

4. John White Geary (1819–1873) was commissioned a brigadier general in the U.S. Army during the Civil War, served as military governor of Savannah, Ga., and in 1866 was elected to the first of two consecutive terms as Republican governor of Pennsylvania. During the administrations of Franklin Pierce and James Buchanan, Geary had served as territorial governor in conflict-ridden Kansas in 1856–1857. Despite his efforts to be impartial, Geary took several antislavery positions that caused him to run afoul of the proslavery legislature. He resigned in Mar. 1857, after receiving death threats and suffering an unsuccessful attempt on his life. At the time he was a Democrat, but in the postwar period he became a Republican.

Ezra J. Warner, *Generals in Blue: Lives of the Union Commanders* ([Baton Rouge, La., 1964), 169–170; *DAB*, s.v. "John White Geary."

5. One of the primary organizers of the Republican Party, Seward during the war had strongly espoused protecting the rights of the freedmen. By the time Andrew Johnson had become president, however, Seward had abandoned a concern for freedmen's rights in preference to a speedy reconciliation with the southern states. Seward had always thought that the division between the North and South was "unnatural and unnecessary," had been willing to consider any expedient to keep the Union intact, and at war's end still thought that restoring the Union was more important than punishing southerners for rebelling. Radical Republicans, like Yoder, naturally disagreed. Albert Castel, *The Presidency of Andrew Johnson* (Lawrence, Kan., 1979), 35; James E. Sefton, *Andrew Johnson and the Uses of Constitutional Power*, ed. Oscar Handlin (Boston and Toronto, 1980), 79–80; Allan Nevins, *The Organized War to Victory, 1864–1865*, vol. 4 of *The War for the Union* (New York, 1971), 76; Van Deusen, *William Henry Seward*, 385.

Tuesday, 17 July 1866

The warmest morning for this season. I am dull and sleepy. This is applicable to body & mind. Mother is busy from early morn till late at night. I would often like to help her do some work. It is often harder work to keep out of work than to *do* it. My attention was again called to day to look at the sore blindness of lovers. Surely some of them have eyes but see not, and ears but hear not. Passingly strange that in making contracts for life that sane persons should make agreements with so little regard to judgements, leaving the feelings rule and reign. Hence so many illmatches! Hence also, when married they are in love with other persons. This attention to others is a fruitful source of innumerable miseries, in an otherwise peaceable families. Fornication and adultery are too common in our land. The good people do not hate them[1] enough. It is said that the Irish Catholics are chaster in that respect than the american protestants! Is this not a topic for examination for proud Americans to ponder? Shall our boasted liberties be so abused by us? Sin is not only a reproach to any people, but it also destroys a nation, but righteousness exalteth it. Craziness is so frequent in this time and place. It must have a cause. Fornication and adultery, are responsible for a large share of it. O, that the public would be better informed on this subject. The demon rum is playing wild in this neighborhood. He hold many a man under his sway. One of our neighbors was last week under his inspiration. He was mad from his habitual devotion at his altar. There are others that are nearly on the brink of the Maniacs hell.

Have the rumsellers no conscience? Have they not sufficient examaples of the results of their doings. Can not legislators check this hellish foe? Must this destroyers forever go forth in the face of the law and slay the wise and the good, both body and soul. When the assassin Booth[2] destroyed the life of our honored chief, it roused the nation to a holy indignation to arrest the destroyer and not only confine him that he might hencefoth be peaceable, but they utterly destroyed him.

But now when the rum burning demon alcohol lurks for the lives of two national chiefs to consign them, not to martyrs graves but to the depth of eternal torment, the nation jokes[3] and laughs at the idea of Johnsons or Seward's drunkenness.[4] What does this mean? Do I dream or is the nation mad? Can not one man do something towards saving a few bright, loving, joyous youth from a disgraceful drunkards grave? The young must be saved. The old can not. When they are once taken captive they are hopeless. Strong stout men who can bare their breasts for the bayonet's pierce, are powerless to refuse the bo[tt]le when presented to them.

Yo[u]ng men ought to be instructed that the use of liquor is disgraceful! They ought to be pledged that they will not handle the unclean thing. But it is asserted by some this is an abridgement of liberty. Who in all the world has liberty to sin? If Liberty mean a right to do wrong then away with it.

Was to Store and post office. Had a letter from "Sam." Mr. Hillegass tried to get into politics, but he failed to day. Some day, when I feel like it he may have his wish gratified. The letter from Lynchburg states that their colored Baptist Church is burned down.[5] Have the rebels done this again? (My pens are too poor to write.) I see the people [of] England as well as those of Switzerland have organize societies to aid the freedmen of the south. What a gigantic machinery. Who can measure the amount of good it is destined to accomplish?

Read highly incouraging letters from different portions of the South. The work is rapidly approaching peace and hormony. Old prejudices are dying out. Love and harmonious action results.

Gilbertsville, Montgomery Co. Pa.
July 17, 1866

Robert R. Corson
    Cor. Sec. Penna. F.R.A.

Dear Sir,

Will you please order to my address several copies of of the Freedmen's Bulletin[6] (June No) for distribution in these parts?

Although the friends of the freedmen are few in these parts, yet these few when properly made acquainted with the wants of the Freedmen and the operations of Penna. F.R.A. in supplying these want[s], they will offer their mites and their prayers to increase its past usefulness, and thus aid in the advancement of a cause which is not inferior to any that has ever appealed to human symphty and consequent benevolence.

I have returned from Lynchburg at the beginning of this month. Knowing that J.W. Shoemaker has reported the general condition of affairs in Lynchburg I will omit it. A letter bearing date 11th inst. informs me that the colored church building in Lynchburg is destroyed by fire.

Yours Tr

Jacob E. Yoder

Did some tailoring work. Though I did not a great deal of it, it would have cost a great deal if I had it done by a tailor.

Catie has returned home this eve. Went to post office. Read the Norriston Register,[7] containing an account of Jefferson Davis's imprisonment.

1. JY originally wrote "it" and then substituted "them."

2. John Wilkes Booth assassinated President Abraham Lincoln.

3. JY originally wrote "is" and then substituted "jokes."

4. JY was referring to the reputation Andrew Johnson had gained as a habitual drunkard when he appeared to be drunk at his inauguration as U.S. vice president in 1864. Although Johnson generally did not drink, in 1866, when his apparent leniency toward the South had antagonized the Radical Republicans, he was accused by the Radicals of being a "drunken tailor" based on disjointed speeches he gave in Feb. and Apr. and thereafter. In addition, a story circulated in Mar. 1866 that a U.S. senator had visited the White House and found Johnson, his son Robert, and his son-in-law all inebriated and that Johnson was keeping mistresses there. While the story fit only Robert Johnson, it reached Henry Ward Beecher, who circulated it as being fact. Where JY got the idea that Seward was a drunkard is harder to determine. In 1862 Beecher had added his voice to those of other newspapermen who wanted to see Seward removed from the Cabinet, so it may be that Beecher's *Independent* may have tarred Seward with the same brush in its late May 1866 article that JY mentioned in his 3 June 1866 diary entry. During Johnson's and Seward's campaign swing in Aug. and Sept. 1866, both were accused in the press of running a barroom and drinking on the campaign train. Howard K. Beale, *The Critical Year: A Study of Andrew Johnson and Reconstruction* (New York, 1930; reprint, New York, 1958), 10–13, 16, 78–79; Beale and Alan W. Brownsword, eds., *Diary of Gideon Welles: Secretary of the Navy under Lincoln and Johnson, Volume II, April 1, 1864–December 31, 1866* (New York, 1960), 453–454, 461; Castel, *Presidency of Andrew Johnson,* 35; Van Deusen, *William Henry Seward,* 342, 461.

5. The *Lynchburg Virginian* reported on 4 July 1866 (p. 3) that a fire broke out in the large wooden factory at Court and West Streets and spread to adjacent buildings including the black Baptist church.

6. The *Pennsylvania Freedmen's Bulletin*, a publication of the PFRA, began in Feb. 1865, suspended publication for Aug., Sept., and Nov. 1866, as well as for July–Sept. and Dec. 1867, and was subsumed by the *American Freedmen* in 1868. On-line search of OCLC, On-line Computer Center, Inc., Dublin Ohio.

7.   Norristown is in Montgomery County, seventeen miles northwest of Philadelphia. The *Norristown Register* was established in 1800 and was a weekly Democratic newspaper. *George P. Rowell and Company's American Newspaper Directory* (New York, 1871), 136.

Wednesday, 18 July 1866

Traveled to Millersville Lancaster Co. Penna. Left home six o'clock P.M. going, on foot three miles, on stage eleven miles, on cars about fifty two miles. The weather has become a little cooler by spells. At Reading an innumerable crowd of people was gathering to attend a democratic massmeeting. Leaving Reading at 12½ P.M. arrived at Lancaster at 3½ P.M. Here I called to see Mr. Killion's family. It is doing well apparently. Saw Mr. Conrad for first time since he professes faith in Christ. With him the possession of religion must be a very different condition from that of slavery in sin. At Lancaster I began to meet old Normal friends. At the Normal I met a great many more than I had anticipated to meet there. Nothing of great importance having occurred and am tired from my trip I will retire soon with an expectation of good sleep which I have not had for a half a week on account of the great heat. It is considerable cooler now. I must stop a few minutes. At Landisville [in Lancaster County] fell in with a polotitian. He has faith in the triumph of the democracy. Conversed on train from Reading with a Lancaster Co. Menonite. He took occasion how he guessed a strangers politics in Philad. a number of years past.

Thursday, 19 July 1866

My lodging place is in Harmony[1] with Mr. J. L. Douglass. Sleep was poor last night. Met again numerous friends, visited in the morning several examination classes. In the Afternoon the State Model School had their closing exercises. These came off with credit to pupils and teachers the sum of the performance was dialogues. One of the dialogues performed was the same one we had three weeks ago in the Lynchburg Colored Exhibition. Twenty of the Model School students will henceforth be transferred to the Normal School, some entering the F others the E Division.

In the evening the Model reunion came off. This was a sociable of model School teachers. There was a goodly number present. Every Normal student that teaches a session in the Model School is considered a Member if he pays his initiation fee which [is] fifty cents. In the course of the evening refreshments were served, consisting of Lemonade, icecream, Cakes, Raisins and candies & c. In this exercise I engaged to freely for the benefit of my stomach.

At the close prof. Wickersham[2] called the roll. Those that were present answered for themselves and [ab]sentees were answered for by others. The information wanted was, If single or married. If not married what the prospects were of becoming such. Also where and what the members are doing. The occasion gave rise to a large fun. Retired at 12, and had a restless night.

1. Harmony Hall at Millersville Normal School.

2. James Pyle Wickersham (1825–1891), who became a nationally known educational leader, started a school at Millersville as a county teachers' institute in 1855, and with his urging and assistance saw the enactment of a state normal school law in 1857. Later that year Millersville became the first normal school in Pennsylvania. Appointed in 1866 as superintendent of Pennsylvania's common schools, by 1874 Wickersham had succeeded in having a school established in every district in the state. He wrote the educational provisions of the state constitution of 1874 and established the school department as one of the five constitutional departments of the state government. Wickersham resigned in 1881 and became first chargé d'affaires (May 1882) and then minister resident and consul general (July 1882) of the United States to Denmark. He resigned from the post in Aug. 1882, however, because of his wife's ill health. *DAB*, s.v. "James Pyle Wickersham."

Friday, 20 July 1866

Weather cooler. Considerable rain at evening in this place. Called to see Mr. Turner at Mr. Frantz['s].

This was the commencement day. Twenty students graduated, one Mr. C. H. Harding, in the classical[1] course, two, Misses. Lizzie Lloyd and Mary M. Martin, in the scientific course, the remaining seventeen in the Elementary course.

This has been the largest class they ever had. I was a little tempted to wish I had changed the number to twenty one, though I was not willing that I had been absent from Va. I rather wished I had been able to have performed the two duties. The Essays and orations reflected credit on the class. The whole day was consumed by the performances.

Prof. Wickersham gave his exaugeral address[2] and prof. Brooks gave a kind of an introductory lecture.

A great many former students had come from near and from far to see the closing scene with this school of the great man that had made this school a centre of so much useful ness and honor. Its history is short but honorable. He took occasion to refer to it briefly. He committed its future administration to Prof. Brooks a man worthy of so high a trust.

Henceforth his services will be more responsible as his labors in the same field will be more extensive. I spent the evening pleasantly with the good Brother Turner. Here I met one of my 62 Normal Friends Mr. Harnish.[3]

1. JY originally wrote "scientific" and then substituted "classical."

2. Because Wickersham had just been appointed superintendent of Pennsylvania's common schools, he was giving his farewell speech or "exaugural"defined as ["rare"]: a discourse delivered at the end of a "term of office." James A. H. Murray, *A New English Dictionary on Historical Principles*, vol. 7 (Oxford, Eng., and New York, 1891), 368.

3. Michael W. Harnish, of Lancaster County, Pa., attended Millersville Normal School in 1860–1861 and 1861–1862. *Catalogue, 1860–61*, 19; *1861–62*, 10.

Saturday, 21 July 1866

Cloudy day. A day of departure. Many a sad and long farewell for Normal Students. Nearly all the students, present and ex, left this morning for their respective homes. Came to Lancaster at nine o'clock A.M. Here met Mr. A. Dotterer,[1] a student of Franklin and Marshall College. He was on his way to attend the funeral of Dr. Gehrhart's wife. I and Mr. Heilman accompanied him. Rev. Mr. Bausman of Reading officiated. He selected for his text, I think 85 chap. and 1st verse.

From the long fatigue to which I was subjected I was not very wide awake so I am unable to judge of the merits of the sermon.

At 3 o'clock P.M. left Lancaster for Reading where I arrived to make train for Pottstown at six and a half. From Pottstown I walked at 9 ¾ o'clock. The same night at 1 P.M., William's second daughter "Aggie"[2] was attacked by a frightfull flightiness. Sleep for the remainder of the night was out of the question. But in the morning her [h]ealth had improved then I took my time at sleep. Read a portion of Pilgrim's Progress in the german language with unusual interest. Attended Methodist Meeting in Brother George's grove. Minister Leopold officiated speaking from the words: The hour is coming when the dead shall hear the voice of the son of God, & c. He spoke of the grave in three relations: the sinner's Grave, the natural Grave, and the holy Ghost's Grave.

After supper came home to Mother. So I am now comple[t]ly at home after an absence of five days. My expenses were seven dollars and sixty cents. Travelling on foot was eight miles, on stage fifteen miles, and by cars one hundred and twelve miles. I think I can go to work now in good earnest, and leave visiting for a more convenient time.

1. JY may have been referring to Abraham Dotterer, son of Jacob and Sarah Dotterer, of Pike township, Berks County, who in 1860 was fourteen years old. Pennsylvania Census, 1860, p. 656A. There was also an Abraham H. Dotterer from New Hanover, Pa., who was mustered into the 11th Regiment of the Pennsylvania Militia on 24 Sept. 1862. Hauze, *Falkner Church History*, 47.

2. JY's older brother William married Mary Ann Gresh. They had nine children; Agnes or "Aggie" was the second child. Fretz, *Genealogical Record of the Descendants of Christian and Hans Meyer*, 526.

Monday, 23 July 1866

Commenced early to repair the pump which was long since not faithful in keeping up the water at night. Worked at it the best part of a half of the day. And now that it is done it seems it is worse than it was before. Wrote a letter to Mary. Practised Penmanship. The many stories that are current concerning Rev. Vancourts finantial disaster prove little more to me [than] the the state of utter human depravity.

The weather is fairer than fair. During my absence last week there was a seasonable rain.

Received a letter from Mary. Made a trip to Boyertown Post Office. Was very anxious to be back till night as I did not know whether Mother had company. Many men came out as if they were determined to detain me.

Mrs. Daniel Moser[1] is very sick mentally and bodily and I think at the soul. She is desperately crazy. Neither she nor those that must be with her can enjoy any rest. Earnest! earnest.

1. There were two married men named Daniel Moser living in Berks County in 1860. The first was a thirty-eight-year-old farmer living with his wife, Deiner, age forty-three, and four children in the Pike township. The other was a fifty-eight-year-old farmer, whose wife, Inda, was fifty-four. They resided in Earl township with their three sons, a daughter-in-law, and a granddaughter. Two other Daniel Mosers lived in Montgomery County in 1860, neither of whom was then married. The eighteen-year-old Daniel was living on a farm where he was a laborer in New Hanover township, and the twenty-one-year-old Daniel also lived and labored on a farm, in this case in Upper Hanover township. Pennsylvania Census, 1870, Berks County, Pike Township, 653; ibid., Earl Township, 196; ibid., Montgomery County, New Hanover Township, 470; ibid., Upper Hanover Township, 993.

Tuesday, 24 July 1866

A very pretty morning. On such a morn God's earth is pretty full of beauty and symmetry. It would seem that all of his servants are faithful and obey all his mandates, except man alone is disobedient yea, rebellious. Did any of the worms or insects frustrate the design of its Creator there would be some shadow of excuse for, but that man should fail to answer the purpose of his existence is passingly strange. "The human heart is desperately wicked." He who will have it purified and keep it such must have and keep a constant war. To him "life is a battle."

In this battle no life is in danger but life is preserved thereby.

I have heard painful news in regard to the relations existing between my pastor and the missionary board that supports him. The board has come the conclusion he is, (what is vulgarly called) "played out." They have discontinued to employ him. He complains greatly the they have so maltreated him. He holds Colder responsible for his unfair treatment. He proposes to leave the church and reunite with the Church of God which he left a number of years ago. Difficulties like these prove a great stumbling to the conversion of the world. I have no faith any more in Coulter [Colder] as a Minister. The prevailing motive in his preaching is to make a living: And I think Colder saw it as well as I did. I think the best that he can do for the present is to go to work that he may make a living. He asked me to go with him to join the Weinbrennarian Church.[1] God be gracious to him and make him wise unto salvation.

Received a number of copies of the Penna. Freedmen's Bulletins. Distributed some of them. Had a letter from Alvin Varner. Read Bulletin and "Harper's Monthly." Collected dues. Brought "aggie" over to Mother. Sisters Amanda and Harriet[2] visited at Mother's. Practice in penmanship is in the programme of to day. This day has been characterized with more activity than some others of the same kind in this month. The true cause of Sarah Waitman's death seems to be unravelled now, her dishonest conduct in acquiring this world's goods. Sent by mail three copies of the bulletin. Made a trip to Boyertown on personal business. Returned at nine o'clock P.M. The prospect of teaching a private school in this vicinity is less encourging.

1. John Winebrenner from Frederick County, Md., was ordained as a Reformed minister at Hagerstown. He became a pastor at a church in Harrisburg, Pa., and because he adopted certain doctrinal beliefs from the Baptists, Methodists, and Mennonites, he was deposed from the Reformed Church in 1828 and organized a new denomination known as the General Eldership of the Church of God in North America, but more commonly called thereafter the Winebrennarians. Bernard C. Steiner, "Maryland's Religious History," *Maryland Historical Magazine* 21 (1926): 16.

2. Harriet Yoder was JY's second younger sister. She was born 31 May 1840, married William A. Mensch in 1861, and lived in New Hanover, Pa. Fretz, *Genealogical Record of the Descendants of Christian and Hans Meyer*, 526.

Wednesday, 25 July 1866

This morning predicts a warm day. Each day is a significant gift of God's. It can be made a blessing or a curse. If poor mortals could only realize that they themselves manufacture their blessings and their curses. Messs. H. Beitaman and Sam Mourer are building [a] fence for Mother. I would assist them but for my *hands*. Penmanship and penmanship is the order of the day and the week. It goes better to day than usual. Wrote a letter to Rev. James Colder and one to J.W. Shoemaker. Assisted fence makers a little.

The general topic of conversation has been, for several weeks past, Rev. Vancourts course of conduct. All the stories that prejudice and opposition could invent and ignorance could believe are in circulation about him. The [s]pirit of prejudice and opposition have some use in the world. But what redeeming qualities ignorance has to compensate for all the mischief it is constantly doing I know not. "Aggie" had promised her mother yesterday to come home "tomorrow." This morning when I have told her she must go home she said: "It is not to morrow." Whatever may be her merit to practical justice, she was right in the abstract. It is not "to morrow." "Tomorrow never comes." It would well for the procrastina[tor] to remember this. Tomorrow is like the horizon. Advance towards it ever so far. It is still a great way in the distance.

Procrastination is meritoriously styled the thief of time. If he would receive all his dues, he might be called the thief of a great many other things. By stealing time he has robbed many a man of a noble life. But for procrastination all would live usefully. Every one see that he omits to do what he should do and commits what he should not do. But by and by he will do better. He means it honestly, he makes the failure in time. Who can fully estimate the value of time. Most valuable, yet most squandered. Thus, man allows himself to be cheated out of the most valuable treasures. Or rather, he does it himself. We are frequently taught to deal honestly with our neighbors. We ought to love ourselves more. If that were effected once then we should deal justly towards ourselves. And not till then will we do it.

Weather is again quite warm.

Read an article in the July No. of Harper's Monthly entitled; National Cemeteries. It is Good. In the same magazine, Read a really good, moral, healthful love story. The characters are George Chatam and Emily Ingersoll. I have not read any thing for a long time with the attention and interest. I hope it will do me practicle good.

Took niece Agnes home. When I fetched her, her sister Elmina[1] cried so unconsolingly. When I returned her "Mina" laughed just as much as she did cry before. They were all glad to be together again after an absence of nearly two days. On my way home was caught in a rain. Stopped at Moses Stauffers. The conversation was various. Retired 9 A.M. [P.M.?]

1. Elmina or "Mina" was the third child of JY's older brother William. Fretz, *Genealogical Record of the Descendants of Christian and Hans Meyer*, 526.

Thursday, 26 July 1866, Fairville, Montgomery Co. Penna.[1]

The morning bids fair. But, it is said, Fair days, like good natured women, must not be praised till afterwards. So I recall my partial praise and bestow it in due season.

"Albert Stauffer is as kicker; he attended prayermeeting at Bill Yoder's" Royers say[s] so. Ignorance befitteth the brute; but for human beings it [is] wholly unbecoming. But low prejudice in this case is united with ignorance. These combined have often spread havoc and desolation in the world. They marshalled armies, and slew[2] the best of heroes for God and humanity. No act was to fiendish for them to do. They then would cover their infamy by saying they had done Gods service. Though God did never delight in their best service they rendered him. But good people are sometimes guilty of such crimes. Let every one beware before he condemn others lest he is the worst cast away.

Left for post office. Received nothing there. Reread "Miss Ingersoll's Pride" in Harpers Magazine. Read an article in Morning Star of July 18th. How a bride refused the cup, and what an effect she had on those present.

The use of liquor is so dangerous, and even so dangerous for acquiring this use. Those who are not yet taken captive by this plunderer of every thing that is noble in his captives, should fight against it. The notice by experience should enlist the energies of every man or woman that has the welfare of humanity at heart, to diminish to use of liquor.

Mother is visiting at Benjamin Holdernen's at Boyertown.

Wrote a letter to C. W. McMahon Appomattox C. H., Va. This teacher of Freedmen in Va. is staying there during this vacation season for the purpose of erecting a school house on the spot where General Lee surrendered his army. This warm weather must be very oppressive in Virginia.

I read in Harpers Monthly Magazine and write alternately.

I am beginning to feel uneasy about my future employment. All the money I have in the world will perhaps equal my expenses for three months. This month what is still left of it and the next I do not propose to do any work that will even pay my board. I will not risk othermen's money. So I must stop my school day studies. I must go to work: that is the only alternative I have and be saving, too. This spending time and money so lavishly must cease. There can but little gain result from it. If I should succeed in becoming a learned man, What use would there be if life would be consumed therein.

While I have resolved to learn writing now and do no work, to go work and do what my hand findeth, is often a temptation. This makes me very desirous to improve in writing. Sometimes I think I do this then again, I think I am very slow at it. Thank God I have Good health. May it long be mine. Made trip to Boyertown and return on foot principally for exercises. Mr. Jonathan[3] accompanied me.

The day closed, as it opened, fair. Thermomater stood about 88°. The warmest we have had this summer was about 102°.

1. JY apparently refers to Gilbertsville here as "Fairville" because of the fair weather described in this day's diary entry. The next day's entry also refers to "Fairville" with "a cool morning" that "promises rain."

2. JY originally wrote "slain" and then substituted "slew."

3. JY probably meant his younger brother Jonathan who was born on 22 Oct. 1845, became a teacher like JY, and never married. Fretz, *Genealogical Record of the Descendants of Christian and Hans Meyer*, 527.

Friday, 27 July 1866, Fairville, Montgomery County, Pa.

A cool morning. It promises rain. At nine o'clock A.M. the funeral of Jonas Steltz's son,[1] a child of eleven years of age, will take place at the house of the deceased's parents.

Wrote, wrote, and wrote. Monotonous work. *J* and *C* were the principal letters I wrote. Mother and Katie have gone to funeral. I am alone master in the house, except it be the flies which are quite numerous.

At half past two o'clock P.M. Mr. Albert Stauffer called in on his way to drive to down to see Revernd S. K. Huber. I went along. We were well entertained.

Left there at ten P.M. Had an unpleasant ride, owing to the threatening rain, the foolishness of the horse, and the unsuitableness of the gears to the carriage. Went along home with Mr. M. to unhitch. Arrived home at 12 P.M. My repeated calls at the door were not heard. Then I made an attempt to sleep on the hay. This was in vain. Now it was one and a half. Repeated my knocking. This time I met with success.

It is folly to return so late.

1. Perhaps JY meant Nathan Stelz, the six-year-old (in 1860) son of Jonas Stelz, who lived in the same township as JY. Pennsylvania Census, 1860, Montgomery County, Douglass Township, 27.

Saturday, 28 July 1866

Rose late. Made a trip to Boyertown. Made inquiry with Messrs. Fred H.

Stauffer[1] and I. B. Hankey[2] in regard to Mount Pleasant Seminary to see how it could be rented. Result of the interview was very unsatisfactory. Postponed the subject for further consideration. Took dinner at Graff's Hotel. Had a short interview with Miss "Lill" Boyer. Returning stopped at Post Office, where demerits of whoredom were discussed.

Money is more valuable than I regard it. I wish I could truly appreciate it.

Read again in the Harpers Magazine.— one article in particular, "Newspaperiana."

Took a grand bath in the creek. At sunset the North wind arose and cooled the warm air around. It prepared the night most splendidly for sleeping. Still I was not so busy in sleeping for I thought I had not done at six next morning when the sound came for breakfast. Reasons for this may be assigned. My attention was employed in active dreams.

Finally the work of the week was writing and reading. One article I read thrice.

1. Fred Huff Stauffer, forty-three years old and a painter, was the proprietor of the Mount Pleasant Seminary in Boyertown. He was the son of its founder, John Stauffer. Stauffer, *Stauffer-Stouffer-Stover and Related Families*, 21; *Circular of Mount Pleasant Seminary*, Boyertown, Pa., (Philadelphia, 1866); Morton L. Montgomery, comp., *Historical and Biographical Annals of Berks County, Pennsylvania* (Chicago, 1909), 1:257; *Boyertown Battallya*, n.p.

2. Isaac B. Hankey (1829–1881) was a graduate of Gettysburg College. After serving as a principal at the Mount Pleasant Seminary in Boyertown, he opened his own school, Kallynean Academy, in Boyertown in 1866 and directly competed with the school that JY would found in August that same year. Montgomery, *Historical and Biographical Annals of Berks County*, 1:257; *Boyertown Battallya*, n.p. Four years later JY's brother apparently was teaching at Mount Pleasant Seminary as JY wrote to Jonathan Yoder on 9 May 1870 and told him, "I am glad to know that you have as large a School at Boyertown as you have. How is Mr. Hankey's school prospering?" Jacob Yoder Letter Book, 3 Mar. 1870–1 Dec. 1870, p. 118, Acc. 35108, LVA.

Sunday, 29 July 1866

Weather fair. Did not go to church expecting to have company from Gablesville.[1] But I did not invite them to come on sunday. Stayed home all day in expectation for this company. But they did not come. At noon I called a few minutes to see Mr. Albert Stauffer. He had to go to sunday school. So I soon departed. At various times during the day I made numerous efforts to write letter. But every attempt so far has proved fruitless. It is now nearly sundown. I will not make another attempt. Three of my brothers have called to day at mother's.

This has been a lazy unprofitable day. I wish I had my own family. Perhaps I was able then to shape the sabbath more according to my taste. Perhaps worse too. I wish the coming week was passed and gone. Attended evening worship at Swamp. The sermon was preached by Rev. Groh from these words: "Wilt thou be made whole?" John 5:6 verse. Sermon was an improvement on the one I heard three weeks ago, especially in Language. I was not greatly edified by it. I look back on this day with shame. Old Keyser died. Money was his great trouble on the mind before death.

1. Gablesville, Pa., was approximately two miles west of Boyertown in Berks County.

Monday, 30 July 1866

Spent the first part of the day in the grove in supplication and prayer. My course of life is far from being satisfactory to[1] me.

As I do frequently fall into grievous sins and am not concerned about the service of my God, I do conclude[2] myself under sin. I am a sinner and not a saint. I am not what I once was. There was a time when religion was my chief concern. It is not now. I can never be a happy sinner. I will not write here what I will do. I will wait till it is done. Then I can record it.

Called at Jacob Bickels.[3] The whole family was binding oats, except the mother. Passed at brother Williams. Here I drank beer and ate apples and pears. Came home till dinner. Passed afternoon at Writing Table. Wrote a letter to Mary. Practised a good deal. Read again Harpers Magazine.

Mother was provoked this morning because I am not going to visit at William Menchs.[4] She is again in good humor. She finds fault with Katie a great many times during a day.

Day is gone again without rain. But a fair prospect is spread out out before us.

1. JY originally wrote "from" and then substituted "to."

2. JY originally wrote "but" and then substituted "conclude."

3. Jacob Bickel may have been the seventy-six-year-old (in 1860) farmer who lived in JY's home community or his son Jacob (age thirty-four in 1860), also a member of the household along with the latter's mother, sister, and two others, perhaps his wife and daughter. Pennsylvania Census, 1860, Montgomery County, Douglass Township, 13.

4. William Menchs was probably JY's brother-in-law. William A. Mensch had married Harriet Yoder in 1861 and lived in New Hanover, Pa. Fretz, *Genealogical Record of the Descendants of Christian and Hans Meyer*, 526.

Tuesday, 31 July 1866

Every indication for rain. I should like rain so much. But if God has decreed us no rain I would not once ask for it. God doeth all things well. He granteth blessing when blessings are best; he granteth chastisements when chastisements are best; For the last few days Mother caught daily more flies in the trap than there seemed [to] be of these peculiar creatures on the premises, yet they are daily increasing. The old saying must have some truth about it, which runs thus: For every one fly killed, ten others will come to attend the funeral.

No doubt there [is] a wise purpose in the indestructibility of flies. If man were endowed with[1] powers to change nature to suit his purposes, confusion would follow. All is right, that is. But man does not do right he does.

Cut Howard Detweiler's hair. Scissors were so dull. The mere mentioning this fact is sufficient to excite sympathy in any one that has any experience in hair trimming.

Mornings mail brought me a complimentary letter from J.W.S. [J. W. Shoemaker] on my recent improvement in penmanship. The same messenger brought a large sized picture of J. P. Wickersham's now State Supt of common schools of Penna.

How I did write again! More than was profitable. If one would judge from the amount of writing I do, he would come to the conclusion that my improvement should be more decided. Wrote a letter to Hiram Stauffer[2] and a note to Jonather B. Geyer.

Fetched a lot of books at brother William's. Among them are my old latin and Greek books. I found I can read some in Virgil yet. But in greek I did not know all the letters any more. I never have had a great start in Greek. I wish I did only know as much about it as I do of Latin. I was also without my good friend dictionary for the last five month[s].[3] I am really happy to meet again with him. I will not for slight reasons part with him so soon again.

A large acquaintance with him creates many friends. Therefore all should covet his acquaintance and friendship. By[4] observing his manners and habits I may improve my own.

Made a visit at Mr. John Dotterers.[5] They were cheerful and sociable. I enjoyed the interview well. Abram and Maria were not at home.

This family is in some ways a model family so far as my judgement goes—in peace, harmony and industry. Wrote a letter to Frank Forrest.

---

1. JY originally wrote "to" and then substituted "with."

2. Hiram Stauffer, age twenty-one, was the son of Reuben Stauffer, of Colebrookdale township in Berks County. JY apparently sought him as a prospective student. Stauffer, Stauffer-Stouffer-Stover and Related Families, 20.

3. This would indicate that JY went to Lynchburg around the end of Feb. 1866. In fact, his name first appears on the list of Freedmen's Bureau teachers for March 1866. Report of Freedmen's Schools for 7th District of Virginia, by Capt. R. S. Lacey, District Superintendent, Mar. 1866, Monthly Statistical School Reports of District Superintendents, July 1865–Apr. 1869 and Jan. 1870, Roll 12, Supt. of Ed., Va., BRFAL.

4. JY originally wrote "He will Teach one how" and then substituted "By observing."

5. John Dotterer was undoubtedly the one living in JY's home community of Douglass township and listed in the 1860 census as a farmer (age fifty-five), with wife, Elizabeth (age forty-six), and children Maria (age twenty-one), Abraham (age nineteen), John (age sixteen), and three younger offspring. Pennsylvania Census, 1860, Montgomery County, Douglass Township, 13.

Wednesday, 1 August 1866

Weather cool this morning rather uncomfortably so. This will brood sickness. Indications for rain are again prevalent. So they were before. There mission was only to disappoint. They may at last disappoint by bringing rain.

I was meditating whether or not the ingenuity of man will some day get control of the clouds and make them bring rain at his command. I came to the conclusion that he would not,—at least not in this period of the world's history; for as long as men[1] are so wholly under the influence of selfinterest as many are as this time, the confering of so great a power would rather be the means of general confusion and and dissatisfaction than it would be that of a general blessing.

Lord in wisdom hast thou laid the foundations of the earth; in wisdom dost thou control its operations. Wisdom is in all thy laws. There is wisdom in our very ignorance.

My labors are so monotonous that I do often get tired and make no improvement. I will go and read awhile. When Caesar invaded England,[2] he found the condition of the inhabitants so infantile, that he obse[r]ved that "these inhabitants are too ignorant for slaves." They must have undergone some[3] modifications since then. For they are not only too wise now to be slave[4] but they are too wise to hold slaves.

Attended Old Keyser's funeral. He had attained to the uncommon age of 86 years, 7 months and 23 day. It was God's will to bless him during life with riches and remarkable good health. Still he had selected this passage for his fune[r]al sermon. "So am I made to possess months of vanity, and wearisome nights are appointed to me." Job 7:3. Rev. Dups of Pottstown officiated. First part of his discourse was the Vanity of Human life. He illustrated the deceptive appearance of life the young voyagers of the sea of life have, but taking a distant landscape scenery. In the second place he spoke of the universal striving for redemption from the bonds of sin. The speaker used good language and possesses more than ordinary elocutionary merit; still his speaking is not so impressive as it might be. His manner is graceful and dignified his personal appearance attractive.

Another report from Vancourt. "He is dead."[5] If half is true what his once loving wife speaks of him, his bodily and spiritual corruption is complete. Such conduct brings not only shame upon the German reformed church but upon the whole Christian Church. Viewing the Matter from a human stand point his influence for evil is larger than a whole noble disinterested Christian life will influence for good. It seems now certain that he had made an attempt to take his own life though his first efforts proved fruitless. Here in Swamp he was successor in the pastorate of the German reformed Congregation to Rev. Hoffman,[6] who had committed suicide, and on whose conduct he heaped so bold sensure. Now himself goes and acts more disgracefully. God may judge him in Mercy. But his poor widow with six children—May He not forsake. He is the father of orphans that do his will.

Visited after funeral at William Mensch's. They are apparently doing well.

Talked freely and copiously with the whole family on current gossip of the day. Of course, they dislike my politics and my labors of the past five months. Those topics as well as my religious belief, which is different from theirs, were not introduced. And so they were quite well pleased with me this time. If circumstances were of such a character, that we could speak freely on these topics our friendship would be more intimate and also more productive of good to both parties. Whoredom, which is so prevalent in these parts, according to "They say," and its freequent results "bad diseases," were spoken off.

Owing to the expectation that Sister Katie and Mary Fryer would come there after supper, I stayed there longer. They came. By the time it was prop[o]sed to leave it commenced raining. Waiting seemed to make the matter worse. And yet leave we would and leave we must. Having failed in their importun[it]ies to keep us till next day, they hunted up old umbrellas (for each one).

We sallied forth at half past eight into the darkness, made worse by the rain. Yet not one dares to wish the rain would stop. Several times during our wearisome trip it seemed as if the rain would be over by the time we would get home. We came home safe in due time with the consciousness that Mary Fryer (She was most familiar with the route) did her part well as a pilot, (though she got sometimes into the gutters and once it was feared we should come beside the bridge), that it *might* have been much worse; for just after we got home the rain came down in good earnest. A good shower followed, yet I wished for more.

1. JY originally wrote "the" and then substituted "men."

2. JY originally wrote "the" and then substituted "England."

3. JY originally wrote "to" and then substituted "some."

4. JY originally wrote "hold" and then substituted "slave."

5. JY must have meant that Vancourt had metaphorically died, as Vancourt resigned from the church sometime before Oct. 1866 and was "deposed from the office and functions of the sacred ministry." In 1885 and 1886 petitions circulated to have Vancourt restored to the ministry. Falkner Church's historian Gary Hauze does not indicate the petitioners were successful, however. He described Vancourt as "one of Swamp's most gifted preachers, so far as oratory is concerned, but who failed to wholly consecrate himself, in heart and life and voice, to the service of his Master." Vancourt died in Gilbertsville in 1889 and was buried in the cemetery in Boyertown. *Falkner Church History*, 49–50.

6. According to Hauze, Andrew Hoffman was from Kreuznach, Germany (in the Palatinate), became pastor of the Falkner Swamp Reformed Church in 1833, and was Falkner Swamp's last minister of foreign birth and education. Hoffman attempted to operate independently of the Reformed Synod, which proved his undoing. He resigned in July 1858 and committed suicide on 5 March 1860, at age sixty-two. (Hauze translated the German on Hoffman's tombstone to arrive at Hoffman's death date.) *Falkner Church History*, 40–43. Curiously, Hoffman was listed in the 1860 Montgomery County census for New Hanover township, dated 7 June 1860, as being seventy-two years old and an "O.S. Pres. Clerg'm." Hoffman's birthplace was given as Baden, Germany (located not far from Kreuznach). His name appears three households after Robert A. Vancourt, also described as an "O.S. Pres. Clerg'm" (both p. 448). The 1850 census (for the same township and county as 1860), however, gave Hoffman's correct age at that time of fifty-two and his birthplace as Germany (p. 174).

Thursday, 2 August 1866

Vegetation wears a new aspect this morning. A little observation proved that the rain did not come far beneath the surface. But the sultry state of the atmosphere promised fair for and addition[al] refreshment.

Went to Post offices at first was "Nix for you this morning." At Boyertown received two letters one from Clem Comly and one from Mary. This was full of interest though not all pleasant news. I know not what to do. And if I had not so high an opinion of the doctrine of obedience to parents I know not what I would do. I think I would advise her to leave at once. There is a time when forbearance ceases to be a virtue. I rather think that time has has come. I know if I was in similar circumstances with any parents I would effect a dissolution *at once* in labors and my presence. Such are trying times. But "it shall not worry" me. As well might you compel to rivers to roll back its waters, as you might keep me from "worrying," when a woman's rights—natural an[d] inalienable rights are so wholly ignored, and placed in its stead comtempt and abuse. And yet apparently I have nothing to say about it. If it is known that I care about it, [it] is only made worse. God where circumstances have rendered impractible and almost impossible the execusion of my will in this matter, let *thine*, which is infallible, *be do[n]e.*

Mother is again displeased with Katie. There is little use for it. Peace and general good will should be the rule in the worst families, and not the exception. Why will persons thus destroy so inwisely their own happiness? Can they never reflect and strike upon some other rule.

Wrote a letter to Mr. Thomas Gable,[1] Cherryville, Northampton Co., Penna. A note from A. K. Shanner,[2] Pottstown offering me a situation as teacher of secondary school of Pottstown. Salary is $35.00/100. This is the most objectionable part. I have no inclination to accept it. If it was forty five I would.

Penmanship was the order of the afternoon, Evening had by A. H. Dotterer.[3] Had a long private interview with him. It will be long remembered without record.

1. Thomas M. Gable was from Northampton, Pa., and attended Millersville Normal School in 1861–1862. *Catalogue, 1860–61*, 10.

2. Aaron Shaner was listed in the 1860 census as a twenty-five-year-old "teacher of common school" in Pottstown. Pennsylvania Census, 1860, Montgomery County, Pottstown Borough, 783.

3. An Abraham H. Dotterer was a private in the 11th Regiment, Pennsylvania Militia, in Sept. 1862. Hauze, *Falkner Church History*, 47.

Friday, 3 August 1866

A cool morning. Wrote a note to A. K. Shaner Pottstown, informing him that I will not apply for the situation in P[ottstown]. Mr. David Erb[1] called in, telling me that Mr. Fred Stauffer desires to see me this evening[2] to rent me his school. Will obey that call though there is little prospect that I can rent it from him. Rent is too high.

Immediately after dinner was to Mr. Mensch's to bring home their umbrellas. They were sociable and gay. Returned at 2½ P.M. Now I am writing. This day I have parted with mustaches. Wrote a note to John Dotterer.

Read the news of the successful operation of the Atlantic Cable.[3] Grand achievment by perseverance. Peace declared in Europe. Good news.

Had a consultation with Mr. F. H. Stauffer. The result was an agreement to let me take possession of Mou[n]t Pleasant Seminary on Monday Aug. 20, 1866.

Wrote a note to Mr. J. W. Shoemaker informing him that I can not attend his school next week, according to engagement.

1. The 1860 Pennsylvania census lists two David Erbs. The first lived in Douglass township, Montgomery County (p. 28), home community of JY. That David Erb was a fifty-four-year-old shoemaker. The other David Erb lived in New Hanover township, Montgomery County (p. 462), and was a thirty-year-old tanner.

2. JY originally wrote "fall" and then substituted "evening."

3. The Atlantic cable had been successfully laid in 1858 as a telegraph link between Ireland and Newfoundland. In 1866 improvements made the cable link permanent. Thomas J. Johnson, *The Oxford Companion to American History* (New York, 1966), 47–48.

Saturday, 4 August 1866

Wrote a note to Mary. Prepared an advertisement for "Boyertown Bauer."[1] Its substance is as follows:

Mount Pleasant Seminary.

This institution, founded 1851, will commence its semi-annual session Aug. 20. This session is subdivided into two terms of eleven weeks with a short vacation intervening.

During this term full attention will be given to the Common English Branches. By special arrangements classes in Elementary Latin, Higher Mathematics, Higher English Grammar, Bookkeeping, History, Philosophy, Physiology, Vocal and Instrumental music, can be accomodated.

The proprietor will spare no efforts to make Mou[n]t P. S. nurserey for the young in which industry, economy, and happiness flourish. While the principal will not remain satisfied, until it will be a school in which they are efficiently taught intellectually, socially, and morally.

None but *regular* students will be admitted and none but *diligent* ones will be allowed to remain.

Boarding per week $3.00
Tuition per qu[a]r. $4.50 to 7.50
Washing, lights and fuel reasonable
For further information apply to Principal Boyertown Aug. 4, 1866

                                   J. E. Yoder, Principal
                                   F. H. Stauffer, Proprietor

Took it to printing office. Visited at various places in B.
Returned home at ten P.M.

1. *Der Boyertown Bauer*, begun in 1858, was the local German-language newspaper (with advertisements in English and a column in "Pennsylvania Dutch"). *Bauer* means farmer in German. *George P. Rowell and Company's American Newspaper Directory* (New York, 1869), 92, 158; *United States Newspaper Program National Union List*, 4th ed. (Dublin, Ohio, 1993), fiche card 4.

Sunday, 5 August 1866

Read Morning Star carefully a great deal of good reading matter.

Attended worship at swamp in the German Reformed Church. A Minister from Ohio officiated. He collects funds for building a church there. Afternoon visited Sunday School at Swamp Creek. Spoke to it briefly and unprepared, and hence unsuccessfully. Mr. A. S. Stauffer called in the evening.

Monday, 6 August 1866

Rose early, wrote short advertisements for Pottstown Ledger, Reading Adler, Berks County Journal.[1] Ran to Boyertown for postoffice. Was too late. Returned till nine P.M.

Wrote a note to Jesse Erb[2]: one to Mary.

Visited afternoon at Peter Lievengood's.[3] Had a good sociable chat. Used too freely strong tobacco. Had a restless night in consequence. What is this tobacco yet destined to do for me?

Mr. Lievengood took occasion to tell me what he thinks of the present condition of things. His views on this subject are of course erroneous but he deserves some credit for what he does know about the world in other respects.

1. The *Pottstown Montgomery Ledger* was established in 1845 and was an independent weekly. The *Reading Adler*, established in 1797 and known as the *Readinger Adler* until 1868, was a German-language Democratic weekly. Presumably the *Berks County Journal* was really the *Berks and Schuylkill Journal*, established in Reading in 1816 and a Republican weekly. *American Newspaper Directory* (1869), 101; *United States Newspaper Program*, fiche card 4.

2. The 1860 Pennsylvania census index shows one Jesse Erb, age fourteen, who was living in the Frederick township, Montgomery County, household of Daniel Stetter (p. 47).

3. Peter Lievengood was listed in the 1860 Montgomery County census (Douglass township), as a forty-five-year-old farmer (p. 14).

Tuesday, 7 August 1866

A cool morning. Rose late. Serious and earnest thoughts passed through my mind concerning yesterdays proceedings. Fixed a little out doors. Public Ledger contradicts all that was in the papers a few days ago about the successful operation of the Atlantic Cable. All dispatches a humbug. So it goes. Who does it?

Made a trip to P. O. but in vain. After returning made hog pen. Practised a great deal penmanship. Wrote a note to Isaac Borneman,[1] Frederick Institute.

When engaged at the hog pen the hen lice made such a terrible raid upon me that I thought for a time they would conquer me. I came off however without any serious injury. I have no doubt but some of the intruders had their limbs lost in[2] the engagement.

Read a brief sketch of General John W. Geary's public life and services. It is is bright. Read its opposite. Not with pleasure though. I did not know before that General Geary was such a *leading* man as he must be. It is not possible that the people of Pennsylvania prefer a Heister Clymer for their Goovner to General Geary. It would be a disgrace for them if they did.

Had an interview with mother respecting her pecuniary affairs. I ended, however, in a different channel. I reminded her of her faultfinding disposition. It was painful to do this: and it was painful to her to hear it. Yet I thought she would profit by it. I did also remind myself, she did not, of paying her duly for my board during my stay with her. It is but right that I should do this.

Read Mr. I. B. Hankey's advertisement in the "Bauer" for his school. It surprised me a little. He seems to be in earnest about building his school. If I knew that he means to keep up his school I would not start my school: for both must fail this way.

Went again to post office. Waited for Mr. I. S. Erb. He had promised to call to see me. But he did not come. I wished *so much* he would come.

1. Isaac Borneman may have been the fifteen-year-old son (in 1860) of Isaac Borneman, a farmer listed in the Montgomery County census for New Hanover township (p. 468).

2. JY originally wrote "by" and then substituted "in."

Wednesday, 8 August 1866

Weather is dry. Called to see A. Dotterer. Wrote a letter to Fletcher Early[1] (colored) Lynchburg. Received a letter from Mary.

Attending prayermeeting at Henry Gilbert's. During services my mind was to much engaged with the things of this world. Called at P. Y. Brendlinger's[2] for students. Had promised two.

1. Fletcher Early was listed in the 1870 Campbell County, Virginia, census, as a thirty-five-year-old resident of Lynchburg who worked in a tobacco factory (p. 540A).

2. P. Y. Brendlinger was listed in the 1860 Berks County, Pennsylvania census (Colebrookdale township) as Peter Y. Brendlinger, a thirty-seven-year-old merchant (p. 164).

Thursday, 9 August 1866

Last night we were favored with a most blessed rain. I was too glad when[1] I heard the joyful noise of the dribbling rain. Retired late. Was disturbed in sleep. Rose early by reason of the intended trip. In my journey to Mother before breakfast I was caught in a shower.

Went out for scholars in the morning. Failed to get any. Learned that Mr. I. B. Hankey is stretching every nerve to get scholars. I suppose I must do the same. I almost got discouraged. Took heart again. Wrote as note to Fred Stauffer to be wide awake. One to Hiram Stauffer. At Noon I left home to make a trip to Englesville,[2] Little Oley,[3] Gablesville, and Boyertown. Returned at ten P.M. Had promised me six pupils for certain and about as many doubtful and as many sure—but not at the present time.

Last night it was feared I would get into the storm at Bills.[4] There was no storm in doors but out doors. Storm came in the afternoon.

Received a letter from Hiram Stauffer. Drunk Ale for medicinal purposes.

1. JY originally wrote "that" and then substituted "when."

2. Engelsville was a small town located one mile southeast of Boyertown.

3. Little Oley was located just south of Engelsville.

4. JY's brother William.

Friday, 10 August 1866

Wrote a note to Jonathan Geyer; one to Aaron Engle.[1] Left in the morning for students. Making for Boyertown, first, then New berlin, Bechtelsville,[2] and[3] Churchville.[4]

Lodged at Wm. Eshbach's.[5] Had the promise of three students. Met some old Friends I had not seen for a year and a half.

Went without dinner. Put in place Ale. Got soar feet. Retired late. Slept badly.

1. Aaron Engle was listed in the 1860 Berks County census (Colebrookdale township) as a thirty-two-year-old butcher (p. 158).

2. Bechtelsville is located six miles northwest of Boyertown.

3. JY originally wrote "Bechtelsville. At the latter place" and then deleted "at the latter place."

4. Churchville was a tiny borough in Berks County approximately six miles from Boyertown. Churchville is now known as Bally.

5. William Eschbach was JY's uncle (his mother's brother) and in 1860 lived in Washington township, Berks County (p. 801). Fretz, *Genealogical Record of the Descendants of Christian and Hans Meyer*, 522.

Saturday, 11 August 1866

Rose early. Had a crow[d]ed conversation with Cousin Aaron.[1] Left at seven and a half A.M. Stopped at Kulps tavern where I met a warworn veteran Mr. James McNuldy. Stopped Mr. Jacob Topps. How welcome I was! They told me that I could make sure of a student at Gideon Moser's. So I did. Thence I repared to Mrs. Moyer, saw Lizzie. They received me cordially. Came home at five P.M. very tired. Used too much tobacco these three days. Sent trunk to Boyertown. Wrote a note to Fred Stauffer.

Traveled on foot the last three days forty miles. The prospect for school is not too flattering. I have changed the time for its commencement from 20th Aug. to 13th Aug.

1. Cousin Aaron was Aaron Eschbach, William Eschbach's son (who was twenty-eight years old in 1860 and a tailor). Pennsylvania Census, 1860, Berks County, Washington Township, 801.

Sunday, 12 August 1866

A cool beginning and ending of the day, and warm midday. Attended divine Morning services at Swamp. Preaching by Rev. Grow[1] from the words: "The kingdom of heaven is not food or drink by righteousness, peace, and joy in the holy ghost."

In the afternoon visited Swamp Creek Sunday School in company with Mr. A. H. Dotterer, who made an address to it. He drew a parallel between the day school and Sunday school.

Called at Brother Williams in the Evening.

1. This was the Reverend Leonard Groh, of Saint John's Lutheran Church in Boyertown.

Monday, 13 August 1866

Rose at early dawn to prepare for a pedestrian trip to Boyertown. Was ready till five. When I arrived at[1] B., the dribbling rain which I left home had grown into a torrent shower.

Broke the fast six and a half o'clock. Fixed up school room. The rain still increased. School commenced with ten pupils, five more than Mr. Hankey had. My spirits were gloomy.—similar to the state of the weather. A classification which was the supposed work of the day was not handled very seriously. So far nearly each one has his own class. Wrote a note Mary. Made a trip home after school. Carrying a lot of books back to Boyertown. Tired I retire[d] at 9 P.M. Received knowledge [of] several new pupils.

1. JY originally wrote "the" and then substituted "at."

Tuesday, 14 August 1866

Rain, rain, and rain all day. Five new pupils. One of them a boarder. I was not quite so low spirited today. I have seen already that so many small children do not bring a benefit to my school and few of them still less. They divide the attention too much.

Fifteen pupils. Prepared a class register to day. Received a bill of charges for school advertisement. It is $1.75. Paid $.50 for erection of German Reformed Church Building in Defiance Ohio. Made fo[u]r trips to store. Received letter Rev. Geo. W. Sisson, Va. A great deal of time is wasted in classifying my school at its present rate of attendance. Met Hankey, Jacob Stauffer, and company. They are all cheerful, sociable,[1] and friendly.

Gave the first lesson in penmanship.

Prepared reading, or elocution lesson and arithmetic lesson and bible lesson. Called at Mr. J. Swineharts. Am again impressed with the necessity of Stringent order in and out of school.

My boarder retired early. He is not a very wild one. If he only does not get homesick.

Very heavy rains late in the evening.

1. JY originally wrote "and" and then substituted "sociable."

Wednesday, 15 August 1866

Clouds are passing away. A most beautiful day! It is really soul inspiring! Had three new scholars. This makes the number eighteen. I have three or four lazy ones, but they keep me busy. The subject for object-lesson was water and rain. Completed Class register and made a programme of recitations. Fred Stauffer's seems to be displeased about something. I dont know what. Wrote a note Aaron

Engel. Mr. Jeremiah Swinehart made me [a] present of a ruler as a "setting out." Made a trip over to brother "Abe" with my "Boarder." Received a good letter from Mary: answered it with a long talk.

Thursday, 16 August 1866

Seventeen pupils. General Information lesson was atmosphere. School worked more satisfactorily than yesterday, one new pupil. Two were absent. Swept room after school. After supper plowed for Mr. Fred Stauffer. Then was in search of a corn-thief in Mr. Jerry Shaffer's cornfield. How he swore at him.

Attended Sunday School Teacher's Meeting. Neglected work for tomorrow.

Wrote a letter to I. S. Erb and Albert Stauffer. Retired 11 o'clock P.M.

Friday, 17 August 1866

Nineteen pupils. Air continued for general information lesson. A good forenoon; but a poor afternoon. David Erb called to see our school. After school went home for books and clothing.

Returned at ten. Fixed lampshade. Then Mr. Fred Stauffer called in; he left twelve o'clock P.M.

Saturday, 18 August 1866

Prepared early for trip up country. By mistake I had to wait. Then I read the address to the National Convention in Philadelphia.[1] I consider the affair a fruitful source of wickedness in our beloved land. We radicals will never stop the strife till right will be victorious. It can not bring them honor. At best they can heap up disgrace for themselves.

Made a trip, in company with Mr. David Erb to Oley & Landes tavern,[2] places which I never saw before, though the farthest is only twelve or thirteen miles distant.

Most person[s] I was after were not at home. Returned five o'clock P.M. Spend the remainder miscellaneous work. Worked for hours at a problem in Partial Payments, but without obtaining the book answer. Weary and dull I committed my body and soul to the watchful care of omnipotence.

1. The National Union Convention that met in Philadelphia on 14 Aug. 1866 offered an opportunity for proponents of Andrew Johnson's presidential style of Reconstruction to coalesce into a unified party that would draw enough Republican votes in the autumn election

ultimately to demolish the Radical party. Behind-the-scenes dissention, however, prevented such unity, and after Johnson's disastrous "Swing Around the Circle" campaign that followed, the 1866 elections allowed the Radicals to take command of Congress and sealed the fate of Johnson and his brand of Reconstruction. Foner, *Reconstruction: America's Unfinished Revolution*, 264–271.

2. Oley and presumably Landes Tavern as well were located in Oley township, situated two townships to the west of Colebrookdale township in Berks County.

Sunday, 19 August 1866

Read "morning star." Many people of Boyertown went to Camp Meeting, in Upper Millford.[1] Visited divine services at Church. Rev. Groh preached.

After noon attended Sunday School. Taught a class of one. Attended preaching in the evening. It was English service.

1. Upper Millford township was located in Lehigh County on the northeastern Berks County border.

Monday, 20 August 1866

Three new pupils. Called at Mr. John Stauffer's. Retired Early. Had a letter from Mary.

Tuesday, 21 August 1866

One new pupil. Four old ones absent. Only 19 present. Some [of] these were at the examination. Two of them were examined. Wrote two notes. Was home after school. Worked till ten o'clock preparing for tomorrows studies. I ho[p]e we may have a good day. Must pay more attention to penmanship in school.

Wednesday, 22 August 1866

Fixed up my room by putting in a desk and old book case. Hemmed a towel. Made a trip to Gablesville. Received a letter from I. Erb. A great Republican meeting was held at Reading. This was a most gloomy day to me.

I was most shamefully humiliated by being stuck with a simple problem in Algebra. I learn more by my teaching than I ever did by teaching.

Thursday, 23 August 1866

Rained almost without clouds. This rain must not be agreeable to the camp meeting folks. School work was more satisfactory to day. Boyertown was the subject for object lesson. Received a letter from Albert Stauffer.

Made a tour to Morysville.[1] Attended Teachers meeting which was doing business for celebration. Or making arrangements for it.

Bought stuff for a suit of clothes. Retired Early.

1. Morysville was located near Boyertown in Colebrookdale township.

Friday, 24 August 1866

Cool morning. Twenty pupils. Elementary sounds of the English Language. The school worked pretty. But Declamation class did not do so well as had expected. There is room for improvement. Gave to Grammar Classes an exercise on noun[s] in the School Room. The one in each class that will write the greatest number till Monday night will get a prize of the value of twenty five cents.

Received a letter from Shoemaker. Answered it.

Saturday, [25] 26 August 1866

Made a trip home, stopping at Gilbertsville.[1] Wrote a note to Mary. Wrote also one to Ed Houck. Fixed class Roll for next week. Called at John Fegley's and J. Swinehart's. Rev Vancourt was here in Boyertown this week. His wife was here and made a great story against him. Now he has an opposite one. Whom shall I believe? Practised Penmanship. I have learned today that I am not persevering enough and not selfconfidented enough to accomp[l]ish any[thing] in the world. I commence a great deal but do not finish enough.

1. JY originally wrote "Boyertown" and then substituted "Gilbertsville."

Sunday, 26 August 1866

A cool fine day. It has been a busy day. Some folks from here were up to the Bower's station[1] camp Meeting. I read a portion of Watt's Improvement on the mind.[2] This suggested many practical thoughts for the school room, which I took note of in my school Memorandum. Mr. Stauffer's had a great deal of company. Wrote one[3] note and two letters; one to Albert Stauffer one to Brother Jonathan.

Attended Sunday [school]. Nobody was present. So I had to open it. I did it with the greatest reluctance. For such reasons as I have, I made a poor thing out of it.

In the morning I had the company of several boys. This evening Miss Annie Stauffer called in. Afterwards I went to tavern to get a drink of brandy as medicine.

1. Bower's or Bower's Station was located in Maxatawny township in northern Berks County.

2. Isaac Watts, *The Improvement of the Mind, To Which is Added, A Discourse on the Education of Children and Youth*, 1st Am. ed. (New York, 1819). The work was originally published in London in 1741.

3. JY originally wrote "to" and then substituted "note."

Monday, 27 August 1866

Six new students. Twenty six in attendance. Not as many new ones as I had expected. This disappointment with the dullness and laziness of some of those that came made my work for the day most discouraging. Oh, how gloomy! Mr. Dotterer[1] is assisting two hours a day. The grammar classes had a trial, to see who could get the greater number of nouns in the schoolroom. They did admirably. The prizes for each class were twenty five cents. The one Mr. Charles Keely in the higher class had written 432 and Jacob Ludwig in the small class 319.

After school went up to brother Jonathan['s] where they, being short of hand, set me to work. Mr. Fred Stauffer brought in german letter to read. At last we were able to read it. Retired at eleven o'clock P.M. Object stones.

1. James Dotterer, from Trappe, Pa., became JY's assistant at Mount Pleasant Seminary.

Tuesday, 28 August 18[66]

Object lesson. Apples. Twenty five pupils. Received a letter from Mary. Wrote one to Mary. All sunshine.

Wednesday, 29 August 1866

Twenty pupils. Object lesson Sugar. Bible lesson Luke Chap. 17. The work not so pleasant. Attended prayer meeting at Henry Gilberts. It was a good time. When I came home Mr. Stauffer handed me a letter which had to be answered yet, which was not finished before Midnight. Retired at 12 3/4 A.M.

Thursday, 30 August 1866

Twenty seven pupils. Trees object lesson. All sunshiny, taken both ways. School worked very well. Was very busy in every way.

Corrected compositions. They are good. Received a book by mail on german penmanship. Stopped the use of tobacco in school room.

Friday, 31 August 1866

Grammar class failed so badly. 24 pupils. Read compositions. They were good. One was too good. Swept school room after school.

Had a letter from Mary. With its requests[1] I can not comply.

1. JY originally wrote "contents" and then substituted "requests."

Saturday, 1 September 1866

Made ready to go Philadelphia. Was too late for stage. Then went to celebration. Weather fair. It was a grand turnout. Nine Sabbath Schools were represented. About two thousand people present. Two good speeches. One Lutheran Minister of Pottstown one[1] by Dechant.[2] Mr. Bower and Dr. Bowman called to see me in the evening.

1   JY originally wrote "of" and then substituted "one."

2. Augustus L. Dechant was a pioneer in the Sunday school movement in the Reformed Church and was severely criticized by the more-conservative members for this innovation. Many Reformed congregants were concerned about the effects of liberal education and distrusted the advent of the Sunday school movement. They feared that by having the Sunday schools for religious teachings parents would renounce their responsibility to ensure their children's spiritual growth. Since the Reformed Church functioned as a religious school six days a week and gave instruction in "the matters of life," these conservatives thought that Sunday schools would become a substitute for that everyday teaching. Moreover, the Sunday school movement espoused a "freer theology" than that accepted by the Reformed Church. Dechant promoted and organized the Union Sunday School, which opened in Apr. 1853 in the public school house near Swamp Creek. As a result, in Mar. 1854 the consistory of the Falkner Swamp Reformed Church prohibited Dechant from preaching there as long as the Lutherans who shared Falkner Swamp Church's facilities would not allow a Reformed minister to address their members.

Dechant and a Lutheran minister both spoke at the Sunday school celebration JY describes in this diary entry. It would appear that the Lutherans embraced the idea of sabbath schools more readily than did the Reformed Church members. JY also embraced the idea of Sunday schools as he attended and taught them. In 1890, Dechant returned to Falkner Swamp

Church and preached a German sermon at the centennial anniversary. Hauze, *Falkner Church History*, 43–44, 58.

Sunday, 2 September 1866

Attending preaching and Sunday school where[1] I heard a class. Wrote a note to G. W. Sisson. A letter to Mary.

1. JY originally wrote "and" and then substituted "where."

Monday, 3 September 1866

Very warm day. Three new pupils. 28 present. General lesson "celebration." All seemed to be stupid as myself. After school I was home for money & c, but I did not receive any. But I was caught in the rain. Wasn't I wet through and through?

Very heavy rain. Received a letter from Robert Turner. Wrote a note to Rev. Colder. Did a great deal of miscellaneous business. Bible Lesson Acts 3, chap. Practised penmanship. Read a good letter in the star. Retired 10:45.

Tuesday, 4 September 1866

Foggy morning. Gloomy too. Well Amanda is absent again! Weather very hot. 28 pupils. Object lesson is a bird which I found last night in my room. Heard of several new students. Mr. Hankey has an assistant. All things passed off pleasantly. But I kept 4[1] pupils in for failing in their lessons. Read the Morning star; it is quite interesting. The Union Convention is in progress at Philadelphia. Labored at Circular.[2] A letter from Eisenberg.

1. JY originally wrote "in" and then substituted "4."

2. This was the 1866–1867 issue of the *Circular: Mount Pleasant Seminary* (Boyertown, Pa.), that Yoder had printed in Philadelphia. A copy of the 1851–1852 circular can be seen at the Schwenkfelder Library, Pennsburg, Pa. It lists the staff, describes the school and its purposes, and gives the requirements for students, as well as religious and cultural aspects of the school and the expenses for attending.

Wednesday, 5 September 1866

Weather fair. School worked to good satisfaction. Thirty pupils. Object lesson, Iron. Bible lesson The Parable of the kings wedding. Had a letter from Mary. Worked at night at circular.

Thursday, 6 September 1866

Read accounts of the opening of Philadelphia Union Convention. Speeches by different Members. Had a letter from Heilman. Twenty nine pupils. General lesson Mainspring in a watch. Bible Lesson "Prodigal son." Wrote a note Mary. Worked late at circular. Attended teacher-meeting.

Friday, 7 September 1866

Twenty nine pupils. Speeches were an improvement on those of two weeks ago. Read in English literature considerable.

Saturday, 8 September 1866

Windy weather. Made out the aggregate of progress and conduct marks for last month. Read "the Guardian" a monthly magazine.[1] Had a letter from Mary. A little fairer prospect for school. Visited and received calls. I stood up nobly against temptation. But when the tempter came a second time, I yielded almost without opposition. Night was full of dreams. I was in argument with Mr. Lewis Worman[2] about Sunday School affairs. To be honest about the matter he flaxed[3] me.

1. The *Guardian*, published in Lancaster, Pa., between 1850 and 1890, was the journal of the Reformed Church. In 1885 it was merged with the *Reformed Missionary Herald* to form the *Missionary Guardian*. On-line search of OCLC, On-line Computer Library Center, Inc., Dublin, Ohio.

2. Lewis S. Worman was a saddler and harness maker in Boyertown. *Boyertown Business Directory*, 1. Copy in editor's possession.

3. To flax is to thrash or beat.

Sunday, 9 September 1866

Rose late. The day is not yet spent. How is it to be spent—in honor, or in dishonor? This Sunday O blessed day! Was in Mennonite Meeting.[1] Listened to the reading of a little politics. Read choice extracts of H. W. Beechers. They are choice too. Oh! valuable is such literature! Subscribed for the Independent. Changed address of Sunday School Times.

Was out a little to enjoy the beautiful weather. How very delightful it is! It could not possible be prettier. The air is so soft and cool. Vegetation is so fresh as in spring but enriched by the ripe fruit. "Breathe there a man with soul so dead whose heart ne'er within him burns," as his eye over vale and hill he turns. Can man look on all this and still be ignorant of God's goodness? God thy works are perfect. But this makes our sin-staind characters appear still more deformed.

God, thou are good to let our eyes behold such beauty. May this privilege not be given in vain to me.

Visited Isaac Steinruck[2] who has leg broken.

1. JY's parents were members of the Boyertown Mennonite Church, and he and his family had attended church there when JY was a boy.

2. Isaac Steinruck (spelled Stinerook in the 1860 census) was a forty-eight-year-old farmer in 1860 who lived in Limerick township just north of Douglass township where JY lived. Pennsylvania Census, 1860, Montgomery County, Limerick Township, 195.

Monday, 11 [10][1] September 1866

Fairwether. Two new students. Thirty two in attendance. Modes of conveyance was the subject for object lesson. 15th chap. proverbs in the bible. This was none of brightest days. Variety o[f] business after school and little of any kind.

1. JY misdated his diary entries from Monday through Friday, 10–14 Sept., correctly dated Saturday, 15 Sept., and misdated again Sunday through Tuesday, 16–18 Sept. 1866.

Tuesday, 12 [11] September 1866

Weather cloudy. My spirit more so. The lessons went too poorly. If it would go so I would not teach out this quarter. I can not tell any body how bad I felt. I don't know where the fault was. It seemed a thousand things conspired together to worry. The never failing students failed. The inclement weather forbid to keep them in. I prayed to God that he would destroy the effects this days conduct [had] in me or the students so that I may not have an evil influence.

Newspa[pe]rs was the lesson in general Information. In the Bible The ten Virgins.

Thirty Pupils were in to day. The attendance was very good for such weather. The failure is so much worse. To effect a climax in worriment, Mr. Brunner[1] came in when the spelling class failed so badly. I do not know what can compensate for such failures. It must be in an unknown way.

Read a part of president Johnson's speeched, delivered at St. Louis.[2] This was not at all intended to cheer me up. What is he about? He talks like a petty politician, soliciting votes. He loses all dignity becoming a president of the U.S.

I fear he is a most dangerous man in our country. If he continues to act yet a while as he does, all his influence will be gone. In that way the country may hope to get saf[e]ty. It seems in no other. Was disappointed in not getting my circulars this evening.

How can I bear up with all that works against me to day. To morrow I think will only come to disappoint me. What will I anticipate evils for tomorrow. Sufficient unto the day is the evil thereof.

Read a letter to Mr. Ward Beecher setting forth B'S inconsistency in politics. Well he does it too.

My health suffers under my present confined labors.

Labored well and long till eleven. The wind is howling through the cracks.

1. William Harrison Brunner was an acquaintance of JY from Millersville Normal School. Brunner attended the school from 1860 to 1862. *Catalogue, 1860–61*, 8; *1861–62*, 8; among JY's papers there is an undated autograph by Wm. H. Bruner, Columbia, Lancaster County, Pa. Yoder Diaries, 1861–1864, Acc. 27680, p. 120, LVA.

2. President Johnson's ill-fated Aug.–Sept. "Swing Around the Circle" campaign to Cleveland, Chicago, Detroit, and Saint Louis and points in between allowed the Radicals to embarrass him by planting hecklers in the crowds along the way. The poorly educated and unrefined president, who had learned his speechmaking in the rough-and-tumble world of backwoods Tennessee politics, was an easy target for his enemies. His 8 Sept. speech in Saint Louis proved to be the worst disaster of the tour. By that time, having long since lost the sympathy of his audiences, Johnson became incoherent and babbled on to the jeers of the crowd. He blamed the 30 July 1866 New Orleans riots—begun by Confederates veterans in the city police who broke up the gathering of a reconvened state constitutional convention by engaging in the "wholesale slaughter" of convention delegates and their black supporters—on Radicals in that city and in Congress. Many northerners thought that it was Johnson's lenient Reconstruction policy that had caused the "massacre." In his "jumbled tirade," Johnson claimed that he had been called Judas Iscariot. When he suggested that the Radicals would find some pretext if they took control of the next Congress to vacate the presidency, someone answered, "Too bad they don't impeach him." On 24 Feb. 1868, the House of Representatives resolved to do so. Foner, *Reconstruction: America's Unfinished Revolution*, 262–265; Eric L. McKitrick, *Andrew Johnson and Reconstruction* (Chicago, 1960), 14, 422–430, 435–436.

Wednesday, 13 [12] September 1866

All the clouds in the heavens have passed away. Those in my mind are still hovering over me. But their stay was not long. The day was bright. It seems strange that such a cloudy day can be followed by such a bright day. Wrote a gloomy note to Mary. Was very greatly disappointed with my circulars. I saw to day a flock of blackbirds wheel about in succession on the top of a hill which formed a most beautiful sight.

Received the first of of the Independent which I read.

Thursday, 14 [13] September 1866

The day was very fair—*so* bright. Called a meeting of the defunct Philomathean literary Society.[1] Five old members met and three new ones.

A sad thing I did, or a thing that I did with great reluctance. I did not take the circulars that Mr. Leaver[2] printed for me.

Object lesson, Roofs of Houses. Bible lesson, Zaccheus. Thirty one[3] pupils. A canvasser for bible was here.

If every day would be as bright as this day my school would be prosperous in a short time. But if every day would be as dark as monday I fear the school would be broken up in less than two weeks.

Attended Teachers Meeting. I did well enjoy it. Spoke to Mr. Jacob Hankey[4] about politics. Visited at Mr. J. Swineharts. Got some new Ideas in regard to Bible lesson.

1. By the mid-nineteenth century, literary societies had become an important adjunct to the regular curriculum at institutions like Millersville Normal School and served as a training ground for writing, speaking, and reasoning. One such society was the Philomathean Society—one of the earliest was established at the University of Pennsylvania in 1813. A *philomath* is someone who loves learning. While Millersville Normal did not style either of its literary societies *Philomathean*, JY mentioned in his 1861–1864 diary that in Mar. 1864 he had made coal oil purchases for the Philomathean Literary Society, no doubt a local group to which he belonged. Yoder Diaries, 1861–1864, Acc. 27680, pp. 110, 111, 113, LVA; Graver, *History of the First Pennsylvania State Normal School*, 220.

2. Samuel Leaver was the editor of the *Boyertown Bauer*. In 1860 he was forty-five years old and two of his children, Catharine (age fifteen) and Henry (age thirteen), were typesetters. His household also contained John Austin (age forty-five), a printer. His oldest child, Mary Ann (age eighteen), however, was listed with no occupation given. Pennsylvania Census, 1860, Berks County, Colebrookdale Township, 173.

3. JY originally wrote "three" and then substituted "one."

4. Jacob Cornelius Hankey was a brother of Isaac B. Hankey who ran Kallynean Academy, which opened at the same time as JY's school and thus competed with JY. Montgomery, *Historical and Biographical Annals of Berks County*, 1:257.

Friday, 15 [14] September 1866

A good day. 26 pupils. Object lesson Building Material. Bible lesson "Freed my lambs."

Swept school room after school. Had several showers of rain. Got assessed, also Mr. Hankey.[1] We had a party five gentlemen and three ladies. I did talk a great deal. This I don't do very often. While a great deal of the conversation was nonsense, I hope it was innocent and healthy for me.

Read the Last Letter of Day in a Foreign country. An interesting sketch of "Copernicus."

1. That is, paid his local taxes. In his 1864 expense records, JY mentioned getting a tax of $0.15 apiece from several people (presumably students in his school) in Apr. and paying a tax of $2.13 "to J. Schweisfort" on 7 May. Yoder Diaries, 1861–1864, Acc. 27680, pp. 111, 118, LVA.

Saturday, 15 September 1866

This was an expensive day. Came to Pottstown with morning Stage to get circulars printed. The printers not anxious to engage the job. I at once embarked for Philadelphia. Returned to Pottstown at 5½ whence I walked over to Fairville, thence to Boyertown where I arrive at 8½, with weary limbs. Received a letter from Thomas Gable. Wrote a note to Williamson & Davis.[1] Read Atlantic Monthly.

Time was to short for my trip to Phila. Folks wished me to stay till Monday, which I could not.

1. JY was most likely referring to Samuel D. Williamson, a white Radical who, along with Samuel Kelso, would soon sit in the Virginia Convention of 1867–1868. Williamson was listed in the 1860 census as a fifty-year-old lawyer living in the western district of Campbell County and a native of Loudoun County, Va. Davis has not been identified. Richard L. Hume, "The Membership of the Virginia Constitutional Convention of 1867–68," *Virginia Magazine of History and Biography* 86 (1978): 484; Harry S. Ferguson, "Participation of the Lynchburg, Virginia, Negro in Politics, 1865–1900" (master's thesis, Virginia State College, 1950), 17; Christian, *Lynchburg and Its People*, 257; Virginia Census, 1860, Campbell County, Western District, 431. See also "Radical Speaking," *Lynchburg Virginian*, 18 Oct. 1867, p. 3, c. 1.

Sunday, 17 [16] September 1866

Weather clear but cool. Attending preaching by Latzel of Pottstown. His Text was Luke 17:17. "Are not ten cleansed. But where are the nine?" He preached long. Unthankfulness was his point in the lesson.

Rambled in the fields in the afternoon with Mr. Schuler.

Read a good deal of Atlantic Monthly.

Attended meeting at New berlin. A very young man officiated whose name is unknown to me.

Took supper at Mr. J. Swineharts. Wrote a letter to Mary.

Monday, 18 [17] September 1866

A blue Monday Again. Two new scholars. Whole number in attendance is 37. Heat is subject for object lesson.

Mr. Leaver gave me a lecturing for not taking my circulars. Mrs. Hankey lectured to Mr. Swavely for my account. Received from A. Stauffer a letter.

This seems to be a troublous time. Mr. J. Shaffer's hired man was attacked last night by a set of robbers.

Weather, which was cool yesterday, has been hot this evening.

Day was closely taken up in work. Ten students were absent. This alone tells that much was wrong. Could I only know what to do with such irregular pupils. If I can not make a changed in this I might as well stop my teaching at once.

Wrote a letter to I. S. Erb.

Tuesday, [18] September 1866

Day begins pleasantly. 31 pupils. Object lesson, Horse. Bible lesson Christs Entrance in Jerusalem. Kept two students in for non-performance. School worked to good satisfaction. Committee on resolution for[1] constitution and Bylaws met.[2]

1. JY originally wrote "met" and then substituted "for."

2. JY was probably referring to his organizational work with the local Philomathean Literary Society. See his 20 Sept. 1866 diary entry.

Wednesday, 19 September 1866

School worked well. 31 pupils. Bible lesson, "In the beginning was the word." Called Weidner's,[1] where I saw Vancourt. Before school called at Brother Abe's. Had a meeting of society. Received a letter from Mary.

Wrote a note to Pottstown Editor.

1. J. L. Weidner operated the Clothing Emporium in Boyertown. *Boyertown Business Directory*, copy in editor's possession. Jacob Weidner was listed in the 1860 Pennsylvania Census for Colebrookdale township, Berks County (p. 168), as a twenty-six-year-old tailor living in William Binder's hotel.

Thursday, 20 September 1866

Twenty 29 students. Object Lesson, Mountains. Bible lesson, Samaritan Woman. Was disappointed in not having received my circulars. Day rather bright and dull. Labored late to draft a constitution and By Laws for Philomathean Literary Society.

Wrote a note to Librarian of Normal Literary Society.[1]

1. When James P. Wickersham began what became Millersville Normal School in 1855, he recommended that two literary societies be formed. One of them was the Normal Literary Society, which was organized in Jan. 1857. Graver, *A History of the First Pennsylvania State Normal School*, 220, 224.

Friday, 21 September 1866

Heavy rain. 26 pupils. Bible lesson Stephen's execution. Object Lesson Salutation. Evening brought sore disappointment and the night sad sins. Wrote a letter to Mary.

Saturday, 22 September 1866

A cold morning. Made a trip over to brother William's on foot. Returned at ten O'clock. Fetched a half a bushel [of] apples from Jeremiah Shaffers. My long expected circulars have come at last. Deceived again with them.

Mr. Albert Stauffer called to see me and [stayed] all night.

Andrew Johnson has now fully come out with his colors. Postmaster[s] are all removed.[1]

1. One of the weapons Johnson could employ in his attempt to gain support for his brand of reconstruction was patronage. Theoretically, by replacing officeholders unsympathetic to his policies, Johnson could help the National Union movement and hurt the Radical Republicans. But he vacillated until after the Philadelphia convention. Early in Sept., while on his campaign swing, he removed twelve hundred postmasters among others. Since all he could find as replacements were Democrats, Johnson further damaged his own cause with his supporters in the Republican Party who resented such appointments. Johnson once again inadvertently aided the Radicals. Castel, *Presidency of Andrew Johnson*, 87–89.

Sunday, 23 September 1866

Talked nonsense a great part [of] the time. Read Morning Star. Attended Sunday school. At night attended prayermeeting when I was very sleepy. Wrote in Miss. Annie Stauffers Album.

The Hill Church[1] celebrated its first Centennial festival. Attendance full. Distributed circulars.

1. Hill Church (later Saint Joseph's), in Pike township, was a Reformed Church that had been Lutheran for a while in the 1700s. It was not far from Boyertown, in neighboring Colebrookdale township. Montgomery, *Historical and Biographical Annals of Berks County*, 1:49.

Monday, 24 September 1866

Twenty eight pupils. Society had a special meeting. Copied constitution for society. Recd a letter from Shoemaker and Frank Forrest. Send away more than a hundred circulars.

Tuesday, 25 September 1866

30 pupils. Government for General lesson. Send away about thirty circulars. Met Jacob Witman.[1] Jacob Holder[2] has again disappointed us. Wrote a note to Independent.

1. Jacob Stauffer Whitman was the first principal of Mount Pleasant Seminary in Boyertown. The school's founder, John Stauffer, gave Whitman charge of the new school after the latter's studies had been interrupted by poor health. JY apparently studied under Whitman and developed scholarly interests closely paralleling Whitman's own. The latter may thus have served as an early mentor to JY. Whitman soon returned to his studies, graduating from Marshall College in 1849, and eventually held important positions elsewhere. A. J. Fretz, A Genealogical Record of the Descendants of Henry Stauffer and Other Stauffer Pioneers (Harleysville, Pa., 1899), 201–206.

2. Jacob Holder may have been the Jacob B. Holder who was living in Earl township, Berks County, just west of Boyertown in 1860 and at that time was a sixty-four-year-old shoe-maker. Pennsylvania Census, 1860, Berks County, Earl Township, 221.

Wednesday, 26 September 1866

Rains all day. 27 pupils. Government for General lesson.

Society met this evening the first time for business. Six members in attendance. Wrote a letter to Mary.

Thursday, 27 September 1866

Twenty nine pupils. General Information. Analasys of Light by a prism. Weather very fair. Received a letter from Mary, one from James Colder [and] Jacob Witman. A. M. was in my school to day and addressed it to very good acceptance.

Friday, 28 September 1866

Twenty four pupils. Bible lesson the Parable of the sower. After School Attended a polictical meeting at swamp over which I presided. Robert Eschbach[1] was the favorite speacker. Arrived home at home eleven and a half P.M. Wrote a note to Shoemaker.

1. Robert Eschbach may have been the Douglass township resident found in the 1850

Montgomery County census who at that time was a twenty-four-year-old shoemaker living in the household of William Mack. He may also have been a relative of JY. Pennsylvania Census, 1850, Montgomery County, Douglass Township, 192.

Saturday, 29 September 1866

Read Morning Star and and Pottstown Ledger. Had a conversation with Mr. East[1] on politics of the day. Wrote a note to William Burr missionary Treasurer.

Rain was threatening all day but it has not come. Made a pedestrian trip to Weaver's Foundry. Here I saw the process of of casting not seen before. Bought a stove for school room.

1. D. K. East may have been Daniel East of Colebrookdale township, Berks County, who in 1850 was a thirty-six-year-old farmer. Pennsylvania Census, 1850, Berks County, Colebrookdale Township, 328. In his 1861–1864 diary, JY mentioned three financial transactions with East, one on 1 Sept. 1862 for an "Antidote for Tobacco," the second on 18 Jan. 1864 for a postage stamp and tobacco pipe, and the third on 3 Mar. 1864, repaying East for a two-dollar loan. Yoder Diaries, 1861–1864, Acc. 27680, pp. 89, 106, 108, LVA.

Sunday, 30 September 1866

A nice day. Attended church in the morning and read Sunday times. After noon taught in Sunday School a female class. Visited afterwards at brother Abe's. Here I am Mr. Joe Borneman.[1] Came home at night fall. Sinned, sorrowed, and repented.

1. Joseph H. Borneman was a Boyertown surgeon and dentist. *Boyertown Business Directory*, copy in editor's possession; Pennsylvania Census, 1860, Berks County, Colebrookdale Township, 170. See also Yoder Diaries, 1861–1864, Acc. 27680, p. 114, LVA.

Monday, 1 October 1866

Twenty nine pupils. Rev. Groh visited school. After school visited Home. Received two letters. One came by way Va. from Hiram Stauffer; one I. S. Erb. Wrote a letter to Clarke School Visitor,[1] one to Mary. Prayed, sinned and sorrowed.

1. *Clark's School Visitor* was a monthly journal originally published in Philadelphia beginning about 1856. It moved in Pittsburgh by 1866 but returned to Philadelphia by 1867 as *Our Schoolday Visitor*. With vol. 16 it became *Schoolday Magazine* and was finally absorbed by *Saint Nicholas: A Monthly Magazine for Boys and Girls* in May 1875. On-line search of OCLC, On-line Computer Center, Inc., Dublin, Ohio.

Tuesday, 2 October 1866

Twenty nine pupils. Received one new student Mr. Abraham Barto. Some of the large students were absent. Ecclesiastical court met to try Rev. Vancourt. His absence prevented action by the court. After supper I helped Mr. Fred Stauffer to cut down corn. This afforded valuable exercise.

Read and copied dialogues.

Wednesday, 3 October 1866

26 pupils. A Democratic mass meeting at Pottstown kept away from school three or more students. A cart wheel in the room for object lesson. Gave out some dialogues for Exhibition. Weather very fair. Received three papers. Read in the independent.

Thursday, 4 October 1866

Thirty one pupils. Weather very cold. Had society. Quite a good meeting. Retired at midnight.

Friday, 5 October 1866

Weather very cold. Twenty pupils. For object lesson How to know what time it is by the clock. The school worked pleasantly.

Received a letter from Mary; one from J. W. Shoemaker. Copied constitution of Philomathean Society.

Saturday, 6 October 1866

Put up a stove. Made out numbers of progress and deportment for last month. Swept room. Set copies. Received dialogues. Wrote a letter *for* Jacob. Made a trip to Gablesville.

Sunday, 7 October 1866

Heard Rev. Mayer[1] preach. Spoke briefly to Little Oley Sunday school. Read Papers. Wrote a letter to I. S. Erb.

1. Lucian J. Mayer was elected pastor of the Falkner Swamp Reformed Church on 26 June 1866, succeeding Robert A. Vancourt who had resigned in disgrace. Mayer served as pastor from 1 Oct. 1866 to 1 Oct. 1887 (having submitted his resignation on 11 Sept. 1887). He died 27 July 1903. Hauze, *Falkner Church History*, 51–56.

Monday, 8 October 1866

31 pupils. Weather very fair. At night attended political meeting. One new pupil.

Tuesday, 9 October 1866

32 pupils. Wrote 3 letters. 1 new pupils. Work of the day satisfactory. Voted for General Geary; I hope not in vain.

Worked till midnight.

Weather Gloomy.

Wednesday & Thursday, 10 [&] 11 October 1866

Gloomy weather, thirty two pupils. Geary has a majority of 17,000.

A letter from Mary.

Friday, 12 October 1866

Thirty one pupils. Copied constitution of Philomathean Society.

Saturday, 13 October 1866

Weather fair. Had exercise in picking Walnuts. Set copies. Attended to Class Register. Majority for Geary 17,125. Read papers.

Practised penmanship.

Sunday, 14 October 1866

Addressed sunday School at Bechletsville.[1] Attended meeting at New Berlin.

1. Actually, Bechtelsville, located just north of Boyertown in Washington township, Berks County. JY crossed the *l* instead of the *t*.

Monday, 15 October 1866

29 pupils. One a new comer. A prospect for more students. Wrote a note to[1] editors of the Journal. Fetched a half a bushel of apples. Carried on a dispute with Joseph Borneman on the subject of the alphabet.[2]

1. JY originally wrote "of" and then substituted "to."

2. On the next page of his diary, JY wrote "Wer," left the rest of the page blank, and then let the diary lapse until 5 Nov. 1866 when he began a new page.

Monday, 5 November 1866

Winter has set in since I wrote last. Labors have been over excessive. Difficulties were met of the most trying kind. Among them were sickness in exhibition, the expulsion of a student, and disappointments &c &c. Had become the victim of sin in various ways. But yesterday I reresolved to fight with renewed zeal against sin. My determination is not yet slackened. Spare time is used in penmanship.

Wrote a letter to Mary.

School numbered sixteen.

Musical Instruments was general Lesson.

Tuesday, 6 November 1866

Weather very fair. 18 students. Prodigal son; bible lesson. Waiter general Lesson. After school visited at Brother Abe's and Mr. William Stauffer's. Received and read Pottstown paper. Geary's Majority 17,198. I am so unused to making diary entries that I am tired of [it] already.

Monday, 12 November 1866

Weather was very fair all last week.[1] Three new scholars. Fourteen pupils in all; leaves was the general Lesson. The bible Lesson was John and Peters defense before the Jewish council after healing the impotent man.

It is more than probable that I will will have to dismiss some one or more of my pupils though so few I have.

1. JY originally wrote "night" and then substituted "week."

Saturday, 17 November 1866

School has been small this week. 14 was the average attendance. The prospect for large numbers coming is not flattering. Was out collecting some. It is a mean business. I charged too much for one.

To day I read considerable of blackstone.[1]

1. Sir William Blackstone (1723–1780) was an English jurist, a revered authority on the common law, and author of *Commentaries on the Law of England*, 4 vols. (1765–1769).

Saturday, 8 December 1866

Weather very gloomy. Busy in cleaning up. Visited Mr. Craft's school[1] in the afternoon. Read congressional news. Seventeen pupils in school this week. Those present are prospering. But the school cannot be said to prosper with such a number. I was attending protracted Methodist Meeting for two weeks preceding the present week, quite regularly. Some eight or ten persons have professed faith in Christ among whom are my brother and sister. I was taught through this meeting that I am not reconciled to God. But if I do not act accordingly this knowledge will not benefit me much. My faith is too small. It is dead—without works. Temptations are to strong, they master me in every attack. How shall I have strength for this foe.

At present I am in a most unsettled condition. This is true in almost every sense it can be taken. I do not know what to do with my school. I do not like to close it in this condition and I do not like to continue it; for it does not pay. I have again a promis of new students unless it is as it was so often before. The clouds are broken to let the last lingering rays of the sun upon our gaze. The weather for the last months has been very pleasant. I such an unworthy mortal am by no means deserving of such comforts as my the climate and my health and food afford.

My correspondence has suffered very much lately. I will and must keep up this branch of my work. Practised Penmanship. Attended meeting at New Berlin. A small Congregation. Wrote a letter to Mr. A. S. Stauffer. Did numerous and various things.

1. Alfred Craft from Pennlyn, Montgomery County, Pa., attended Millersville Normal School in 1864–1865. *Catalogue, 1864–65*, 11.

Sunday, 9 December 1866

Visited with Mary at Mr. Daniel Engels.[1] Conversation with Mr. Engel was on Religion. Attended Sabbath School after noon. Preaching in Church by Groh [in] evening. Mr. Francis Weaver[2] took supper with us.

Saw Mary home from Church. Returned home at ten and a half.

1. In 1850 Daniel K. Engels was listed in the census as a thirty-three-year-old cooper, with Mary A. Engels, age thirty-seven. In 1860, he was listed as a forty-three-year-old storekeeper and Mary was forty-seven. Pennsylvania Census, 1850, Berks County, Colebrookdale Township, 317; ibid., 1860, Berks County, Colebrookdale Township, 159.

2. Francis Weaver may have been the son of Francis Weaver who lived in the East Earl township area of Lancaster County. In 1850, the younger Weaver was fifteen years old and working on his father's farm. Ten years later his father had retired. The census that year gave the younger Francis's age as twenty-three and listed him as a day laborer living in the household of his brother David B. Weaver. Pennsylvania Census, 1850, Lancaster County, Blue Ball, 36th Election District, 190; ibid., 1860, Lancaster County, East Earl Township, 190. In his 1864 diary and papers, JY noted that he had received fifteen cents in tax from F. Weaver, among others. Yoder Diaries, 1861–1864, Acc. 27680, p. 118, LVA.

Monday, 10 December 1866

Three new pupils. Bible lesson. The Blind Man Healed. Object Lesson, "Cold." Nineteen Puples. The work of teaching was pleasant. At night debated with Joseph Borneman the Question: "Should Woman have the elective franchise?" Read papers. Prepared work for next day.

Tuesday, 11 December 1866

Weather very cold. Read Sunday S. Times. God guide me this day by thy unerring counsels. Read considerable.—Practised penmanship. Exercised in as great variety of ways. Retired late.

Wednesday, 12 December 1866

Weather fair and very cold. Made a speach in favor of women's rights question. Busy *all* day.

Thursday, 13 December 1866

A letter from Harrison Landis. Weather *very* cold. Busy—too busy. School commenced very pleasantly with a full number of twenty. Read Independent. Corrected Compositions.

Friday, 14 December 1866

Speeches good in school. After School attended a party at Charles Hagys. The performance consisting principally of Charades was interesting and profitable. But one feature of the party was detestable. It broke up at twelve. Returned home at one o'clock cold and crabbed. Retired at two.

Saturday, 15 December 1866

No work done of any value. Dozed time away. After Supper we played charades. After eight called to see mary. Spent time pleasantly. Retired at 2 P.M. with the expectation of snow when rising.

Sunday, 16 December 1866

Ground is white for first time this season. This can be called with truth ugly weather. The snow is drifting somewhat while it is falling—falling it is most rapidly. In the changes of nature we are more and more impressed with this infinitude of God. We are but slow to learn God's Attributes as we are to learn his law. And after we have learned it we are so slow to practise it.

We are so slow in "passing from animalhood to manhood." We begin an animal and are to end a[1] spirit. If life goes right at all it is a hot battle between flesh and the spirit. While the spirit is not in the ascendancy there is no rest no satisfaction. When the [flesh] triumphs the decision is not final. There is no lasting peace on that basis. If quiet permanent quiet shall reig[n] the spirit must triumphantly reign. It is hard[l]y worth the while for an ordinary man to venture any reflection on the philosophy of life. It is so misterious, so complicated, so important. Yet our intimate concern with it makes it our duty to investigate and reflect for ourselves. Notice the differences in the lives of men. Which of them are the nearest right a[nd] which of them are the furthest from right? Whose conduct is it safest to follow?

In my career their have been dark periods. I am in one now. Sometimes I know what would be best this course or that. There is considerable dissatisfaction all around. The question comes up often in my mind; "Shall I not or should I not change my manner of living?" Yes, what shall I do? Would that God would decide it for me speedily.

Attended Rev. Mayor's preaching. Read one of W. Beecher's sermons. Visited at Mr. Jeremiah Swineharts.

I am still sleepy for the lose of sleep during last week.

1. JY originally wrote "and" and then deleted "nd."

Monday, 17 December 1866

A slushy day. Only fifteen students present on account of it. Received numerous and various impressions of the propensities and weeknesses of human nature as it is exhibited in conduct from the infant to the aged.

In such a school as this world affords, can one live on without improvement in valuable practical knowledge? No, lest he dash through it with his eyes shut. But how much can I learn from my own failings? This is the most important question. May I not have learned to be more in earnest in all I do. Action is what is wanted everywhere. "Habits of Animals" was the general Lesson. 4 Chap. of Ephesians was the Bible Lesson. Played Charades with students after supper.

Visited stove and mechanics shop, So I must do my work late at night.

Tuesday, 18 December 1866

Weather milder. One new student Mr. Moyer. General Lesson "Tools of Animals." Bible Lesson John the Baptist's Preaching. Busy as busy can bee. Received a letter from Good Shoemaker. Wrote one letter to him, one to J. V. R. Ludwig one. Received two tons of coal. Planned an exhibition. Called on Mr. Henry Fegley who has just returned from School in Philad. Carried in coal. Feel very good this eve. Mr. George Witner of Oley[1] stayed with [us] for supper.

Read papers. Wrote this with a Gold pen.

1. George Witner, of Oley township, Berks County, was listed in the 1850 census (p. 8), as a forty-nine-year-old farmer. His son George was twelve years old.

Wednesday, 19 December 1866

Three out of school on account of chatechical instruction.[1] Church after school. Society after church. Saw Mary home after society. Set copies afterwards.

1. That is, instruction in Christian doctrines, morals, and discipline for those preparing to become members of the church.

Thursday, 20 December 1866

Full school. Received a letter from Henry Rhoads, Frederick Penna.[1] Attended spelling School 3 miles off at night. Thermometer zero.

1. There were two men named Henry Rhoads listed in the 1860 Pennsylvania census for Montgomery County. The more likely correspondent of JY was the Henry Rhoads given as a twenty-seven-year-old farmer living in JY's home community of Douglass township, not far from Frederick, which was also located in Montgomery County about six miles east of Gilbertsville. A second Henry Rhoads resided near Pottstown and was described in the census as a fifty-one-year-old "R.R. Boss." Pennsylvania Census, 1870, Montgomery County, Douglass Township, 234; ibid., Pottsgrove Township, 489.

Friday, 21 December 1866

School has speeches. Saw Mary in the evening and had the company of Mr. Hallman.

Saturday, 22 December 1866

Students have left for their respective homes on account of next week's vacation.

Walked to Swamp to teachers institute. It was a lame concern. It is doubtful whether destitution of knowledge can be considered a reproach to those that are engaged in teaching, yet it is nothing [less?] than a disgrace for a teacher not to exert himself to gather knowledge especially if he possesses so little.

While these Institutes are far from perfection in their manner of proceedure, marked improvement is noticable from time to time.

I took part in the exercises. By my mind was dull on account of my disregarding the laws of health during the week. Took supper with my dear mother. Repaired to Boyertown after eight o'clock where I met Mr. Orlando Fegley[1] who is now a Medical student at Phila.

1. Orlando Fegley was born 8 June 1841 in Boyertown, Pa., graduated from Pennsylvania College (now Gettysburg College) in 1863 and from the University of Pennsylvania Medical School in 1867, and died in Allentown, Pa., in 1900. Ewing Jordan, comp., *University of Pennsylvania Men Who Served in the Civil War, 1861–1865: Department of Medicine, Classes, 1864–1882* (Philadelphia, [1930]), vol. 2, pt. 2; Pennsylvania Census, 1850, Berks County, Colebrookdale Township, 321.

Sunday, 23 December 1866

Weather gloomy. Attending preaching by Rev. Grow. The Subject was "Sound in faith." He produced good reflections. Read papers. Visited at Joseph Borneman's. A great deal of the conversation was not dignified. Took supper at my brother's.

Passed the evening in reflection and reading.

Had a letter from J. W. Shoemaker. Also the first school visitor in its enlarged form. Send a note to School Visitor. Thoughts on marriage come frequently into my mind and oftener [than] they are invited to come. These are grave if not great thoughts. I can not dispose of them. The more I reflect the more perplexed I become. For a man of means I[t] may be an easy matter to take to himself a "help mate" or a to-be-helped-mate but for one of my circumstances it is too momentous to take the step. But what makes the subject still worse not to decide on this matter in the affirmative is also a burden to me. How many thousand questions come into this considerations? Can I improve myself for usefulness after I am married as well as I can now? Can I support a family in a way that is satisfaction to all parties concerned? Can I live a virtuous life without marrying? Do I not disappoint a good woman by not marrying? I can not decide.

One thing I do decide on—my manner of life must undergo a change for the better in different ways. Their is much room for improvement i[n] so many places.

Monday, 24 December 1866

Rain in the first part of the day. But 11 o'clock P.M. witnesses a cloudless sky. Made out number of progress [reports] for last month. Fixed and mended a great deal. Bought material for a coat. Wrote a letter to Harrison Landis. Wrote five for J. L. Weidner. O. L. Fegley visited me.

The old year is vanishing rapidly, a few more vicissitudes of day and night will transport us to another year. In thoughts this day is not rich nor is it noted for transgressions as so many are.

Tuesday, 25 December 1866

Christmas Day. But not a blessed one I saw in times gone by. It is cheerless dull lonesome day. It brought no special joy whilst I can not say that that is intolerable. If I never had seen any really blessed Christmas I would not complain. The contrast is so great. Once this day was not to me as other days. It was blessed, because it was celebrated as a good on which God conferred the greatest blessing on mankind that heaven contained. The fashion to make presents is imitated by christian nations. But how often is the true design realized?

Attended a sermon by Rev. Grow. The Subject was Christ or—"Thy king cometh unto thee, meek." Matthew Chap 21 verse 5.

I was reading during the greater part of the day a variety of literature. Flora got dinner ready. Mr. Stauffer's were away. Tended the cattle.

Mr. I. S. Erb promised to see me in the afternoon but did not redeem his promise.

Winter reveling in fields. This christmas is neither "white nor green." It has just snow enough to make [it] look very dreary. But the gloomy season of snow will not always abide, the cheerful spring will come in its due season.

The nation is not in sorrow—it is prospering. Progress is going on everywhere. This century may yet look for great achievements.

Wednesday, 26 December 1866

A various day in employment. Visited. Intertained company. Attended funeral of Father Werstler[1] a man of 82 years, and prayermeeting at Gilberts.

Death is in the land. A teamster met with an accident this morning near Boyertown whose recovery is doubted.

I begin to be concerned about my soul's salvation because I am so unconcerned about it. I can not see why I am so unconcerned so indifferent. So easy. When I hear a stirring appeal to piety or when I reflect on the importance of living—radical religion, I resolve and reresolve to go work but such resolves vanish like smoke with their beginning. So demoralized a strong will can become. This eve I have been called on in meeting to exhort but I was dumb. In this meeting I had given formerly signs [of] fair promise but promise only. That was why I refused to speak. I will not make any promises when there is so little hope of fulfillment. There seem to be many people who, like I esteem their salvation of minor importance, but unlike in knowing what they must do and how they must go at it. If this serving God were not made so unpopular then it might be easy to serve him. What seems to be almost impossible to suffer the greatest persecution at the hands of Church members. Is it possible that what is good and holy can be so perverted and degraded? How long will this stupor remain on my soul? When will God arrest me in my course, as he did Paul, in my useless course?

1. Father Werstler may have been Jacob Werstler who was a seventy-five-year-old farmer living near Boyertown in Colebrookdale township in 1860. Pennsylvania Census, 1860, Berks County, Colebrookdale Township, 154.

Thursday, 27 December 1866

Snow greeted my first out door vision. But this falling of snow was but short duration but the blowing of snow extends beyond the day. The biting cold wind is almost insufferable. Swept the school room, thoroughly blacked stove, mended desks and repaired doors and engaged in other fixings.

The welcome "Independent" was read with its usual interest. This is delightful amusement. Who can do without such as visitor? I read it to Mr. Stauffers family. I[t] is particularly interesting this week again.

This cold weather materially affects my arrangements. No visiting can be done. School room can't be scoured.

My religious impressions this day have been more remarkable than usual. This I love. It is my delight to have my thoughts on spiritual and heavenly things when my hands do their destined work. May I be more successful daily to turn my thoughts on noble subjects. The things of time are so inferior in their value and tendency.

Christmas is past and New Year is coming. This induces us to take a retrospective glance and anon to the future. What awaits? What will the future reveal to mortals? No answer. There is a cover over the future through which the mortal eye cannot penetrate. It is like a thick fog. We can only see a little ahead as we march on.

My wish is that all mortal beings might have the same health and shelter for this night as I have.

Friday, 28 December 1866

Weather very cold and windy. Reading was the chief work of the day. Just before sunset I started for brother's. Enjoyed the Evening talking with them.

Saturday, 29 December 1866

Returned at 3 O'clock. Then scrubbed the school room. Called to see mary.

Saturday, 6 [5][1] January [1867]

Made trip to Philad.

---

1. JY dated this entry "Saturday, Jan. 6" although it was really the 5th.

Monday, 7 January 1867

Twenty students. Practised for coming Exhibition in school hours. The prospect for it is encouraging. Read Atlantic Monthly Magazine.

Tuesday, 8 January 1867

Weather very cold. All students present which were twenty two. Practised dialogues f[a]r in[to] the Evening. Read several articles in the atlantic monthly. Made an attempt to compose for exhibition. Failed.

Friday, 11 January 1867

I have been quite closely engaged in school the just past school week in making selections for exhibition in addition to practising what have been selected before. The attendance was better this week than it was since I took charge of school room duties. My health has been declining slowly but gradually since I took charge of this school from too much labors indoors with an inadequate exercise and intemperate living.

This day I have had more well regulated exercise and moderation.

In the evening I have had a discussion on morals with Mr. Jos. Borneman.

Wednesday, 15 January 1867

Weather very cold, nothing uncommon transpired. Practising and assigning peices for Exhibition kept me busy a great part of the day. I was provoked frequently by lazy and careless boys.

Sunday, 27 January 1867[1]

Last night I held a literary entertainment with my pupils. The hall was over crowded. About four hundred souls were present. Received about twenty one dollars. This sum is more than expenses. Have been in church this morning. Rev. Mayer officiated. Have derived but little benefit from it. This afternoon I have visited at my brother's. This evening I have labored to[o] at the rearrangement of the house.

Weather has been very cold incessantly for more than a month.

In the preparation for entertainment of our exhibition I neglected my health.

When I look back upon my conduct I can not take any pleasure in it.

1. JY mistakenly wrote 1866 rather than 1867 in the entry.

Monday, 28 January 1867

Horrible dreams last night. Was too intemperate in eating. Busy in rearrangeing what was deranged in exhibition. The school though small was working well.

I had fully purposed to tell Mr. Stauffer to look about for some one else as a teacher. Wrote J. W. Shoemaker. Wrote to Pottstown Ledger.

Tuesday,[1] 29 January 1867

Resolved fully to day to quit the business of teaching at the close of this term. I have been home this evening. I was not home for about five weeks. The work of the school was pleasant. The students generally do not do as much work as they ought to do. If they could only realize what privileges they do enjoy. Thermometer stands zero.

1. JY mistakenly wrote "Wednesday" rather than "Tuesday."

Saturday, 2 February 1867

Weather milder than it was for many weeks. A little rain. Had my pictures taken with Mr. Shuler. Took off my whiskers. To day Mr. L. C. Fegley [took] the last of my boarding students. This was enough to make a man of pride feel cheap. Well what can I do? Nothing; just submit to fate.

Could I only close up my work at once! By going on to stop one quarter hence I must make the failure worse than it really is.

In a pecuniary point of view I have most signally [singly] failed. Still I dare not wish that I had not undertaken this work. Every one must pay "lehr" money.

A Copy of Programme.

Literary Entertainment

of

Mount Pleasant Seminary

Boyertown, Penna

Saturday Evening, Jan. 26. 1867, at 7 o'clock

Order of Exercises

Music

Prayer

Music

Opening Remarks   James Dotterer

The Little Fanatic —   Dialogue   Three Characters

Tableau —   Rain Bow

The Man with an Axe to Grind —   Dia[logue]

Music   Two Characters

The Last Words of a dying Child

                                — Recitation   C. T. Stauffer

Tableau —   Revenge

True Fidelity —   Dia.   Four Characters

Tableau —   Barber Shop

Doctor and His Patient —   Dia.   Two Characters

Music

Oratorical Extracts

Winter —   Dia.   Two Characters

Tableau —   President as he was and as he is

The New School Master —   Dia.—   Three Characters

Music

The Apothecary Cross-Examined — Dia.   Three Characters

Tableau —   Freedmen's Bureau

Selection of a School Site —   Dia.   Twelve Characters

Tableau —   Joan Arc

School Examination —   Dia.   Five Characters

Music

Select Reading "Uptown"   Theo. Fegley

Killed with Kindness   Dia.   Five Characters

Women's Rights —   Charade

Demons of the Glass —   Dia.   8 Characters

Music

Broken Hearts —   Declamation —   Theo Fegly

Sentiments —   By the School

Music

Doors open at 6½ o'clock P.M.

Admission   10 cents

Music by the Boyertown Brass Band

Monday,[1] 4 February 1867

Weather gloomy. A little rain. School full except chatechumens[2] absent. Those present unusually diligent. I have be[en] again very impressively reminded of the importance of temperance in all things and earnestness in the struggle of righteousness against the sins which so easily beset us. I made good resolves. Of course it would be better or more desirable to record noble conduct put in practice already than[3] to record merely plans to be noble. Without resolves there is failure the[n] there can be nothing wors.

Mr. Stauffer thinks I must remain here another quarter after present. I can not. I have been engaged in warm debate with Mr. Jos. Borneman, on the question: "Is that law right that distributes property to nephews and nieces not equally but to each family according to what the parent would have been entitled if living." Spoke in the negative and believe so too. Wrote a letter to Mr. Reuben Beitaman. I am very much tired of teaching. I do not make expenses now. Who could like such a proceeding?

Saw a drove of horses that came yesterday from the West. One of them is valued by the owner four hundred dollars. Set my copies with unusual care. Was out shopping.

George "Black" made a mistake in correcting Mr. Henry Moser's words in Orthography. My papers have not come to day as they should have.

Practised penmanship.

1. JY wrote "Wednesday 4 February 1866," although it was actually Monday.

2. Catechumens are those receiving instruction in Christian doctrines, morals, and discipline in preparation for becoming members of the church.

3. JY originally wrote "the" and then substituted "than."

Tuesday, 5 February 1867

Very busy day. The school may be ever so small still I will be busy. Life is pleasant when it runs as it runs now. If God will only keep me so busy evermore that I may be kept out of mischief. Useful employment is the best safeguard against wickness.

Received a present of pulswarmers[1] from Mary. Returned the favor with a work on object lessons. Received a letter from J. W. Shoemaker; one from L. C. Fegley, also a Frank Lesly's Ladies Magazine.[2] Read an anecdote to the school in the place of a general Lesson.

Reviewed several pages of the most difficult problems in Brook's Mental

Arithmetic.[3] These gave me not a little exercise.

Read Biographical sketches of Pitt, Blackstone, Byron, and Sam Johnson,[4] and various fugitive pieces.

Made some selections for compositions. Wrote a letter to Wm. Y Eisenberg. Set copies. Made numbers.

1. Pulse-warmers or wristers are warm knitted coverings for the wrist.

2. *Frank Leslie's Ladies' Magazine*, also called *Frank Leslie's Lady's Magazine*, began publication in 1854 as *Frank Leslie's Ladies' Gazette of Fashion and Fancy Needle Work*, becoming the *Ladies' Magazine* in Sept. 1857. *The National Union Catalog, Pre-1956 Imprints*, vol. 182 (London, 1971), 655.

3. Edward Brooks, *Methods of Teaching Mental Arithmetic, and Key to the Normal Mental Arithmetic* (Philadelphia, 1860).

4. William Pitt (1708–1778), English statesman; George Gordon Byron (1788–1824), English poet; and Samuel Johnson (1709–1784), English author.

Wednesday, 6 February 1867

Wether very fair. The most active day in school I've had for a long time. Lectured to the school on various topics namly, neatness, order and virtue as assigned subjects for compositions.

Saturday, 9 February 1867

Made a trip to Pottstown. Weather very slushy. Received a set of photographs, and frame for Wickershams picture. Received a letter from J. E. Bowman, N.Y. Wrote J. Shoemaker, and Rev. R. Cruikshank. I was canvassing Pottstown to ascertain whether it will be possible that an audience can be gathered to make an entertainment. The result has proved rather unfavorable.

Saw Mr. Ludy[1] brought up before the squire and bound over to appear before court by a young lady. Called to [see] Mary. Enjoyed to visit greatly. Read Mr. Henry Rhoad's speech in the state legislature on the Constitutional amendment. Much rain in the first part of the eve. Wind come up at 11 o'clock and cold weather.

1. The 1860 Pennsylvania census listed one Ludy family in the Boyertown area with sons: Esther Ludy, mother of Alfred (age twenty-two) and Urias (age twenty), both of whom were laborers. They lived in the household of Iphraim Wenzel, a cooper. Pennsylvania Census, 1860, Berks County, Colebrookdale Township, 173.

Sunday, 10 February 1867

Weather very cold. Visited Bauer Dentist. Read Buchanan Read. Attended preaching by Leberman, the Secretary of the German Reformed missionary Society. His subject was the causes of hinderance in prosperity of the church. The service was instructive.

Read an excellent sermon of Beecher's in the Independent.

I do greatly regret the loss of my whiskers, for the newly shaved parts pain me much.

Monday, 11 February 1867

Sixteen or seventeen pupils present. The work went slowly. Mondays are always worse than other days. Some lessons were however well enough. Read Independent after school. Was argueing for hours with Jos. Borneman on Geography. In consequence of this debate my business at home had to be done at late hours. Practised some penmanship. Conversed on love affairs with Mr. Al Craft. Dreamed furious in the night by reason of immoderate use of Tobacco.

Tuesday,[1] 12 February 1867

Morning red. Evening dirt, I should guess.[2] But the evening has been if possible prettier than the morning. School small. It is most difficult to keep such a small school in spirit. Had a letter from W. Y. Eisenberg. Pottstown Papaper came to day. At Supper had an argument with Mr. Stauffer on the subject of infant baptism. He commenced it. I should think he dont think any the better for having introduced it. I handled him roughly.

Would I could impress my students with a due sense of the value of education. They learn it when it will be too late.

1. JY wrote both "Tuesday" and "Wednesday" for the day of this entry.

2. JY was paraphrasing the Bible, Matthew 16:2, "When it is evening, ye say, It will be fair weather: for the heaven is red. And in the morning, It will be foul weather to-day: for the heaven is red and lowring." The saying, a well-known weather proverb, is commonly stated: "Red sky at night, sailors' delight. Red sky at morning, sailors take warning." Stuart Flexner and Doris Flexner, *Wise Words and Wives' Tales: The Origins, Meanings and Time-Honored Wisdom of Proverbs and Folk Sayings, Olde and New* (New York, 1993), 155.

Wednesday, 13 February 1867

Weather fair. Had a letter from H. Landis. Read School Visitor. Attended Prayermeeting at Henry Gilbert's. Examined my finantial affairs. It makes me feel bad to think about it, when in reality I run in debt daily. Mr. Henry Bauer[1] has gone to the spirit land to day.

 Though he was sick for some weeks death met him unexpectant.

Mr. Fred Stauffer believes that the county superintendency is a humbug, or "the greatest humbug there is." It is deplorable enough that such things can be believed after the office has been created so many years. If good men were the functionaries the people were convinced differently. The superintendent[2] of this County was in this district to-day.

1. The only Henry Bauer listed in the 1860 Pennsylvania census as living in the Boyertown area was a twenty-four-year-old carpenter, who had a twenty-one-year-old wife and two small children. Pennsylvania Census, 1860, Berks County, Colebrookdale Township, 156.

2. JY originally wrote what looks like "suptende," and then substituted "superintendent."

Thursday, 14 February 1867

Busy. Rainy gloomy day. Work passed off pleasantly. Received Independent, Sunday School Times, Programme of Trappe anniversary.

Henry Moyer[1] stayed with me all night. His company was pleasant. He explained his soldier's[2] life.

1. Henry M. Moyer was listed in the 1860 census as a thirty-five-year-old farmer, living in Montgomery County with his father, his wife, and three children. Pennsylvania Census, 1860, Montgomery County, Upper Salford Township, 1026. He was also a member of the Falkner Swamp Reformed congregation and had served in the 11th Regiment, Pennsylvania Militia, during the Civil War. Hauze, *Falkner Church History,* 48.

2. JY originally wrote "social" and then substituted "soldier's."

Friday, 15 February 1867

The school goes slow. Speeches were good what there were of them. Some few were however not prepared. Attended Mr. Holdaman's Sale after School. Swept School Room, passed a part of the Evening [at] Dr. Borneman's. Read Resolutions of sympathy with Mrs. Mintzer[1] of Pottstown on the late death of her husband. Meritorious works will be appreciated once though often too late. Gen Hancocks father[2] died lately.

Why is human nature so prone to chime in with public sentiment? "He who gathers laurels while living will find his wreathe soon fade away."

How little do I accomplish in life? Yet how much work is before me? My efforts are too general. More concentration of mind I want. More speciality[3] of purpose, perseverance in what is begun.

Friends can not be relied upon, one rely upon ones self.

1. There were two Mintzer families listed in the 1860 census for Pottstown: Joseph Mintzer was a thirty-six-year-old hardware merchant whose household included his mother, his wife, and six children. The other Mintzer family was that of forty-eight-year-old Henry Mintzer, a grocer, who lived with his wife and eight children. Pennsylvania Census, 1860, Montgomery County, Pottstown Borough, 788–789, 799.

2. Benjamin Franklin Hancock (1800–1867), father of Union Maj. Gen. Winfield Scott Hancock (1824–1886), was a lawyer in Norristown, Montgomery County, Pa. He died on 1 Feb. 1867. William Cathcart, ed., *The Baptist Encyclopaedia: A Dictionary* . . . (Philadelphia, 1881), 1:492.

3. JY originally wrote "specially," and then deleted "ly" and substituted "ity."

Saturday, 16 February 1867

Mist interspersed with rain. Cleaned school room for the most part alone. The labor was hard on one not inured to bodily exertion. When it was done, I was fully rewarded in the satisfaction the clean room gave. The sore legs it entailed were not a burden. Read and attended to Saturdays work generally.

Received a letter from Rev. R. Cruikshank and S. S. Times.

At Night called to See Mary.

Sunday, 17 February 1867

Fair weather. Read a sermon by Beecher on "Fishers of Men." It is of course good as usual.

My present state of mind is indescribable. Yet I have the inclination to take a note of some of the most prominent features. I am thrown down to the lowest depth of humility from a naturally proud turn of mind. If all my Debtors should pay me to day I could not discharge all my debts. What [is] worse than all, I have a very low estimate of my ability for business of any kind. But thank God I have health and strength. While I have these I can make a living for myself. But judging from the past it goes bare at that. When I was quite young I adopted the Honesty policy in business. I have now my doubts whether a poor man can follow it out and make a respectable living. Still I am resolved to hold on to it. Just here is the trouble. [How] can a man keep up when he exacts nothing and is necessarily drawn from continually by this corrupt world.

Mr. Stauffer asked me again to stay after this quarter. What have I told him but that I will not?

Attended Mayers Preaching twice. I was not pleased with it. Read papers. Mary stayed here for supper.

Blank; blank is my life at present when will it be other wise?

I've had a good talk with Ferrel on Religion. He knows a great deal more than I thought.

Yoder Diary, 20 February–8 April 1867.

The following section of the diary is taken from an incomplete set of diary pages in private hands. Copies are in the editor's and the Library of Virginia's possession.

Wednesday, 20 February 1867

Dreadful snow. School small in consequence. Nothing new of great importance has transpired, except our dog swallowed a good dose of Essence of perpermint without producing any apparent effect upon his usual sleepy bearing. At night called at Dr. Borneman's Office where puzzles were proposed and solved, various topics discussed, and stories related. Read a love story.

When a school is as small as mine it is a difficult matter to keep the dignity and ambition that should characterize all the actions in which the young are participants.

I am really proud of some of the materials I have. If there was only more of it.

Thursday, 21 February 1867

Snow all day. Snow everywhere. But I do enjoy to see the snow come down. If anything I do like mo[st] it is to see the rain to come down in gentle regularity in summer after a protracted drought. But as the snow ceases to fall all its charm is at an end. If power it has then over the imagination, it is that which is akin to hatred. For the spotless covering will soon depart and not only expose the sombre appearance the ravages of winter have spread far and wide, but also by contrast and of itself make the aspect of nature unlovely.

Received a letter from J. W. Shoemaker and Sunday School Times.

Visited at Lewis Wormans. Conversation was brisk. Read our State legislative Proceedings on the constitutional amendment. Good speeches were made. Even in opposition Mr. Deise would deserve credit if his effort were is a good cause. But the good work is begun: neither Deise nor any other man can hinder it so much to prevent [it] from becoming a law. It is astonishing to me that there is a single man to be found who was educated outside the precincts of the late slave states. Rejoice ye son of labor in the sunny fields. The oppressor reigneth not forever. Rejoice ye lately despised "abolitionists." It is on the other hand not less astonishing to see this little bank of abolition[ist]s pride themselves in their profession, who but so short years ago need but be named to be despised. In this again is manifested that God prospers the righteous, and puts the wicked to shame.

Friday, 22 February 1867

Beautiful morning. The yellow rays playing upon the silvery sheet dazzle the eye. "Fixing" had to be attended in the first place. Read various fugitive pieces in the papers. Made a tour through town; but did not find the business men at home. On returning met Dr. Borneman at whose office an entrance was made and an observation taken of his at the time casting frameworks to set on artificial teeth. The operation is an entirely new new one; hence something is to be learned by it. S[o] I did a part of the work.

Well, this is the twenty ninth birth day of mine. After I will have seen again as many as I now have, my earthly race will have been run. Yes maybe long ere that. What new changes does this suggest—are any improvements necessary? Is any thing to be taken up or is any old practice to be laid down. There are enough of either. Where is the beginning to be made?

What new thing have I acquired during the past year? In answer to this question, I have learned more of human frailty than of meritorious knowledge and in no one less than in my own.

From noon till supper I worked with Mr. Borneman, Dentist polishing several sets of artificial teeth. Liked the new business well. But by this thoughtless conduct neglected some of my own work. Still in the way of learning I have surely done well.

11½ o'clock P.M. Just returned from Entertainment given by the so-called Philomathean Literary Society. The audience was good. In the performance I will not pass any remarks, while it would be my inclination rather to notice its[1] defects than its merits. I know it is easier to notice errors than it is to avoid them.

Wrote a letter to J. W. Shoemaker in regard to Entertainment at Pottstown.

1. JY originally wrote "its the" and then deleted "the."

Saturday, 23 February 1867

Little work done in the Morning besides making out monthly report. Prepared a dose of medicine for our age stricken canis. It is the third dose that he swallowed during the week. Each one seems to make him more vigorous. A great portion of the day is gone but little is left to show that he was here.

Medicine worked admirably. One hour after its ministration perfect cure was effected.

Independent came and was partly read.

Wrote J. Dotterer. Fetched a pair of pantaloons from the tailor's. Ascertained my weight to be one hundred thirty eight which is six pounds more than two months ago.

Reports of[1] last nights entertainment are not very flattering. Have called again for the third [time] for this day at Dr. Bornemans.

1. JY originally wrote "from" and then deleted "rom" and added an"o."

Sunday, 24 February 1867

Retired late last night. Read the Independent. The Bill making Louisiana a territorial government till the people of that state shall have formed a constitution in conformity to the general consti[tu]tion has passed the lower house.[1] The cause of this legislation is wholesale murder committed in that state with interference by the state to punish the perpetrators.[2] Justice may sleep but she never dies. But she seem[s] to have had a pretty long sleep. Wrote a letter to Tillman Stahler[3] in Pennsylvania style. Wrote a note to Mary. Visited at my brother's. Attended Rev. Groh's preaching. Read school Journal.

I was tempted to close school immediately. Have not indulged the thought yet.

1. On 12 Feb. 1867, the U.S. House of Representatives passed a bill (H.R. 1162) reported from the committee investigating the New Orleans riot of 30 July 1866 that imposed a new civil government in Louisiana to be elected by African Americans and loyal whites. While the Senate considered the bill several times, it let the congressional session end without taking any action on the bill. Foner, *Reconstruction: America's Unfinished Revolution*, 274; F. and J. Rives, comps., *The Congressional Globe: Containing the Debates and Proceedings of the Second Session of the Thirty-Ninth Congress* (Washington, D.C., 1867), 1128–1133, 1164–1175, 1223–1224, 1302–1304, 1511, 1518.

2. On 30 July 1866, after several days of threats and brisk sales of firearms, a riot broke out in New Orleans when a parade of African American supporters of a reconvened constitutional convention to enfranchise the freedmen was attacked by angry white onlookers. The

blacks ran for cover in the convention hall and were fired on by the police and the mob, who then broke into the hall and began an indiscriminate carnage that soon spread to the streets. African Americans were hunted down and attacked on streetcars, in shops, and on the street. By the time federal troops arrived several hours later, 34 blacks had died and 119 had been injured. White Unionist members of the original convention who were attending the reconvened session suffered losses of 3 dead and 18 wounded. Among the police 20 were injured and 1 white supporter killed, probably at the hands of his cohorts. President Johnson blamed Radical Republicans for the tragedy and expressed no regrets for the massacre. Foner, *Reconstruction: America's Unfinished Revolution*, 262–263; Ted Tunnell, *Crucible of Reconstruction: War, Radicalism, and Race in Louisiana, 1862–1877* (Baton Rouge and London, 1984), 103–107; McPherson, *Ordeal by Fire*, 519–520; Giles Vandal, *The New Orleans Riot of 1866: Anatomy of a Tragedy* (Lafayette, La., 1983), 180. For a fuller account of the riot, see Vandal, *The New Orleans Riot of 1866*, chapter 6, "The 'Bloody Details' of July 30."

3. The 1860 Pennsylvania census index lists only one person with a name similar to Tillman Stahler: Tilghman Stahl (according to the census itself) who was a twenty-nine-year-old farmer living in Lehigh County, about twenty miles north of Boyertown. Pennsylvania Census, 1860, Lehigh County, Upper Milford Township, 419.

Monday,[1] 25 February 1867

Only eleven pupils present. Work went on as usual. Had no time left with these few. "Mirror" was the subject for General lesson. After school settled with the Boyertown printer. Visited at John Fegley's. Wrote several notes. Read, mused and reflected. Determined to adopt for my use one of Thomas Jefferson's Rules of Life. "Never spend your money before you have it."[2]

1. JY wrote "'Wedn' Monday" for this entry.

2. Jefferson wrote that advice to his namesake Thomas Jefferson Smith on 21 Feb. 1825. Paul Leicester Ford, ed., *The Works of Thomas Jefferson* (New York and London, 1905), 12:405–406.

Tuesday, 26 February 1867[1]

Weather is springlike. Only ten in school. How slowly time drags along. Have some news of new scholars; but now it is too lalte. The doom is sealed. The best of luck to mount Pleasant in my absence!

1. JY wrote "1857" for this entry.

Thursday, 28 February 1867

Read Independent. It afforded me pleasure to read a long letter about Lincol[n]'s character. Received a letter from Albert Stauffer and one from J. Dotterer. Wrote one to A. Stauffer. This is a fair ending of Feb. as was its beginning. Reconstruction is going on all right. American progress is taking pace with American ideas. If I had only time and mea[n]s I would do little than study history as it is developed now. This I regret greatly. Poverty is surely[1] unhandy to me now if not also disgraceful.

1. JY wrote "surely#" but left no explanation of what he meant.

Friday, 1 March 1867

Weather is gloomy. School work rather dragging. Declamation did no credit to itself. Had ten pupils. Still I could hardly get through. Swept school ro[o]m after school. After supper played a few games at checker with Al. Never played any before about a week ago. I rather like [it] not so much as an amusement as a mental discipline. Read Norristown Free Press.[1] In particular one of Nasbys letters.[2] Now it is ten o'clock P.M. and soon will be in the land of Dr[e]ams.

1. The *Norristown Free Press* was established in 1829 and merged with the *Norristown Herald* (established 1799) in 1837 to form the *Norristown Herald and Free Press*. Published once a week, the paper was Republican. *George P. Rowell and Company's American Newspaper Directory* (1871), 136; *United States Newspaper Program*, fiche card 32.

2. Petroleum V. Nasby was the pseudonym of David Ross Locke, journalist and political satirist. In Mar. 1861, he created the fictional character of Nasby, an ignorant, lazy, hypocritical, prevaricating country preacher, to satirize Copperheads—Northerners who sympathized with the South during the Civil War. His writings were quite popular. *DAB*, s.v. "David Ross Locke."

Saturday, 2 March 1867

Bathed, played checker, attended public sale at Geo. Landis'.[1] Read a lecture on Spermatorrhoea,[2] and visited Mary. Returned late at night.

1. There were two men named George Landis residing in the Boyertown area in 1860. The first was a fifty-eight-year-old tanner, living with his wife Catherine, five children, and a daughter-in-law. The other was a sixty-six-year-old farmer, living with his wife Mary and six children. Pennsylvania Census, 1860, Berks County, Colebrookdale Township, 153, 166.

2. Spermatorrhoea refers to abnormally frequent or excessive involuntary emission of semen without orgasm.

Sunday, 3 March 1867

Attended Clemmer's preaching. Visited at Henry Borneman's.[1] Minister Mayor took supper with us. Life is a burden to me. So many dark prospects never before loomed up for me in the future. No money in the purse, liabilities greater than assets. No employment. No prospect for getting any. A strong inclination. Oposition in the family. My health not very flattering. Have no inclination to do constant manual labor and no apt[it]ude for shrewd business. Stop school as a *failure* when this fact is in its most obvious stage to every observer.

BOYERTOWN

How truly I can bear witness to the fact that when Satan leaves his strongholds and reenters, he hold[s] his ground with so much more tenacity! I am discouraged to any thing. Resolutions have failed to often. This old expression presents itself with great force to my mind. "The way to hell is paved with good resolution."

I wish God would force me into some mode of procedure. Wish I could only now see what he wants me to do. Some radical change must soon take place in my "modus operandis."[2]

My ancient pride is wounded quite badly. This moment I suffer from disobedience to what I well enough knew should have been obeyed at all hazards.

For my own part I would be willing to take hold at any common work, and I could make a living by it but I could not study with it nor could I lay up anything. I have contracted a wrong habit in regard to my mode of doing business. I am to liberal. How can I be otherwise as I must be if I will keep pace with the world around. I am affraid I am too honest.

Attended Mayers preaching. "His subject was Take heed therefore how ye hear." Gallanted Mary home through[3] rendered so terrible on account of it unexpectedness. Came home before and read or reread the Spermatorrhoea lecture. Though early retired, fell asleep late.

1. The 1860 Pennsylvania census listed a Henry H. Borneman living in the Boyertown area who was a thirty-six-year-old watchmaker. In June 1864 an H. Borneman paid JY $1.25 "for a day's labor." Yoder Diaries, 1861–1864, Acc. 27680, p. 114, LVA.

2. JY originally wrote "operandis," and then made a slash through the "e" and put equal signs at the top and bottom of the slash to undo his deletion.

3. JY escorted Mary home through some event of nature (presumably a sudden violent thunderstorm) so horrible that words failed him.

Monday, 4 March 1867

Rose with a harrassing cold whose unpleasantness increased as the day increased. Felt miserable all day. Much company at night. Accomplished little. Taught my brother Grammar who stayed the night with me.

Tuesday, 5 March 1867

Took games at checkers. A letter from Muth.[1]

1. The 1860 Pennsylvania census index lists a Daniel and a Frederick Muth in Berks County, along with about a dozen others surnamed Muth in Lehigh and Lebanon Counties.

Wednesday, 6 March 1867

Called to see Mary where I enjoyed myself well.

Thursday, 7 March 1867

Received my papers. Independent & S. S. Times.

Friday, 8 March 1867

Composition day. Nearly all responded creditably to the call. After school went home with Mr. Moyer one of my students. The march was about 3½ miles. Made a short call at a[1] neighbor's. Spent the evening in a pleasant social chat with [a] good old friend.

1. JY originally wrote "the" and then substituted "a."

Saturday, 9 March 1867

Took dinner with my[1] eighteen year confidant.[2] He has a wife and family. How every thing changes! Came home at 3 o'clock P.M. Called at Borneman's and Mr. J. Swinehart's. Read a good sermon in the Independent. This sermon I will read often. Its subject is activity. Rev. Mayer took supper with us. Had a letter from J. W. Shoemaker.

Did not go to see Mary according to promise. Bought material for c[l]othing. Am all alone. Alfred went home yesterday.

1. JY originally wrote "one of" and then substituted "my."
2. JY originally wrote "confidants" and then deleted the "s."

Sunday, 10 March 1867

Weather is Gloomy. Read the Norristown Herald. Company was at Stauffer's to noon. Called to see mary in the morning. Eating walnuts make me feel drowsy. Read Independent on woman's rights—pro and con.

Attended prayermeeting at William Stauffer's by which I trust I was benefited.

Monday, 11 March 1867

School small and misery everywhere. As blue as blue can be. Hope for better things.

Tuesday, 12 March 1867

School commenced in the greatest dissatisfaction. But what is the use to be grieved with things that you cant alter? Take things by the smooth handle. Mr. F. Weaver kept me from work an hour and a half trying to sell me a book.

Solved riddles in the school visitor, &c.

Wednesday, 13 March 1867

Weather still gloomy. School worked pleasantly. Read School Visitor. Artemus Ward[1] alias Charles Browne, The American humorist, died lately in England. Eleven[2] pupils. Had an interesting lesson on phisiology.

1. Artemus Ward was the pen name of Charles Farrar Browne, a widely read humorist and lecturer, who died 6 Mar. 1867. His writings during the Civil War won the admiration of Abraham Lincoln, and he also became a close friend of the young Samuel Clemens (Mark Twain). *DAB*, s.v. "Charles Farrar Browne." JY added "Charles F. Browne" above the line and then marked through the second "Browne."

2. JY originally wrote "ten" and then substituted "eleven."

Thursday, 14 March 1867

This evening I have closed school without notice and contrary to Mr. Stauffers wishes. This was a great struggle. Attended church at eve. Wrote Shoemaker.

Friday, 15 March 1867

Made out bills and collected them. Went to the borough election voted and independent ticket. But it was not elected. Dr. Bowman called on a visit.

Saturday, 16 March 1867

Accomplished not much. Mended umbrella. Read the Independent. A most terrible snow storm confined me to the house all day. Played checkers with Dr. Borneman. I see now that I might have spent that time more profitably in some useful employment. It is truly painful to find out how poorly I have come out with my teaching here these thirty one weeks. I have lost more than a hundred dollars. Otherwise I have nothing to complain [about]. My students have done well. God bless them all, is all I ask now.

Sunday, 17 March 1867

If it keeps on snowing long at this rate an under snow railroad will be necessary for those that must go out. Church bell is ringing away but the people can hardly come out, especially when there is so little attractive as there is. Read Morning Star. Good things too. This is indeed an age of changes, novelties and trickeries. Not only the School teacher should possess a pair of "big eyes." Every one should have them. If for no other reason than to distinguish the genuine from the false pictures he meets everywhere. What more than any one thing alone else prevents me from being successful in life is the want of concentration of mind for a long time.

Spent a pleasant moment at William Stauffer's this afternoon. At noon Mr. Fred Stauffer pressed the subject of infant baptism to my consideration. I showed but little respect for his innate prejudice and still less for wrangling on the definition of "family" which he would have mean a house contai[ni]ng children. The weather is of the severest winter kind. If possible I will go to meeting, yes to Methodist meeting. Methodism is still unpopular in this community. There is some use in prejudice as there is for any thing else in this or any other world, but my wits are [unable] to assign any use for a[1] prejudice against a thing that has so nobly refuted "all manner of evil that was said against it falsely"[2] and shown its admirable practicability over any of the other churches here!

Well but so it [is]. Who can help it? This is a queer world anyhow. It will be humbugged. But ministers should be last of all the humbuggers or[3] hucksters of human wellfare[4] and human souls.

Read Beecher's Sermon on industry again, for the third time. I will often read it over again because it is *invaluable*.

1. JY originally wrote "such" and then substituted "a."

2. JY was paraphrasing the Bible, Matthew 5:11, "Blessed are ye when men shall reproach you, and persecute you, and say all manner of evil against you falsely, for my sake."

3. JY originally wrote "of" and then substituted "or."

4. JY originally wrote "welf" and then substituted "wellfare."

Tuesday, 26 March 1867

Last week I spent at Harrisburgh at a religious convention by the Free Will Baptist church.

This morning I came to Philadelphia. Am tired. Feel bad. It is my own fault. God give grace to me to be moderate in all things. Took dinner with John H. Martin in 22 Str. Met Shoemaker at 3½ P.M. and Charles Harding.[1] Now I am ready to go to work and work I will if God grants me health.

My conduct this day is not admirable. It is a good ways from it. May this day be the end of it.

Practised some penmanship. The start is good. The end will show itself.

This morning I have come to Philadelphia to study penmanship and elocution under J. W. Shoemaker.

1. Charles Harding was from Philadelphia and attended Millersville Normal School from 1861 to 1863. *Catalogue, 1861–62*, 10; *1862–63*, 10.

Wednesday, 27 March 1867

Snow again in morning. Took first lessons. The start promises much. Read a part of Sheakspeares Hamlet. Wrote a letter Al Craft, one to Rev. James Colder. Practised penmanship and elocution. Was on street much in Fore Noon. I feel not as yesterday, mean but very good [in] every way. Was not spending money as yesterday.

Now I have good paper, pens and ink, what excuse will there be for poor writing? Wrote a letter to Jonathan Yoder.

Thursday, 28 March 1867

Do not feel well do; because I have eaten to much since here in the city. Wrote a letter Miss Fannie Harvy in Lynchburg. Practiced but little penmanship. Had no lesson in it for want of time, S——'s time. Read Sheakspeares Hamlet Prince of Denmark. Committed Hamlets address to the players. Read Philadelphia Ledger. Made a trip out to Penna depot in 31st St. Speaker Colfax[1] is not here tonight according to expectation.

Read a part of Ezekiel. More spiritual nearness I must have to God to keep me out [of] mischief and sin. So terribly I am spoiled that it is a great work to keep me within the limits of moderation and temperance.

A conductor on a street car arrested for refusing a colored person to come on the[2] car. A change in legal affair[s] and a good one, too. Democrats not not like this law. Now, if I had any influence among them I would advise not to try to keep the negro down by[3] legislation or any other [means] to prevent him from equaling them, but with might and main to try to elevate themselves above the Negro in real worth: "there is enough room up higher." In this way establish their superiority. Such superiority will be an enviable one. What has not the spirit of prejudice done that is bad. Well so it goes and perhaps it can not be helpt.

1. Schuyler Colfax (1823–1885) was an Indiana Republican who served in the U.S. House of Representatives from 1855 to 1869 and as Speaker from Dec. 1863 to Mar. 1869, when he became vice president of the United States. His involvement in the Crédit Mobilier scandal that broke in 1872 (wherein $20 million of Union Pacific Railroad moneys were diverted to the promoters' pockets) ended his career. *DAB*, s.v. "Schuyler Colfax."

2. JY originally wrote "the st," and then marked through "the" once and through "st" three times.

3. JY originally wrote "so" and then substituted "by."

Friday, 29[1] March 1867

Weather clear but cold. Was over to Walnut [Street] for Shoemaker. Recited[2] Hamlet with some satisfaction. Practised Penmanship to some extent. Attended a dramatic exhibition by Mr. McLuvie's school. Retired at twelve.

1. JY dated this entry "Friday March 28, 1867," although it was actually the 29th.

2. JY originally wrote "that" and then substituted "recited."

Saturday, 30 March 1867

Shaved, bathed, had a splendid letter from Mary. Read Independent. Recited Penmanship at 7½ A.M.; Read 1. P.M. The practice was not as good to day as it might have been. In reading the teacher observed especially my harshness of voice. Hope he will benefit me greatly in this respect. Oh I begin to see a great many deficiencies I did not before. But this is just what I want to do so that I can correct them. If we can see errors in our conduct as errors we will abandon them.

Afternoon Shoemaker and I spend shopping. In the evening I attended the second concert by the Mendelssohn Society in the musical Fund Hall, Locust St.

between 8th & 9th. Music is considered first class they gave. Ticket which cost $1.00 presented me.

Read some in Our School Day Visitor.

Retired at Midnight.

Sunday, 31 March 1867

Rose at 8. Took breakfast immediately. Visited Freewill Baptist Church on 8th & Parrish. Rev. Boyer preached from Romans, 8th, first part of 24th verse. "For we are saved by hope."[1] This people have only lately adopted the name of Freewill Baptists. Formerly they were known as United Brethren. They worship in an upper room as Paul did. They have no church edifice. May God bless they abundantly where they need it most. I will go there soon again.

Slept three hours in the middle of the day. Read Our School Day Visitor and Independent. Wrote a letter to Mary.

At 7½ P.M. attended Church at 11th & Wood Strs.

Rev. Smily is its pastor. This is the first Congregational church I have seen and the first Congregational Minister I have, to my knowledge. The first occular and oraeular impressions agree with my previous I had received from the branch of God's Church upon earth. I do not see what could prevent this church from becoming very influential in our future history. The pastor says Good friend Shoemaker is the most eloquent man in this city. He preached a good discourse from the subject[2] Christ's temptation in the wilderness recorded in Matthews Gospel, 4th Chapter. He deduced some very practical reflections from it. His principal attention was given to the two combatants. He considered the scene as a field of conflict. He made himself the herald of victory from that battlefield come to proclaim the blessed news of the Gospel. He regards this transaction as the most important conflict ever existed in the universe. Here the Christ bruised the serpents head. Retired at 11½ P.M.

1. JY originally wrote "hoped" and then deleted the "d."
2. JY originally wrote "subjects" and then deleted the "s."

Monday, 1 April 1867

It is now 7½ o'clock and April fool was not after me. Spent sleepless hours last night. Rose at 6 o'clock. Recitation hours will come between 3 & 6 P.M. Wrote letter to Dr. Bauman.[1] Received [one] from Al Craft. Practised a long while penmanship and Elocution. Recited several new pieces in Elocusion. Had another present from Shoemaker of a ticket of Henry Bible Class Concert of North Presbyterian Church in Marshal St. Read Ledger—mostly miscellaneous items. The day was most fine in weather. Ideas flow lazily So I will go to concert, expecting more fluency on returning.

Received Morningstar.

Attended a Bible Class Concert on Marshal and Sixth in the North Presbyterian Church. Miss Hinkle read about two third of the time. She read beautifully.

1. Dr. Bauman has not been identified, although JY listed an Augustus Bauman and a John W. Bauman in a series of names on the front endpaper of his 1869–1870 diary. Yoder Diaries, 1869–1870, Acc. 27680, LVA.

Tuesday, 2 April 1867

Read a part[1] of Hamlet which is to be performed in Chestnut St. Theatre. Committed a piece in Kidd Elocution.[2] Rambled about[3] the Sts with Mr. Shoemaker in search of a Room. Found none that. Attended Chestnut St. Theatre. James Murdock impersonated Hamlet. And did do it *well*. But when the play had reached beyond eleven o'clock I began to get tired. At twelve minus a half an hour, the king, queen, Laertes and Hamlet lay on the floor expiring and the curtain fell. Wrote a letter to Brother Jonathan.

1. JY originally wrote "propor" and then substituted "part."

2. Robert Kidd, *Vocal Culture and Elocution: With Numerous Exercises in Reading and Speaking* (Cincinnati and New York, 1857).

3. JY originally wrote "abouts" and then deleted the "s."

Wednesday, 3 April 1867

Practiced one hour penmanship before breakfast with but little profit. Studied but little the remainder of the fore noon. Afternoon took a short lesson in Elocution, the remainder I spent in making a tour to the Fair Mount Water Works.[1] This was the first time I had ever visited this important appendage to Philadelphia. I should now think I never had seen Philadelphia if I had not seen this spectacle. It is at once picturesque and artistical and scientific. How wonderfully every thing is adapted to man's comfort and happiness. How true it is that all creatures shall be subject to man. When I returned at Six O'clock a letter from Mary was handed me containing a letter [from] Lynchburg or Liberty Va. from Alvin Varner. After supper took a short lesson in rehearsing. It [w]as satisfactory to myself and teacher. Retired early.

1. The Fairmount Water Works were originally designed by Benjamin Henry Latrobe between 1798 and 1800 to supply Philadelphia with clean water from the Schuylkill River and began operation in Jan. 1801. Frederick Graff, the works' engineer, made further improvements to the system including adding a reservoir on Morris (later Fairmount) Hill. By 1824 the waterworks and their handsome buildings had become the pride of the city, and it was said that a visit to Philadelphia without seeing the Fairmount Water Works was like visiting London without seeing Westminster Abbey. Russell F. Weigley, ed., et al., *Philadelphia: A 300-Year History* (New York and London, 1982), 226–230.

Thursday, 4 April 1867

Weather fine as every day this week. Read Independent before breakfast. It is good. Election in Connecticut is given in favor of democracy. I had not expected this. Though [it] is a loss to the Republican Party it can hardly be considered a gain to the Democratic party.[1] Republican [party] is just as strong to in Connecticut to day as it ever was. The republican party took a bolder stand than before. If they had sacrificed principles and labored for partisan purposes as the other party everywhere does, then the trash that forsook it to feed upon bread & butter would have stayed. So let men rather go than principles. Give not up the right. Victory will crown it so sure as truth is truth.

Wrote a letter to Henry M. Moyer. Ransacked the Philadelphia Ledger from notices to rent rooms for Shoemaker. Found none. Wrote a letter to D. H. Keck.

Practiced and recited elocution not to very great satisfaction. But the writing was good. Was over to Chestnut for Mr. Shoemaker.

Mr. Shoemaker has as pupil he charges four dollars for one lesson of two hours. Wrote a letter to Geo. W. Sisson, Latrobe Westmoreland County Penna.[2] Had a long conversation with the ladies of the house on religious matters. Came to no profitable conclusions except that it[3] is clear that human nature is very depraved.

1. JY referred to the 1867 congressional and gubernatorial elections in Connecticut in the spring of 1867. The state, like the country, was divided over the issue of President Johnson's brand of reconstruction versus that of Radical Republicans in Congress. The Democratic Party's wins resulted from a split among Connecticut's Republicans and the fact that the state's moderate Democrats' prevented prominent Copperheads from taking a major role in the campaign. Thus the moderate Democrats took three of the four congressional seats and the governorship by narrow margins in each race. Gambill, *Conservative Ordeal: Northern Democrats and Reconstruction*, 127; Beale, *The Critical Year*, 385; Albert E. Van Dusen, *Connecticut* (New York, 1961), 240–241.

2. Like JY, Sisson had left his Freedmen's Bureau school post in Lovingston, Va., and returned to Pennsylvania.

3. JY originally wrote "the" and then substituted "it."

Friday, 5 April 1867

Was to see the Academy of Natural Science[1] Located Samson & Chestnut Sts. This was the most pleasing sight I ever[2] [saw]. The wild animals and birds possessed the most interest for me. This establishment alone has enough charms to pay for a pretty long trip to Phila.

1. The American Philosophical Society was formed in 1727 and became the preeminent scientific association in North America by early in the nineteenth century. From the Society came several other Philadelphia institutions including the Academy of Natural Sciences founded in 1812. By 1876 the Academy had amassed a 30,000-volume library and voluminous collections of various specimens such as fish, animals, reptiles, shells, and birds, the last considered the largest such collection in the world at the time. Weigley, *Philadelphia*, 55, 241–242, 447–448.

2. JY originally wrote "every" and then deleted the "y."

Saturday, 6 April 1867

Was disappointed in not receiving any letters. Wrote two, one to Theo. S. Fegley and one to Al Craft. Practised long in penmanship. At night in the barber shop a new idea came into my head. In business I must act a little more like other men. Must look more to my interest. I will mature this thought more in the future.

Sunday, 7 April 1867

Weather delightful. Attended Sabbath School and Church in morning in 1st Freewill Baptist Church in Philadelphia.

Read Sunday Dispatch, and lines entitled a token of friendship. More radical reformitory measures were considered. At night Gallanted to ladies to Seventh and Arch Sts Presbyterian Church. Sermon was based on "Faith which worketh by love." It was good. I have this day received more favorable impressions of the Presbyterian church than I had entertained before.

He preached a bible sermon.

Monday, 8 April 1867

The day commenced pleasantly. The noise is great in comparison [to what] it was on the Sabbath.

THE FREEDMAN'S

SPELLING-BOOK.

PUBLISHED BY THE

AMERICAN TRACT SOCIETY,

NO. 28 CORNHILL, BOSTON.

Yoder Diary, 1869–1870.

Little is known about Yoder's activities from 8 April 1867, when his diary abruptly closes with him in Philadelphia studying with his former classmate and PFRA superintendent Jacob W. Shoemaker, until Yoder's return to Lynchburg in the fall of 1868 as the new PFRA superintendent for the Lynchburg area. Freedmen's Bureau records document Yoder's administration of the black schools in a six-county area from 1868 until 1871, but the second volume of the Library of Virginia's diary does not begin until 15 November 1869 and on 14 November 1870 suddenly ends.

Monday, 15 November 1869

Looked at rooms with a view to rent for house-keeping.

Got wood.

Consulted with Booker Purvis[1] in regard to former difficulties about reporting. Result gives him no satisfaction.

Asked Mr. Bitting[2] to give an address to our proposed Teachers institute. He has consented.

Read "Church Manual," J. M. Pendleton D.D.[3] Was much pleased with it. I love it.

Attended Protestant Methodist Conference.[4] The subject under consideration. The Union of this Church with the Methodist Episcopal Church.

Read an article in "The Republican" on Religious education of the Colored People. It is a sign of Progress. God bless this spirit. Let us have more of it.

Taught Mr. Lindsey Hayden[5] in Grammar. Called on four of the Schools in Lynchburg. Had letters from Keck and McMahon.

Wrote J. E. McGoldrick[6] sending him fifteen dollars.

Had a speller sent me by my brother.

Wrote L. S. Worman.

---

1. Booker Purvis was a black teacher of freedmen at Mount Zion in Campbell County, taking over the school in Mar. 1869 from Ella Leftwich who then moved to the New Glasgow school in Amherst County. Monthly Statistical School Reports of District Superintendents, Feb. 1869, Roll 12; Booker Purvis, Mount Zion Church School, Campbell County, Report of 29 Apr. 1869, and Ella Leftwich, New Glasgow School, Amherst County, Report of 29 Apr. 1869, in Teachers' Monthly School Reports, Nov. 1865–Apr. 1869, Roll 15, Supt. of Ed., Va., BRFAL.

2. Charles Carroll Bitting, born in Philadelphia, Pa., in Mar. 1830, served various pastorates in Virginia, beginning in Hanover County in 1855, followed by one in Alexandria during the Civil War. Sometime after 1866, when the Sunday School Board of the Southern Baptist Convention, for which he had been secretary, moved from Greenville, S.C., to Memphis, Tenn., Bitting became pastor of the First Baptist Church, which JY attended. Bitting left Lynchburg for Richmond in 1871 to become secretary of the American Baptist Publication Society for the Southern States. George Braxton Taylor, *Virginia Baptist Ministers, Fourth Series* (Lynchburg, Va., 1913), 329, 335; Mary Sue Diuguid Davis, *Centennial Celebration, First Baptist Church, Lynchburg, Virginia* ([Lynchburg, 1915]), 15.

3. James Madison Pendleton was a Baptist minister, an educator, and one of the founders of the Crozer Theological Seminary in Upland, Pa. Pendleton wrote the *Church Manual, Designed for the Use of Baptist Churches* in 1867. *DAB*, s.v. "James Madison Pendleton."

4. The Virginia Protestant Methodist Conference opened its sessions in Lynchburg on 12 Nov. 1869. *Lynchburg News*, 12 Nov. 1869.

5. Lindsey Hayden was a black teacher of freedmen located variously at Body Camp and at Bunker Hill in Bedford County. He graduated from Hampton Institute in 1877. Schedule of Schools Under the Pennsylvania Freedmen's Relief Association, Quarters Ending 31 Dec. 1869, 31 Mar. 1870, and 30 June 1870, Letters Received, 1 Jan.–24 Aug. 1870, Roll 5, Supt. of Ed., Va., BRFAL; "Record of Hampton Graduates Known to Be Now Teaching," *Southern Workman* 7 (Jan. 1878): 6.

6. J. E. McGoldrick was a PFRA teacher at Liberty in Bedford County, Va., during the autumn and winter of 1869–1870. He resigned in mid-Mar. 1870 after he "got himself into some trouble at Liberty with the School committee." JY reported to PFRA secretary Robert A. Corson on 21 Mar. that McGoldrick had in fact fallen "in love with one of his pupils," who unfortunately was married. In a letter JY wrote in Oct. 1870, he reported that McGoldrick was then "in Phila. with his wife." Yoder Letter Book, 3 Mar. 1870–1 Dec. 1870, pp. 29, 38, 52–55, 61, 63, 67, 70–71, 80, 95, 156, Acc. 35108, LVA; Schedule of Schools Under the Pennsylvania Freedmen's Relief Association, Quarters Ending 31 Dec. 1869 and 31 Mar. 1870, Letters Received, 1 Jan.–24 Aug. 1870, Roll 5, Supt. of Ed., Va., BRFAL.

Tuesday, 16 November 1869

Decided to start house-keeping. Called on Major Willard[1] to invite him to address Teachers Institute. Could not find Mr. Hodgkinston at home.

Mr. Jones' son[2] shot himself while playing with a pistol.

Read "Taming a Shrew."[3]

Had a letter from L. Cass. Fegley, 413 North 19th Street Phila.

Started a local teachers Institute.

Read "the Press."[4] General Wool[5] is dead and burried.

Mr. Varner called here on his way home from Liberty.

I do hate cordially his bragging. If he treats other men as he does me in language he does more h[ar]me than two honest men can do good. This is [a] sober thought. I hope, however, he does better out of my presence.

1. H. H. Willard was a local lawyer whose office was located at 135 Main Street. *Lynchburg Business Directory, 1873, Containing a List of Every Branch of Business . . . Compiled by L. N. Lunsford & Co.* (Lynchburg, 1873), 70.

2. Samuel Jones, son of Charles T. Jones, accidentally killed himself with a pistol. Christian, *Lynchburg and Its People*, 273.

3. William Shakespeare's play *The Taming of a Shrew*.

4. Presumably JY was reading the *Lynchburg Press* (the city's second newspaper with this name), which was established in mid-1869 by J[ohn] P. Wright and Company and edited by George P. Button. Lester J. Cappon, *Virginia Newspapers, 1821–1935: A Bibliography with Historical Introduction and Notes* (New York and London, 1936), 121.

5. John Ellis Wool (1784–1869), American army officer, commanded Union forces in Virginia, 1861–1862. He prevented the Confederate capture of Fort Monroe and occupied the city of Norfolk. He was promoted to major general at age seventy-two and retired in 1863. *DAB*, s.v. "John Ellis Wool"; Patricia L. Faust, ed., *Historical Times Illustrated Encyclopedia of the Civil War* (New York, 1986), 842.

Wednesday, 17 November 1869

Had letters from T. Y. Scott,[1] Armistead and "Many Parents of Lowry's Crossing."[2] Wrote Mark R. Lloyd.

Listened to discussion on politics at Victors and Ambler's.[3]

I see again how irresponsible the Colored People are.

Had letters from Corson, Allen, Johnson[4] and Matthias.[5] I do not know that I [have] had six letter[s] before in a day.

Wrote Bauman and Jonathan Worman, Corson.

Attended lecture by Bitting & Bible Class.

Received Boots and Books from home.

Read a part of Shakespere and Physiology.

Received check "No. 89" of Corson.

1. Thomas Y. Scott was a black teacher of freedmen at Yellow Branch in Campbell County. Schedule of Schools Under the Pennsylvania Freedmen's Relief Association, Quarter Ending 31 Mar. 1870, Letters Received, 1 Jan.– 24 Aug. 1870, Roll 5, Supt. of Ed., Va., BRFAL.

2. Rosetta Armistead was a PFRA teacher in 1869–1870 at Lowry's Crossing in Bedford County, Va. Rosetta Armistead to Ralza M. Manly, 30 June 1869, Unregistered Letters Received, May–Nov. 1869, Roll 9; Schedule of Schools Under the Pennsylvania Freedmen's Relief Association, Quarters Ending 31 Dec. 1869 and 31 Mar. 1870, Letters Received, 1 Jan.–24 Aug. 1870, Roll 5, Supt. of Ed., Va., BRFAL.

3. The Victor and Ambler book and stationary store in Lynchburg was operated by thirty-five-year-old Henry C. Victor and thirty-nine-year-old John J. Ambler. *Lynchburg Business Directory, 1873*, [4], 68; Virginia Census, 1870, Campbell County, Lynchburg, 530A (Ambler), 536 (Victor).

4. JY had two teachers named Johnson on his roster. Priscilla (Percella) Johnson was a PFRA teacher first at Pleasant Hill and then by Jan. 1870 at Lapsley's Run, both in Botetourt County. Henry H. Johnson, from Brooklyn, N.Y., taught at a school at Holcombe's Crossing in Bedford County. Ralza M. Manly to Capt. R. S. Lacey, 1 Jan. 1869, enclosing pay for Percilla Johnson et al., for teaching in Dec. 1868; Schedule of Schools under the Pennsylvania Freedmen's Relief Association in the State of Virginia, Quarters Ending 31 Dec. 1869, 31 Mar. 1870, and 30 June 1870, Letters Received, 1 Jan.–24 Aug. 1870, Roll 5; Monthly Statistical School Reports of District Superintendents, Jan. and Feb. 1869, Roll 12, Supt. of Ed., Va., BRFAL.

5. The name A. J. Mathias is found on a list of unidentified names on the front endpapers of JY's 1869–1870 diary. Yoder Diaries, 1869–1870, Acc. 27680, LVA.

Thursday, 18 November 1869

I am not a saint yet.

This morning I went to Depot at 3½ o'clock to go to Liberty. Painfully the train left me behind. Took a review of Dry Goods sent here last year. Attended to some business accounts.

Visited Mr. Brooke[1] in company of Miss Whitaker.[2] Had more conversation on politics than for a month previous. I am more and more inclined to conservatism, though I would not be a democrat at home.

I read the good the Old Independent. Read some "Hamlet."

Had a letter from James H. Dotterer.

Wrote Varner and Miss Couch.[3]

This has been Thanks-Giving Day. But the thanks were all invisible. It was unobserved except by Post Office Revenue Office and Banks—nominally.

I would now be ready to conclude this to be a very wicked world if I were not very wicked myself.

I am pleased to learn that at an early day, steps will be taken to open free schools.

1. This may be Lewis P. Brook, a fifty-three-year-old local white Radical who had been born in Pa. and who was president of the Lynchburg Manufacturing Company. In 1871 he ran for city council on the "Peoples Ticket." Virginia Census, 1870, Campbell County, Brookville Township, 419; *Lynchburg News*, 7 Dec. 1869, 19 May 1871. In a letter to PFRA secretary Robert Corson of 18 Apr. 1870, JY mentioned a Mr. Brook whom he described as a "member of city council and native of Pottsville, Pa." Yoder Letter Book, 3 Mar. 1870–1 Dec. 1870, p. 106, Acc. 35108, LVA.

2. The sisters Anna and Ada Whitaker were both teaching in Lynchburg at this time. Anna would become JY's wife in June 1871. Schedule of Schools Under the Pennsylvania Freedmen's Relief Association, Quarters Ending 31 Dec. 1869, 31 Mar. 1870, and 30 June 1870, Letters Received, 1 Jan.–24 Aug. 1870, Roll 5, Supt. of Ed., Va., BRFAL; Virginia Bureau of Vital Statistics, Marriages, Lynchburg City, 1859–1901, Jacob E. Yoder to Anna F. Whittaker, 28 June 1871, p. 13, LVA.

3. Fannie A. Couch was a PFRA teacher from Pottsville, Pa., who taught freedmen at Fincastle in Botetourt County, Va. Before coming to Virginia, she had taught in Murfreesboro, Tenn. Schedule of Schools Under the Pennsylvania Freedmen's Relief Association, Quarters Ending 31 Dec. 1869, 31 Mar. 1870, and 30 June 1870, Letters Received, 1 Jan.–24 Aug. 1870, Roll 5, Supt. of Ed., Va., BRFAL.

Friday, 19 November 1869

Wrote Mathias, Mark R. Lloyd, I. Erb. Had a letter from Lloyd and Manly.

Published and u[n]published Manly's address tonight, as Mr. Manly tells me that his journey is "unavoidably deferred."[1]

Mr. Scott stays with me to night.

1. R. M. Manly to JY, 19 Nov. 1869, Letters Sent, Vol. 4 (54), p. 63, 10 Nov. 1869–28 Mar. 1870, Roll 3, Supt. of Ed., Va., BRFAL.

Saturday, 20 November 1869

Had to attend to consultations of the House Keeping affairs. Made out seven subscription lists for new school-house.[1]

Called at different places. Found at last Mr. Hodgkinston at home.

Began an article on Education for the press.

Wrote Mac,[2] and two letters to McGoldrick, I. S. Erb & Mrs. R. Lanning.[3]

Had letters from Couch, Mac, Varner, J. L. Bauer, Worman, Manly and Lanning.

1. Several African American citizens in Lynchburg originally asked the Freedmen's Bureau in Dec. 1868 that they be given the use of one of the barracks buildings at Camp Davis as a school. From that request evolved the formation of the Educational Association of Lynchburg (also known as the Howard Educational Association) and the construction of the Polk Street School to which JY refers here. Just before the dedication of the new edifice JY wrote to Robert A. Perkins, one of the Association's members, that if Perkins could do so he should have the attendees at the ceremony give contributions toward this "the first free school for hundreds of miles around." In this way, the donors would immortalize themselves: "Five hundred years to come what race will ransack the archives of Lynchburg to see who to [sic] took the lead in giving a free School School[-]House to Lynchburg. Not a few white men will then with Shame Confess the truth about this matter. You and I will watch then their search with what kind of an interest you may imagine." JY to Robert A. Perkins, 7 Mar. 1870, Yoder Letter Book, 3 Mar. 1870–1 Dec. 1870, pp. 14–16, Acc. 35108, LVA.

2. "Mac" was probably Charles W. McMahon.

3. Rosetta Lanning was a PFRA teacher at Coolwell in Amherst County, Va. JY to R. M. Manly, 27 Apr. 1870, Unregistered Letters Received, Dec. 1869–Aug. 1870, Roll 10; Schedule

of Schools Under the Pennsylvania Freedmen's Relief Association, Quarters Ending 31 Dec. 1869, 31 Mar. 1870, and 30 June 1870, Letters Received, 1 Jan.–24 Aug. 1870, Roll 5, Supt. of Ed., Va., BRFAL.

Sunday, 21 November 1869

Taught Sabbath School. 13th Chapter was the lesson. Then attended service at 2nd Presbyterian.[1] There was a funeral. Subject: "It is well." 2nd Kings 4th Chap 26 verse.

Formed the acquaintance of some young men. Yesterday I saw the smallest man I ever saw. His name is "Col. Sheffin" Bedford County, Va.

Explained scripture to Mr. Hayden.

Continued Last nights article for the Press.

Attended 1st Presbyterian Church.

Read a part of Richard the III.

1. Second Presbyterian Church was located on the corner of Church and Ninth Streets and was built in 1851–1852. *Chataigne's Lynchburg City Directory, 1875–76*, 15; Chambers, *Lynchburg: An Architectural History*, 167–169.

Monday, 22 November 1869

Squared a business account with Mr. Jones.

Completed Press article. Started to visit Miss Lanning's School. After Riding 4 miles I found that it is seven miles further than I thought it it was, & so I turned round on the Spot.

Wrote Mr. John Bauman, Varner, Morgan,[1] Corson.

Had letter from Manly, Corson, Burton,[2] Stauffer.

Wrote Chockly,[3] Corson, "Adams & Bro."[4]

Mr. Hollins of Mrs. Lanning's school called.

1. Royal J. Morgan was an African American Lynchburg resident and a member of the Educational Association of Lynchburg Board of Trustees for black schools. In Nov. 1869, he and his associate Nelson James were awarded the contract to do the plastering and furnish desks for the new Polk Street School. Morgan was also active in local Radical politics and served as treasurer of the Court Street African Baptist Church. Z. A. Cozzens to Manly, 25 May 1869; R. J. Morgan to Manly, 19 Oct. 1869; R. A. Perkins to Manly, 14 Nov. 1869; Royal J. Morgan and Nelson James to Manly, 6 Dec. 1869, including "Bill of Materials for the Erection of a School," Letters Received, A–V, 22 Apr.–31 Dec. 1869, Roll 4; Educational Association of Lynchburg, Board of Trustees, 1 Jan. 1870; Morgan to Manly, 1 and 6 Jan. 1870; Perkins to Manly, 13 Jan. 1870; Morgan to Manly, 19 Feb. 1870, Unregistered Letters Received, Dec.

1869–Aug. 1870, Roll 10, Supt. of Ed., Va., BRFAL; Account 185, Court Street Baptist Church, 25 July 1871, Lynchburg, Va., Accounts, 8 July–22 Aug. 1871, Registers of Signatures of Depositors in Branches of the Freedman's Savings and Trust Company, 1865–1874, Records of the Comptroller of the Currency, Record Group 101, NARA; *Lynchburg Virginian*, 8 May 1871, p. 3.

2. Roderick S. Burton was a native white PFRA teacher first at Buchanan and then at Pattonsburg in Botetourt County, Va. Subassistant Commissioner's Monthly Report, Oct.–Nov. 1868, Monthly School Reports of Assistant Subassistant Commissioners and Agents, Jan. 1868–Jan. 1869, Roll 13; District Superintendent's Monthly School Reports for Dec. 1868, Jan. and Feb. 1869, Monthly Statistical School Reports of District Superintendents, July 1865–Apr. 1869 and Jan. 1870, Roll 12, Supt. of Ed., Va., BRFAL.

3. Virginia A. Chockley was a white PFRA teacher at Amherst County Court House. Sometimes JY referred to her humorously as Mrs. Chocklett (chocolate). Subassistant Commissioner's Monthly Report, Jan.–Nov. 1868, Monthly School Reports of Assistant Subassistant Commissioners and Agents, Jan. 1868–Jan. 1869, Roll 13; District Superintendent's Monthly School Reports for Dec. 1868, Jan. and Feb. 1869, Monthly Statistical School Reports of District Superintendents, July 1865–Apr. 1869 and Jan. 1870, Roll 12; Mrs. V. A. Chockley, Amherst County, Report of 29 Apr. 1869, in Teachers' Monthly School Reports, Nov. 1865–Apr. 1869, Roll 15, Supt. of Ed., Va., BRFAL; JY to Robert R. Corson, 4 May 1870, listing the teachers in his district including "Mrs. V. A. Chocklett," Yoder Letter Book, 3 Mar. 1870–1 Dec. 1870, p. 110, Acc. 35108, LVA.

4. The I. H. Adams and Brothers lumber and coal business was located at the Upper Basin in Lynchburg. *Lynchburg Business Directory*, *1873*, 8, 10.

Saturday, 27 November 1869

This morning I arrived from a trip to Fincastle.[1] Started on Tuesday Morning. The rain made it an unpleasant trip to Liberty. Once I had to jump off the train. Stayed the day at Liberty with McGoldrick. At night went up to Bonsack[2] at night. The Hotel Keeper is a straight forward conservative.

Next day I went by stage to Cloverdale.[3] He[re] I called on Mr. Scott's[4] school. Was well pleased with the School. It is a working School.

From here I walked to Fincastle ten miles in three hours. Met ladies and Lloyd.

Next day visited their school. It is only 40 strong. In this respect it is not doing as well as it might. At night had an educational meeting. It was a success. The people are alive to the subject of education. Hence they prosper otherwise. There are a large proportion of the colored people possessors of their own houses. This is a beautiful county, and a peculiar people. This valley looks like Lancaster County Pa. Conversed with the most honorable colored man I ever saw Samuel Pogue.[5]

Friday I returned to Bonsack by Stage to Bonsack. This place I left this morning at 5 O'clock.

Had letters from Manly, Spencer,[6] Armistead, Mrs. Smith,[7] Dear Sisson and Jonathan.

Had telegram from Manly.

Wrote Manly, Morgan, Armistead.

1. Fincastle was the county seat of Botetourt County.

2. Bonsack was located in Roanoke County near the Botetourt County line.

3. Cloverdale was in Botetourt County near the Roanoke County line.

4.   Samuel Scott was a teacher at the Cloverdale School. District Superintendent's Monthly School Reports for Jan. and Feb. 1869, Monthly Statistical School Reports of District Superintendents, July 1865– Apr. 1869 and Jan. 1870, Roll 12, Supt. of Ed., Va., BRFAL.

5. In Oct. 1869, Samuel Pogue was a PFRA teacher at Lapsley's Run in Botetourt County. Report of Nov. 1869, in Teachers' Monthly School Reports, Sept.– Nov. 1869, Roll 17, Supt. of Ed., Va., BRFAL.

6. Laura Spencer was an African American PFRA teacher at the Court Street Church School in Lynchburg for part of the 1868–1869 school year. District Superintendent's Monthly School Reports for Jan. and Feb. 1869, Monthly Statistical School Reports of District Superintendents, July 1865–Apr. 1869 and Jan. 1870, Roll 12, Supt. of Ed., Va., BRFAL.

7. This was more likely Mrs. Lucinda Smith, a PFRA teacher who taught at Lovingston and at Pleasant Valley (Dec. 1868) in Nelson County. Pauline Smith (who signed herself "Miss") also taught in Pleasant Valley during the 1868–1869 school year. Lucinda Smith later taught at "McIver's Station" (McIvor's Depot) and at Coolwell in Amherst County. Subassistant Commissioner's Monthly Report, Oct.–Dec. 1868, Jan.–Feb. 1869, Monthly School Reports of Assistant Subassistant Commissioners and Agents, Jan. 1868–Jan. 1869, Roll 13; Mrs. Lucinda Smith, Lovingston School, Nelson County, Report of 31 Mar. 1869, in Teachers' Monthly School Reports, Nov. 1865–Apr. 1869, Roll 15; Schedule of Schools Under the Pennsylvania Freedmen's Relief Association, Quarters Ending 31 Dec. 1869, 31 Mar. 1870, and 30 June 1870, Letters Received, 1 Jan.–24 Aug. 1870, Roll 5, Supt. of Ed., Va., BRFAL.

Sunday, 28 November 1869

Met Miss. Attwood.[1] Attended Sunday school twice preaching at Baptist Church. Attended Missionary Meeting at Baptist. Wrote Wilson,[2] Burton, McGoldrick, Mrs. Smith, Varner.

Rec'd letters from Manly and Burton.

1. Phebe A. Attwood was a PFRA teacher in Lynchburg in 1869–1870. Schedule of Schools Under the Pennsylvania Freedmen's Relief Association, Quarters Ending 31 Dec. 1869, 31 Mar. 1870, and 30 June 1870, Letters Received, 1 Jan.–24 Aug. 1870, Roll 5, Supt. of Ed., Va., BRFAL; JY to Robert R. Corson, 4 May 1870, listing the teachers in his district, Yoder Letter Book, 3 Mar. 1870–1 Dec. 1870, p. 110, Acc. 35108, LVA.

2. H. A. W. Wilson was a PFRA teacher at Arrington in Nelson County. Schedule of Schools Under the Pennsylvania Freedmen's Relief Association, Quarters Ending 31 Dec. 1869, 31 Mar. 1870, and 30 June 1870, Letters Received, 1 Jan.–24 Aug. 1870, Roll 5, Supt. of Ed., Va., BRFAL.

Monday, 29 November 1869

Got coal. Borrowed Money before breakfast. Visited all the Schools; some with Manly and others alone. Visited four of City council. Saw School house lot.

Tuesday, 30 November 1869[1]

Rose at 2½ [A.M.] Came to Goods Crossing[2] before day light. Started out in search of J. E. Morris[3] school immediately.

Begged my breakfast at eight o'clock. Hunger is a good cook indeed. Spoke to School and left at at 11 o'clock. Come to Lowrys xing at at one. Visited Mrs. Armistead's school about 4 minutes, returned to Depot in time for freight train. Walked thirteen Miles.

Had letter from Varner. Wrote Varner.

1. JY mistakenly wrote 29 November 1869 as he began this entry, and then realized his mistake and wrote 30 November 1869 on the next line.

2. Goode is in Bedford County.

3. James E. Morris was a teacher at Ebenezer in Bedford County in Apr. 1869 and at Lowry's Crossing, also in Bedford County, during the 1869–1870 school year. James E. Morris, Report of Apr. 1869, in Teachers' Monthly School Reports, Nov. 1865– Apr. 1869, Roll 15; Schedule of Schools Under the Pennsylvania Freedmen's Relief Association, Quarters Ending 31 Dec. 1869, 31 Mar. 1870, and 30 June 1870, Letters Received, 1 Jan.–24 Aug. 1870, Roll 5, Supt. of Ed., Va., BRFAL; JY to Robert R. Corson, 4 May 1870, listing the teachers in his district, Yoder Letter Book, 3 Mar. 1870–1 Dec. 1870, p. 110, Acc. 35108, LVA.

Wednesday, 1 December 1869

Had letters from Foster, T. Y. Scott, Varner, Mac, Wilson, & c. Burton.

Wrote Mrs. Lanning.

Visited Mrs. Laning's School. Seven miles from the rail road.

The opposition to her school bitter.

Met a man who deplores the education of the "niggers." He should deplore his own ignorance. If so he would be nearer the mark.

Attended lecture at Baptist Church.

Thursday, 2 December 1869

Visited Schools in town.

Wrote Mrs. R. Armistead to quit school.

Had letters from Morris and McGoldrick.

Worked at the financial report.

Wrote Corson at Length.

Visited ladies.

Miss Harvey made another desperate effort to get a position as teacher. Apparently she has failed again. The leading men had a long consultation with me about her. I gave my word against her every time.[1] Tried to get Patent Slating.

1. Fannie Harvey had served as a Freedmen's Bureau teacher from Feb. 1868 until at least May 1869, at which time she was employed at the Jackson Street School where JY himself was teaching. Whatever she did to offend JY is not revealed, but clearly JY's displeasure with her did not have a long-term effect. When the public schools opened in Lynchburg in Apr. 1871, Harvey became principal of Public School No. 8, located in her house on Franklin Hill. Indeed, Orra Langhorne, writing in 1880 when Harvey was teaching in the now-public Polk Street School where JY was the principal, described Harvey as "one of those truly called to to [sic] teach, and a glance at her attentive, orderly scholars shows the observer that she realizes the importance of the teacher's office." In fact, she had renounced "the switch or ruler, which so often forms the badge of office with instructors" for decorating with plants and minerals, "the nature of which 'Miss Fanny' carefully explains to her pupils, and the interest the children show in collecting such things testifies to the confidence and affection they feel for their teacher." Subassistant Commissioner's Monthly Report, Oct.–Dec. 1868, Jan.–Feb. 1869, Monthly School Reports of Assistant Subassistant Commissioners and Agents, Jan. 1868–Jan. 1869, Roll 13; J. E. Yoder, Millie Phelps, and Fannie Harvey, Jackson Street School, Lynchburg, Report of May 1869, in Teachers' Monthly School Reports, May–Aug. 1869, Roll 16, Supt. of Ed., Va., BRFAL; Langhorne, "Visit to Colored Schools," 77–78; Sheriff, *Sheriffs Lynchburg City Directory, 1876–1877*, 14.

Friday, 3 December 1869

Weather is colder. Read in Crabs Synomyms.[1]

Wrote Miss Leftwich.[2] Prepared to go to Appomattox C. H. came too late for train. Took a look at the selling of tobacco.

Visited Misses. Whitakers Schools.[3]

Some naughty boys are throwing in window lights at Miss. Ada Whitaker's school even in school hours. Five or six have been battered in.

Mr. Harry Saunders[4] and Mr. Cobbin of Yellow Branch have been visiting me. They gave a dissatisfactory account of Mr. Scott's school.

Read Synonymes.

Attended Prayermeeting at Baptist Church.

1. George Crabb, *English Synonymes Explained, in Alphabetical Order; with Copius Illustrations and Examples Drawn from the Best Writers* (Boston, 1819).

2. Ella Leftwich was a PFRA teacher at Mount Zion in Campbell County in 1868–1869 and at New Glasgow in Amherst in 1869–1870. Subassistant Commissioner's Monthly Report, Sept.–Nov. 1868, Monthly School Reports of Assistant Subassistant Commissioners and Agents, Jan. 1868–Jan. 1869, Roll 13; District Superintendent's Monthly School Reports for Dec. 1868, Jan. and Feb. 1869, Monthly Statistical School Reports of District Superintendents, July 1865–Apr. 1869 and Jan. 1870, Roll 12; Miss Ella Leftwich, New Glasgow, Report of 29 Apr. 1869, in Teachers' Monthly School Reports, Nov. 1865–Apr. 1869, Roll 15; Schedule of Schools Under the Pennsylvania Freedmen's Relief Association, Quarters Ending 31 Dec. 1869, 31 Mar. 1870, and 30 June 1870, Letters Received, 1 Jan.–24 Aug. 1870, Roll 5, Supt. of Ed., Va., BRFAL; JY to Robert R. Corson, 4 May 1870, listing the teachers in his district, Yoder Letter Book, 3 Mar. 1870–1 Dec. 1870, p. 110, Acc. 35108, LVA.

3. At this time Anna Whitaker was teaching in the Normal School in Lynchburg and her sister Ada (Adaline) Whitaker was at the Madison Street School. Anna F. Whitaker, Normal School, Lynchburg, and Ada Whitaker, Madison Street School, Lynchburg, Reports of Nov. 1869, in Teachers' Monthly School Reports, Sept.–Nov. 1869, Roll 17, Supt. of Ed., Va., BRFAL.

4. The 1870 Virginia census index gives only one Saunders in the area who might have been Harry: Henry Saunders, age fifty, a black farm laborer living in the Otter township area of Bedford County with his wife and three children (the oldest age thirteen). Virginia Census, 1870, Bedford County, Otter Township, 287A.

Saturday, 4 December 1869

Had a great deal of company. Made a plan[1] to finish the New Glasgow School House.

Had a letter from Corson.

Wrote J. Bauman, Jonathan, and Keck, McMahon and Varner.

Col. Wood called here.

1. JY originally wrote "a great plan" and then deleted "great."

Sunday, 5 December 1869

Attended Sunday School. It was very small. I had the whole school in my class.

It was rainy. No Service at most of the Churches. There must be a great many fair-weather Christians in this place.[1] Afternoon attended preaching at the Colored Methodist Church.

Col Brown's[2] funeral services were performed. He came to his death by an accidental discharge of a gun.

Had a letter of Forrest.

At night attended service at Methodist Protestant church.

A large part of the day I read synonyms. I appreciate this study very highly because I am deficient in this branch of education. Am very sorry that I did not before make this a study. This book was recommended to me years ago but never had an opportunity to get it.

1. JY's friend Charles C. Bitting encountered this phenomenon at First Baptist Church one night when the time came for the prayer meeting and no one was there but his wife and himself. When Caroline Bitting noted at eight o'clock that no one else was present, Bitting told her "It is time to begin." They then sang a hymn, Bitting led a prayer, and they had begun singing a second hymn when a few congregants entered. The newcomers "were surprised to find the meeting in progress with no one present save the pastor and his wife." It took only a few more occasions like this to bring "the people to greater promptness." Taylor, *Virginia Baptist Ministers, Fourth Series*, 335–336.

2. Col. William B. Brown, characterized as "an old and honorable citizen," was accidentally shot through the leg at Fisher's store and died on 3 Dec. 1869. The site of the store was probably Cyrus Fisher's establishment at 176 Main Street where he sold guns and cutlery. Christian, *Lynchburg and Its People*, 273; *Lynchburg Business Directory, 1873*, 29.

Wednesday, 8 December 1869

Since Sunday wrote Corson twice, Manly, Morgan, McGoldrick. Had letters from James Lynch,[1] Mrs. Armistead, Manly, Corson, R. Herb, Jonathan, Kate.

Made differents lists about school to Corson.

Wrote an article to Paper entitled Ignorance.

Morgan tried my patience much about the tent cloth which he stole last year.

Gave a lecturing to Mr. Scott for his negligence at School. He stayed with me last night. Wrote Varner.

Commenced reading "Ivanhoe."[2]

Manly says the New Glasgow appropriation is accepted.

Wrote Mr. Whorton[3] New Glasgow.

1. A James Lynch was listed in 1879 as a black laborer residing on Diamond Hill. R. A. Smith, comp., *J. P. Bell & Co.'s City Directory of Lynchburg, Virginia, 1879–'80* ([Lynchburg, 1880]), 130.

2. *Ivanhoe*, a novel by Sir Walter Scott.

3. Alexander Wharton, of Amherst County, was listed in the 1870 census as a thirty-nine-year-old mulatto farmhand, who had a wife and five children. Virginia Census, 1870, Amherst County, Temperance Township, p. 564A.

Thursday, 9 December 1869[1]

Read a part of Ivanhoe. Wrote a long letter to J. H. Fritz,[2] to Jonathan, John Bauman, Wm L. Bowman.[3] Read two Independents.

Gave a lesson to ladies in German. Gave a lesson to James Perry.[4]

Put up a stove in Miss Attwoods room.

Spent the last cent for wood I had.

Read the evening press.

Had a letter from Bauman and McGoldrick. Wm. L. Bowman called and I was absent. I was so sorry for it.

1. JY mistakenly dated this entry as "8 December," repeating the date of the previous entry. It was actually 9 December.

2. Jonathan Harry Fritz, of Somerset County, Pa., was a class- and roommate of JY at Millersville. He was enrolled in 1865–1866. *Catalogue, 1865–66*, 11.

3. William L. Bowman was a tobacco manufacturer who resided at the corner of Eleventh and Wise Streets. *Chataigne's Lynchburg City Directory, 1875–76*, 33; Virginia Census, 1870, Campbell County, Lynchburg, 549.

4. In 1873 James Perry was listed as an African American barber at the Orange House. *Lynchburg Business Directory, 1873*, 74, 81.

Friday, 10 December 1869[1]

Read a part of Ivanhoe and Independent.

Had letter from Lynch, Manly.

Wrote Mark Lloyd and Morgan.

I had a check from Manly for $77 to aid the Building of Yellow Branch School House and Repairing Madison St. School House.[2]

Manly sends me a letter which originates from Yellow Branch.

Attended Prayermeeting at the African Baptist Church.

1. JY mistakenly dated this entry 9 December.

2. JY wrote to R. M. Manly late in Oct. 1869 to report that early in the month he had established a school with fifty-three students at Yellow Branch in Campbell County. He requested the aid of the Bureau in building a new schoolhouse to accommodate the others who wanted to attend. On 9 Dec., JY wrote again, thanking Manly for the check to build at Yellow Branch and to repair the Madison Street School in Lynchburg. He was able to report in mid-Jan. 1870 that in fact the Yellow Branch School had been completed and that a local man Griffin Phillips would open the school on 18 Jan. JY to R. M. Manly, 28 Oct., 9 Dec. 1869, 8

and 14 Jan. 1870, Unregistered Letters Received, Dec. 1869–Aug. 1870, Roll 10, Supt. of Ed., Va., BRFAL.

Saturday, 11 December 1869

McGoldrick did not come, according his promise. Check from Philadelphia did not come as was expected and promised.

The box I sent the Ladies was carried the the wrong place.

The good[s] now in possession of Morgan and promised to me "on his honor" are not received. The coal which was ordered to the ladies did not come till afternight.

I drew $77 at Bank. Bought wood for myself. Paid Richard Coles.[1] Loaned money to the ladies. Paid coal.

Wrote notices for Educational Meeting. Fetched Stove pipe for ladies and carried the same to Stove Store. Fetched the goods sent to Ladies at Island Depot.

Read in Ivanhoe and the Press.

Busy all day.

1. Richard Coles was a black laborer who resided on Franklin Hill. Sheriff, *Sheriffs Lynchburg City Directory, 1876–1877,* 44.

Sunday, 12 December 1869

Disappointments commence early this morning. A change in the time table of O. and A. R. R.[1] left me behind the train I[2] intended to go to New Glasgow on a promise made several days ago.

Attended Sabbath School afterwards preaching by Rev. Foreman.[3] At the close of service some one took my ha[t] while I stepped up to give my contribution. Of course I got [back] a more worthless hat than my own.

Visited the ladies afternoon. Took a walk with Miss Whitaker.

At night attended preaching by Rev. Bitting. The room was too hot. I had no benefit from the sermon.

Had letters from Manly.

Wrote Manly, Wharton, and James Lynch.

1. The Orange and Alexandria Railroad had merged with the Manassas Gap Railroad in 1867 to form the Orange, Alexandria, and Manassas Railroad. It covered 148.8 miles in Virginia from Lynchburg, via Charlottesville and Gordonsville, to Alexandria. Poor, *Manual of the Railroads of the United States, for 1868–69,* 198–199.

2. JY originally wrote "where" and then substituted "I."

3. William W. Foreman, a forty-seven-year-old African American, was the pastor of the African Methodist Episcopal Church on Jackson Street. He and his wife, Ruth A. Foreman, were born in Maryland. Virginia Census, 1870, Lynchburg, 49; *J. P. Bell & Co.'s City Directory of Lynchburg, Virginia, 1879–'80*, 86. See also Lynchburg School Board Minutes for 2 July 1877, vol. 2, 24 Jan. 1877–24 Dec. 1881, p. 23, Lynchburg School Board, Lynchburg, Va. For a short history of the Jackson Street AME Church, which met for a while at Camp Davis in 1866, see Lib Wiley, *Alongside the River: A History of Lynchburg's Congregations* ([Lynchburg, 1986]), 8–9.

Monday, 13 December 1869

Made several little purchases.

Made trip with horse and buggy to Yellow Branch School.

Mr. Scott is one of the lowest type of humanity.

He had done too desperately mean by the people. He robbed them of at least $25 dollars.

I met Maj. Robert C. Saunders.[1] This is a Virginia Gentleman. He is wealthy, intelligent and a planter. I took supper with him. He invited me to stay with him at night. I declined his hospitality because I desired to be home.

I left his place at 7 O'clock. Arrived at Lynchburg after midnight.

It was a most charming moonlight night. The distance 18 miles. It was too great to be pleasant. A letter McG.

1. Robert C. Saunders (1827–1902), son of Judge Fleming and Alice Watts Saunders, of Bleak Hill, Franklin County, and Flat Creek, Campbell County, was a former Virginia legislator and former Confederate soldier and quartermaster. His home was at Evington in Campbell County, approximately twelve miles southwest of Lynchburg. Early, *Campbell Chronicles and Family Sketches*, 109, 113; Nathaniel Claiborne Hale, *Roots in Virginia . . .* (Philadelphia, 1948), 77, 81–82.

Tuesday, 14 December 1869

Sorrow and sadness broods over me. Not yet received my money from Society. And I need it on everyhand.

Wrote Mrs. Lanning. Mr. McGoldrick.

Read a large part of Ivanhoe.

Wednesday, 15 December 1869

Nothing but rain and gloom. This Gloomy night did not bring me a cheerful letter.

Had a letter from Manly.

Thursday, 16 December 1869

No letter from Corson with Check, but a letter in regard to Christmas presents.

Two letters from Varner. Put a partition in Baptist Church.

Sent Corson a telegram for Money.

Wrote Manly.

Had lots of company. Teacher meeting at night.

Read the Press.

Friday, 17 December 1869

Rec'd Christmas presents.

Wrote Corson, Worman, Dotterer.

Had a letter from Corson.

The Sexton brought a part of the tent cloth.

Attended Young Men's Prayermeeting. Sorted presents.

Saturday, 18 December 1869

No money again. Borrowed another $5.00. Divided the Christmas gifts and sent those coming to Miss. Leftwich, Mrs. Smith and Mr. J. E. McGoldrick.

Was Crowded all day with Company.

Had letters from J. E. Morris, and Lloyd.

Wrote Morris, Lynch and Saunders.

Sunday, 19 December 1869

Made a trip to Corncord School[1] to organize a School which I did. The assembly was small on account of the bad roads. The distance is nine miles.

Took dinner at Mr. Moore's, a northern man. Came home at night.

Had a letter from Corson containing a check for $646.66. So long I had waited for it. Worked till midnight on writing, packing Christmas presents.

Attended preaching by Bitting at night. Sermon was every good.

Wrote Varner, Wilson, Leftwich, Chockly.

1. Concord School was located in Campbell County along the border of Appomattox County.

Monday, 20 December 1869

Sent Christmas presents to Pamplins,[1] Wilson, Mac and Dean[2] by express.

Sent P. O. Money orders to Couch, McGoldrick, Varner.

Sent in Registered letter money to R. S. Burton.

Paid Goodman,[3] Victor, Wood, Perkins Whitaker, Whitaker, Attwood, Stevens,[4] Richardson,[5] Armistead, Fanny Adams.

Read press. Had visitors and what not?

Wrote McGoldrick, Couch, Armistead, Lanning, Chockly, Corson.

Inquired for Board at Mrs. Murrays.[6]

Had letters from Mac, Varner & Chockly. Had a talk with Col. Wood.

1. Pamplin's Depot, later called Pamplin City, was in Appomattox County on the border of Prince Edward County about twenty miles southeast of Lynchburg.

2. Clara A. Dean and Eliza P. Dean were teachers at Farmville. The former was from Fabius, N.Y., and the latter may have been as well. Schedule of Schools Under the Pennsylvania Freedmen's Relief Association, Quarters Ending 31 Dec. 1869, 31 Mar. 1870, and 30 June 1870, Letters Received, 1 Jan.–24 Aug. 1870, Roll 5, Supt. of Ed., Va., BRFAL.

3. J. Goodman and Son (owned by E. and J. Goodman, of Baltimore, Md.) was a clothing store at 122 Main Street. *Lynchburg Business Directory, 1873,* 33.

4. Esther A. Stevens was a PFRA teacher during the 1869–1870 school year. Schedule of Schools Under the Pennsylvania Freedmen's Relief Association, Quarters Ending 31 Dec. 1869, 31 Mar. 1870, and 30 June 1870, Letters Received, 1 Jan.–24 Aug. 1870, Roll 5, Supt. of Ed., Va., BRFAL; JY to Robert R. Corson, 5 Apr. 1870, listing the teachers in his district, Yoder Letter Book, 3 Mar. 1870–1 Dec. 1870, p. 78, Acc. 35108, LVA.

5. Fannie Richardson was a PFRA teacher at Arrington in Nelson County during the 1869–1870 school year. Ibid.

6. Jane Murray, the widow of Thomas, operated a boarding house at 189 Main Street. *Chataigne's Lynchburg City Directory, 1875–76,* 92.

Saturday, 25 December 1869

A gloomy Christmas day. Rain commenced at Noon. Work is suspended generally. Carousing is carried on extensively. It looks more like a fourth of July at home than Christmas.

Bought Christmas Presents for Ladies. Paid $6.00.

Read a large portion of Midlothian.[1]

Read Papers.

Lectured Mr. Hayden[2] on his want of energy.

Took a drink of liquor to facilitate circulation.

Read an article in the daily News about the shooting that occurred on Friday between a Cavalryman and a Citizen. The Citizen is dead. "The Citizens should shoot down this squad of men as mad dogs." This advice I do not like; yet I know not that the men referred to deserve anything better.[3]

Society seems to need protection against the Soldiers.

Wrote Manly.

1. *The Heart of Midlothian,* a novel by Sir Walter Scott.

2. JY probably was referring to Lindsey Hayden, who was teaching at Body Camp in Bedford County, although JY wrote what looks like "Sorden" and made a correction that could be interpreted as "Storyden."

3. A group of four drunken soldiers became disorderly and the police arrested two of them while the others got away. The escapees went back to their camp, gathered up some guns, and returned to town to "kill any policeman, or any 'd———d rebel' who should dare interfere with them." In the course of the soldiers' rampage, the police pursued them, accompanied by various others including William Boley, who lived near Campbell Court House. One of the soldiers took aim and shot Boley, who later died. The two soldiers then made good their escape from Lynchburg. According to local historian W. Asbury Christian, had the responsible soldier been caught, a lynching would have occurred. *Lynchburg News*, 24, 29, 30, 31 Dec. 1869, 1, 4, 15, 21, 22, 24–27 Jan., 3, 4, 7, 9, 10 Feb., 4 Apr. 1870; Christian, *Lynchburg and Its People*, 273.

Sunday,[1] 26 December 1869

No intercession to the rain. I was absent from Sunday School. Was at divine service at my own Church.[2] The minister read a sermon by Spurgeon[3] "The Lord giveth songs in the night."

Read Midlothian. Wrote Wm. Banister.[4]

Attended preaching at Baptist at night.

1. JY originally wrote "Monday, no Sunday" when starting this entry.

2. JY did not join College Hill Baptist Church until 1878. At this time, he may have been attending a Methodist church, possibly Centenary Methodist Episcopal Church on Church Street between Tenth and Eleventh Streets. Chambers, *Lynchburg: An Architectural History*, 319.

3. Charles Haddon Spurgeon (1834–1892) was an English Baptist minister and author.

4. William F. Bannister was a PFRA teacher at Mountain View in Botetourt County for part of the 1868–1869 school year and at Brookville in Botetourt in 1869–1870. District Superintendent's Monthly School Reports for Jan. and Feb. 1869, Monthly Statistical School Reports of District Superintendents, July 1865–Apr. 1869 and Jan. 1870, Roll 12; Schedule of Schools Under the Pennsylvania Freedmen's Relief Association, Quarters Ending 31 Dec. 1869 and 31 Mar. 1870, Letters Received, 1 Jan.–24 Aug. 1870, Roll 5, Supt. of Ed., Va., BRFAL.

Monday, 27 December 1869

Rain again. Changed my boarding place to Mrs. Murray. Concluded "The Heart of Midlothian." Forrest Staid with me. Got one half a ton of coal.

Had many callers.

Had a letter from Corson.

Heard lessons.

I have not completed my essay on Methods of teaching Grammar.

Tuesday, 28 December 1869

Callers commenced early. Among them are Wilson, Boling, Kelley.[1]

Wrote Purvis & Whorton.

1. William Kelly was an African American stonemason who resided on Polk Street near Sixth Street in Lynchburg. On 1 Aug. 1877, he represented black citizens before the Lynchburg School Board. *Chataigne's Lynchburg City Directory, 1875–76*, 76; Sheriff, *Sheriffs Lynchburg City Directory, 1876–1877*, 63; Lynchburg School Board Minutes, 24 Jan. 1877–24 Dec. 1881, 2:31.

Sunday, 9 January 1870

Crowding of work and illness[1] oblige me to omit a record of a remarkable portion of my life. I am not well now. Went to Church this morning but had to leave it soon.

Wrote Dan George, Corson & Manly. Read a speech by Father Hyacinth[2] on Education. Had a conversation with ladies on religion. Commenced a work on "Personal Religion."[3]

Attending preaching by Rev. Bitting at night. Suffered from this proceedure physiologically.

Misses Whitaker are made sad by the death of their father.[4]

1. JY informed Manly on the previous day that he had not been able to send three delinquent teachers' reports because of his "late illness," and on 10 Jan. noted in the diary that he was dosing himself for neuralgia. JY to Manly, 8 Jan. 1870, Unregistered Letters Received, Dec. 1869–Aug. 1870, Roll 10, Supt. of Ed., Va., BRFAL.

2. Charles Loyson, known as Père Hyacinthe (1827–1912), French priest, Carmelite, and "a forceful and well-received preacher at Notre Dame de Paris." In 1868, he left Catholicism in protest against a proposed definition of papal infallibility, was excommunicated in 1869, and married one of his American converts. He founded his own schismatic body at Paris in 1879, which eventually failed. Paul Kevin Meagher, Thomas C. O'Brien, and Consuelo Maria Aherne, eds., *Encyclopedic Dictionary of Religion* (Washington, D.C., 1979), 2:2170–2171; *The New Schaff-Herzog Encyclopedia of Religious Knowledge* (Grand Rapids, Mich., 1950), 7:52.

3. Possibly Henry Boardman, *The Great Question: Will You Consider the Subject of Personal Religion?* (Philadelphia and New York, ca. 1858).

4. George Whitaker was born on 24 Feb. 1799 and died on 6 Jan. 1870. On 26 Feb. 1826, he married Mary Colegrove who survived him. Whitaker family gravestones at Ashford, Conn., Cemetery; Whitaker family members, interviews by editor.

Monday, 10 January 1870

Numbered receipts for last month. Read a part of personal Religion. Visited the New School House. Conversed with Mr. Curle[1] and Mr. Kelsoe.

Heard Mr. Prides Lesson.

Had a letter from A. Varner.

Attended a business meeting of the Church. The business was extensive. It adjourned at ten o'clock.

Bought a remedy for Neuralgia. Took the first dose of it.

1. William Curle was a black carpenter who worked in the Upper Basin in Lynchburg and lived in Amherst County. *Chataigne's Lynchburg City Directory, 1875–76*, 46.

Tuesday, 11 January 1870

Squared my book accounts. Studied Book Keeping. Bought Wood. Collected $20 for Mr. Varner.

Read "Oemenical Council" in Harpers.[1]

Mr. J. D. Lanning was here.[2]

Wrote Jesse[3] & Varner. Numbered Blank Book. Heard a class in German.

Heard James Perry's Lesson.

1. JY refers to an article in *Harper's Weekly* about the Ecumenical Council held in Rome on 8 Dec. 1869. The article compared the prospects of this council with the last one, the Council of Trent, held in the mid-sixteenth century. The discussion included reference to the "protest" of Father Hyacinthe and to the concern of liberal Catholics that needed reforms would not be frustrated by the pope and his council. *Harper's Weekly* 13 (11 Dec. 1869): 794.

2. Rosetta Lanning ceased teaching her school at Coolwell in Amherst County at the end of the Jan.–Mar. 1870 quarter. Her husband, John D. Lanning, taught in her place for the remainder of the school year. Schedule of Schools under the Pennsylvania Freedmen's Relief Association in the State of Virginia, Together with Rental Account for the Quarters Ending 31 Mar. 1870 and 30 June 1870, Letters Received, 1 Jan.–24 Aug. 1870, Roll 5; Rosetta Lanning, Harris Creek School, Coolwell, Amherst County, Reports for Feb.–Mar. 1870, in Teachers' Monthly School Reports, Feb.–Mar. 1870, Roll 19; John D. Lanning, Harris Creek School, Coolwell, Amherst County, Reports for Apr.–May 1870, in Teachers' Monthly School Reports, Apr. 1870–June 1871, Roll 20, Supt. of Ed., Va., BRFAL; JY to Mrs. R. Lanning, 3 Mar. 1870;

JY to Robert R. Corson, 5 Apr., 4 May 1870, listing the teachers in his district, Yoder Letter Book, 3 Mar. 1870–1 Dec. 1870, pp. 8, 78, 110, Acc. 35108, LVA; Virginia Census, 1870, Amherst County, Amherst Township, 403. See also JY to Mrs. Rosetta Lanning, 1 Apr. 1870, Yoder Letter Book, 3 Mar. 1870–1 Dec. 1870, pp. 68–69, Acc. 35108, LVA. John and Rosetta Lanning, along with their three children, had been born in New Jersey. In the census taken in Aug. 1870, John was described as a fifty-year-old farmer, while Rosetta was thirty-three and keeping house.

3. JY was probably writing to his brother Jesse, who was twenty-three years old. In Mar. 1870, he wrote to Jesse twice about the fifty dollars he owed him, apologizing the first time for not having paid him sooner and the second time, when he sent the money, for needing to have twenty dollars paid to Mr. Mathias, a debt that he had not thought he owed. He also asked Jesse not to "loose patience" with him. Fretz, *Genealogical Record of the Descendants of Christian and Hans Meyer*, 527; JY to Jesse Yoder, 3 and 17 Mar. 1870, Yoder Letter Book, 3 Mar. 1870–1 Dec. 1870, pp. 3, 19, Acc. 35108, LVA.

Wednesday, 12 January 1870

Wrote receipts. Copied two general reports.

Heard four lessons.

Read the Messenger.[1]

Had letters from Mac, Corson, Wharton, Lloyd, and Dr. Christian (P. H.).[2]

Wrote Mac, Varner, Wharton, Leftwich.

Contracted for Wm. H. Richardson to go to Holcombe Rock to open a school.[3]

Attended lecture at Baptist.

1. JY may have been reading the *Reformed Church Messenger*, which began in York, Pa., in 1827 as the monthly *Magazine of the German Reformed Church*. In 1832 it became the *Messenger of the Reformed Church* and two years later was converted to a semimonthly. In 1838, it was transferred to Chambersburg as the *Weekly Messenger of the Reformed Church*, before moving again, this time in 1864 to Philadelphia. The name changed several times over the years, by 1867 being known as the *Reformed Church Messenger. The National Union Catalog, Pre-1956 Imprints*, vol. 485 (London, 1977), 412.

2. Dr. P. H. Christian's medical practice was located at 61 Ninth Street. *Chataigne's Lynchburg City Directory, 1875–76*, 42.

3. On 18 Feb. William H. Richardson began a primary school at Holcombe Rock, located in Bedford County along the James River, approximately twenty-five miles west of Lynchburg. William H. Richardson, Holcombe Rock School, Bedford County, Report of Feb. 1870, in Teachers' Monthly School Reports, Feb.–Mar. 1870, Roll 19, Supt. of Ed., Va., BRFAL.

Thursday, 13 January 1870

Read Independent. It is as good as ever.

Drew $624.[17]/100 at Bank. Paid out nearly all of it—some hand to hand, others by Post Office Money orders; other by mail in Registered letters. Wrote Miss. Couch, McGoldrick, Mr. Varner. Had letters from Varner, Mrs. Chockly & Shoemaker. How glad I was to hear once more from him!

The Yellow Branch School House is completed.

Wrote Maj. Saunders and Mrs. Chocklett.

Many of the colored men are still leaving for the south. Some of the Tobacco manufacturers are heeding the cry for better wages.

Friday, 14 January 1870

Copied four letters for the Educational Society. Went to Liberty in the Evening Train. Conversed with McGoldrick till 1½ O'clock at night. Had restless night.

Saturday, 15 January 1870

Came home in the Evening Freight from Liberty. Copied seven letter[s] for Educational Society. Had letters from Mac, J. W. Bauman, two from Manly.

Wrote Manly & Corson.

Sunday, 16 January 1870

Attended Sabbath School at Cold. [colored] Methodist School, preaching by Bitting and Preaching again at night by (P. E.) Brown at Court Street:

Had an interview with Mr. Wm. H. Stuart[1] on education.

Wrote Keck, Harry Saunders, Alex Wharton and McMahon.

1. William H. Stewart was a teacher of a freedmen-supported school at Long Mountain Church in Campbell County in the early months of 1869 and in Lynchburg in 1870. Monthly Statistical School Reports of District Superintendents, Feb. 1869, Roll 12; William H. Stewart, Long Mountain Church School, Campbell County, Report of 30 May 1869, in Teachers' Monthly School Reports, May–Aug. 1869, Roll 16; Schedule of Schools Under the Pennsylvania Freedmen's Relief Association, Quarters Ending 31 Mar. and 30 June 1870, Letters Received, 1 Jan.–24 Aug. 1870, Roll 5, Supt. of Ed., Va., BRFAL.

Monday, 17 January 1870

Copied five letters for R. A. Perkins.

Visited Pe[r]kins', Attwood's, Anna's, and Miss Stevens' schools.

Wrote Banister, Pogue, Capt. Sheaffer.

Got a Post Office Money Order for Miss. Anna. Read 70 pages of "Stepping Heavenward."[1] It is good and racy.

Had a letter from Miss Jackson.

Mr. Perkins school is disorderly. All talk at the same time, when none should talk without special permission. The same is true in regard to leaving of Seats.

Heard Mr. Prides lessons. Instructed some of the boys how to form a debating Society.

Read a part of Personal Religion.

I am still the servant of sin! When will I be master of my passions? I try try to hate sin. Yes I do. But how can I commit the sins that I hate! I can not understand myself in this matter.

1. Elizabeth Prentiss, *Stepping Heavenward* (New York, 1869).

Tuesday, 18[1] January 1870

Visited New Glasscow School. Got the people interested to repair their house. Politics broke down the interest in the school. How such ignorant people can blunder. They let little differences of opinions ruin their immortal interests. Nothing but education will help this people. Religion alone will not do it. Met a conservative colored man who is prospering. His name is Horace Holaway.[2] Read "The Daily News" and "The Republican." Virginia is not yet in the Union. Last Friday the House passed a bill admitting the state to Representation. It was expected the Senate would concur yesterday in the same action, but no so. The debate is still going on.[3]

Listened to Miss Ada reading "Steppings Heaven-ward." This book is good. It gives a good picture of frail Human Nature. To err is human as it is common. When can man get above this erring humanity? Had a letter from Varner.

Wrote E. Leftwich. Weather is lovely this eve. It was gloomy this morning.

So many of the colored people leave this state. What effect will this have upon the general welfare? The people begin to ask. Classes kept me in the cold till late. I feel the effects.

1. JY mistakenly dated this entry "January 17," repeating the date of the previous day's entry.

2. The 1870 Virginia census listed Horace Holloway as a sixty-five-year-old farmhand living in Amherst County with his wife and twenty-one-year-old son, William. Virginia Census, 1870, Amherst County, Temperance Township, 565.

3 The House of Representatives passed a bill admitting Virginia into Congress on 14 Jan. 1870. The Senate passed the bill with amendments on 21 Jan., and three days later the House concurred in the amended bill. President Ulysses S. Grant signed the bill into law on 26 Jan. 1870, thus bringing Reconstruction to a close in Virginia. Richard G. Lowe, *Republicans and*

Reconstruction in Virginia, 1856–70 (Charlottesville, 1991), 181; *Congressional Globe*, 41st Cong., 2d sess., 1870, 502–503, 670, 740, 821.

Wednesday, 19 January 1870

Spoke with Maj. Saunders. Got coal for Misses. Whitaker's School.

Wrote some articles of constitution for the Boys. They are about starting a debating society.

Attended preaching or Lecture by Bitting. Afterwards anniversary of Sabbath School at the Centenary. Performances were very creditable.

Studied some Geometry.

Read some "Personal Religion."

Thursday, 20 January 1870

Wrote Jonathan, L. Smith, Wilson, McMahon.

Met Supt. Manly before breakfast; accompanied him to the depot.

Copied a letter for squire Talaiferro.[1]

Mr. Berry Reed called. Bought wood & coal for Baptist Church.

Studied Some Geometry.

Independent is very rich, above usual.

Read a part of Stepping Heaven-ward.

Attended committee meeting to frame a constitution for the Hanibal Lyceum.[2] Foreman and Perkins attended it.

Heard Perry and Kelley's Lesson. Started fire so often and still the room is cold.

Read Pottstown Ledger.

1. In 1870 Squire Taliaferro was thirty years old, worked in a tobacco factory, and had a wife, Eliza. The next year, he helped organize the city's Radical Republicans for Lynchburg's city council races and ran himself, but unsuccessfully, on the Radical ticket. Virginia Census, 1870, Campbell County, Lynchburg, 532A; *Lynchburg News*, 9 May 1871, p. 3; 26 May 1871, p. 3; 27 May 1871, p. 3.

2. The new debating society.

Friday, 21[1] January 1870

Visited Perkins School. Staid 1½ hours. Heard a good reading class. Most of the Geography's were poor. Too much confusion, loud talk and leaving of seats at any[time]. 45 pupils present.

Visited Ada's School. 1½ hours. 60 pupils. Heard several classes. School is lacking in arithmetic.

Visited Miss Anna's school. Composision [and] reading was in order. They were not above ordinary good.

I gave them Bees to write about next time.

Looked at the new school-house.

Attended prayermeeting at the Baptist Church. It was cold and lifeless except Brother Ford's remarks *on* the Worth of Souls. He has the appearance of a Christian man.

Visited briefly Messrs. Johnson and Hayden's School[s].

Read the Independent. Worked some examples in Geometry. Read some in the Ledger.

Had letters from Couch, Lynch & Saunders.

Took cold again by a cold water bath.

1. JY dated this entry January 20, although it was actually the 21st.

Wednesday, 26 January 1870

Since Sunday I made a trip to Tower Hill and Allen Creek.[1] This has been a famous trip. Monday Morning Mac and self set out on foot to Tower Hill. The distance is twelve miles. Arrived there at 12½ noon. Then visited Mr. Lythgoe's school,[2] and the new school. We were hospitably entertained at Washington Johnsons.[3] Conversed long on school matters and politics. Saw but few human beings in this twelve mile's trip. Dr. Christians son, as we passed him in the fields plowing, th[u]s unceremoniously addressed Mr. McMahon; "McMahon You are a scriptural man; can You tell me why the confederate states are like the poor man at Dives gate?"[4] "No" was the reply. The interrogator thus responded: "Because they were licked by dogs."

Passed Hon. Thos. Bocock's[5] farm.

Att Tower Hill many of the colored people are land owners. Still they will do very little to support their school. Will not harmoniously work to build their house when the Government gives them $100 towards it.

Was very thankful to God on Tuesday morn when the clouds passed away. At Eleven I started on horseback for Bent Creek.[6] Arrived here at [12] o'clock. A very black ferryman took me over the river.

With all speed I walked to lock "40" four miles distant. He[re] I left the canal[7] to hunt up Miss Ellen Wills school which is about three miles and a half distant. Lost my way. Turned back three times. By the assistance of a boy I found the place at last after walking about six miles. She has no school now. Had the most excellent supper I had for a long time.

A[t] Eleven O'clock wa[l]ked three miles to Canal. Was two hours before the packet.[8] Arrived here 8 o'clock this morning without Sleep. God brought me home safe at last.

Had letters from Varner, McGoldrick & Berry Ried. Wrote Varner and McGoldrick.

Attended Experience meeting[9] at the Baptist Church.

Virginia is once more admitted into the family of states.[10]

1. Tower Hill was located east of Lynchburg in Appomattox County and Allen Creek was located along the James River in Nelson County on the border of both Amherst and Appomattox Counties about twenty-five miles from Lynchburg.

2. Thomas J. Lythgoe taught a school at Tower Hill in Appomattox County. On 30 May 1870, Lythgoe wrote to R. M. Manly that the parents of his students were asking him to continue teaching as most of the pupils were "'Big Lads'" who would otherwise be idle. "The people are so anxious for a school that I cannot very well refuse them." Unregistered Letters Received, Dec. 1869–Aug. 1870, Roll 10; Schedule of Schools Under the Pennsylvania Freedmen's Relief Association, Quarters Ending 31 Dec. 1869, 31 Mar. 1870, and 30 June 1870, Letters Received, 1 Jan.–24 Aug. 1870, Roll 5; Lythgoe to R. M. Manly, 6 Oct. 1869, Letters Received, A–V, 22 Apr.–31 Dec. 1869, Roll 4; Manly to Lythgoe, 12 Oct. 1869, Letters Sent, Vol. 3 (53), p. 532, 12 June–10 Nov. 1869, Roll 2, Supt. of Ed., Va., BRFAL.

3. The 1870 census lists Washington Johnson as a forty-nine-year-old African American farmer, living in Appomattox County with his wife, Judith E., and three children, the younger two at school. Virginia Census, 1870, Appomattox County, Clover Hill Township, 38.

4. JY was referring to the biblical parable told by Jesus of the rich man (commonly called "Dives," which is Latin for "rich man") who "feasted sumptuously every day," while at his doorstep lay the poor man Lazarus, who was covered with sores and who wanted to be fed with the crumbs from Dives's table; "moreover the dogs came and licked his sores." Herbert G. May and Bruce M. Metzger, eds., The Holy Bible: Revised Standard Version . . . (New York, 1962), 1269, Luke 16:19–22, n 16.19–31.

5. Thomas Salem Bocock (1815–1891) served in the House of Delegates, 1842–1844 and 1877–1879, in the House of Representatives of the U.S. Congress, 1847–1861, in the Provisional Confederate Congress, 1861–1862, and as Speaker of the House of Representatives of the Confederate Congress, 1862–1865. He also served as a delegate to the Democratic National Conventions of 1868, 1876, and 1880. Bocock was present at the State Capitol on 27 Apr. 1870 when the floor collapsed, but sustained only a leg injury that was "not serious." Emily J. Salmon and Edward D. C. Campbell, Jr., eds., The Hornbook of Virginia History: A Ready-Reference Guide to Virginia's People, Places, and Past, 4th ed. (Richmond, 1994), 133, 154, 155; Biographical Directory of the United States Congress, 1774–1989: The Bicentennial Edition, 636–637; Lynchburg News, 28 Apr. 1870, p. 3.

6. Bent Creek was in Appomattox County along the James River opposite Nelson County.

7. In 1832, the James River and Kanawha Canal Company was incorporated to replace the James River Company and complete a canal along the James River to the navigable waters of the Ohio River. The first division, from Richmond to Lynchburg, was finished in 1840. The second division, from Lynchburg to Buchanan, was opened in 1851, making a total of 160 miles of canal, 90 locks, and 37 miles of slack water navigation. The third division was never completed. The canal flourished through the 1850s but never really recovered from the Civil War. In 1880, a railroad company purchased the canal and eventually laid tracks on the old canal towpath from Richmond to Lynchburg. Wayland Fuller Dunaway, *History of the James River and Kanawha Company* (New York, 1922), 90–91, 131–132, 157–158, 166–167, 205, 233–239, 239 n.

8. A packet boat was a shallow-draft riverboat that carried mail, freight, and passengers.

9. An Experience Meeting is a religious meeting at which one or more persons relate their conversion experiences.

10. On the day of this diary entry, President Grant signed the legislation readmitting Virginia to Congress. Salmon and Campbell, *Hornbook of Virginia History*, 53.

Thursday, 27[1] January 1870

Visited Mrs. Smith School. 52 pupils present. Was pleased with the School. Spoke to the School. Walked home 12 miles to do business at Bank before 3 o'clock. Came too late though completely exhausted. Lectured on Arithmetic before the Educational Society.

Had letters from Corson, Varner & Manly. Wrote Corson, Manly.

1. JY dated this entry 28 January 1870, but it was actually 27 January 1870.

Friday, 28 January 1870

Read Stepping Heavenward. Well was stepping Heavenward. So am not I. Am drowsy. Slept till after nine o'clock this morning. Am fretful. Rec'd & wrote letters. Rec'd 1½ doz of "the New Era."[1] It promises to be a live[ly] paper. This is the first issue.

Attended the Young Men's Prayer meeting. Attendance larger than usual so was the interest manifested.

Read the Press.

1. A new Republican paper published in Washington, D.C., the *New Era* struggled for survival. In Sept. 1870, the black activist Frederick Douglass purchased a half interest in the paper, renamed it the *New National Era*, and became its editor. Despite his efforts, the paper continued to lose money and despite a later name change to the *New National Era and Citizen*, it ceased publication in Mar. 1874. William S. McFeely, *Frederick Douglass* (New York, 1991), 273, 286.

Saturday, 29 January 1870

The day commenced gloomily. At noon the clouds moved away. Am full of visitors all day. Hayden, Johnson, Wharton, Richardson, & Stuart called.

Read again "Stepping Heavenward."

Well that is a good book. In reading such a book I conclude I am nothing in the way of Intelligence & feeling & believing. What a picture of humanity.

Thursday, 10 February 1870

Since I wrote the above, I passed through sickness, sin and sorrow. Made a trip to Botetourt County. Held the second Teachers institute last week in Lynchburg. The next is to be held on the second week of May at Liberty Va.

We have had the principal Snow of the season this week.

Colored people are still Emigrating from this state. I hear nothing particular of immigration now.

Senator Johnson of this state is reported to be a strait republican.[1]

Rev. C. Bitting did not come to the Institute as he had promised. Now he makes the sorry excuse that he forgot it.

My temptations seem to become more numerous daily. There is little of God in all my thoughts. I forget to pray and to do any other good thing. But to be sinful and to do wicked acts I do not forget. I am as vile a sinner as I ever was. What shall deliver me from the power of sin in whose chains I lie? So often I have abused the grace of God given me for redemption. God bring about my salvation at all hazards. I cannot afford to be lost for nothing that this world can give. I have good impressions this morning. But what do they amount to when past experience teaches me that they will not be embodied in actions? "Laziness is the essence of all moral evil," says some one. I am desperately lazy now a days. The present state of my health occasions this. Still it is not the less an evil.

1. John Warfield Johnston (1818–1889) was elected a U.S. senator as a Conservative on the readmission of Virginia to Congress in 1870 for a term ending on 3 Mar. 1871. He was reelected on 15 Mar. 1871 and again in 1877. He lost another bid for reelection in 1883, resumed his law practice, and died in Richmond in 1889. *Biographical Directory of the United States Congress, 1774–1989: The Bicentennial Edition*, 1273.

Monday, 14 February 1870

To day I have been unusually well employed. Fixed my last month accounts; made payments, wrote numerous letters, visited some schools in town. Attended business meeting of the Church. The important topic of business was the expulsion of Sister E. Whitehead.[1] No vote was taken when I left at Nine O'clock. It should have been taken two month ago; if I understand Christian discipline.

I had a letter of rebuke from Col. Corson last Thursday for not raising more money. It is just. It presses hard on me.

1. This is probably the Mrs. E. Whitehead who was a charter member of College Hill Baptist Church in 1876. She may have been Mrs. Edgar Whitehead (Sallie M.), who was listed in the 1870 census as living in Amherst County, with her husband and two young sons. It is unknown why or whether she was indeed expelled from the church. Adon A. Yoder et al., *View Book, College Hill Baptist Sunday School, Lynchburg, Virginia: A Pictorial Journey Down the Years 1875 to 1915* ([Lynchburg, 1915]), [29]; Virginia Census, 1870, Amherst County, Amherst Township, 422A.

Tuesday, 15 February 1870

Had an application for a new teacher at Stonewall Church.[1] Made an agreement to send there J. M. Powell.

Wrote Corson, Ellen Wills, Couch, Priscilla Johnson.

1. The location of a Stonewall Church in the six-county area for which JY was responsible has not been determined.

Saturday, 19 February 1870

My health is not good. Last night I staid with Brother Kenneday.[1] He is in great affliction. He has just started life for himself. He has nothing in the world—no parents. A short time ago has been laid up with an aneurism. His pain is almost unsupportable. The physicians seem to give the case over.

I have been bored to day by Richardson & Phillips.[2] Phillips seems to be as slow teacher. Conversed with the ladies after supper. I have been generally well employed this week. Attended to Mrs. Whites petition for rent. The day before yesterday wrote some dozen letters.

1. This may have been the J. W. Kenneday listed in the 1870 Lynchburg census, which was taken on 27 June. He is the only male Kenneday given in the census index. At the time, he was a twenty-one-year-old blacksmith's apprentice, living in a household with the Lewises. Samuel Lewis was twenty years old and worked at the post office, while James was sixteen and employed in a tobacco factory. Both of the Lewises were African Americans. Virginia Census, 1870, Campbell County, Lynchburg, 541A.

2. William Griffin Phillips was from Yellow Branch and began teaching there when the new school building was finished on 17 Jan. 1870. JY to Manly, 8 Jan. 1870, Unregistered

Letters Received, Dec. 1869–Aug. 1870, Roll 10; Schedule of Schools Under the Pennsylvania Freedmen's Relief Association, Quarter Ending 31 Mar. 1870, Letters Received, 1 Jan.–24 Aug. 1870, Roll 5, Supt. of Ed., Va., BRFAL. Phillips was not listed in the quarterly report dated 30 June 1870, nor was his name on the Apr. and May 1870 lists of teachers for whom JY requested pay. JY to Robert R. Corson, 5 Apr., 4 May 1870, listing the teachers in his district, Yoder Letter Book, 3 Mar. 1870–1 Dec. 1870, pp. 78, 110, Acc. 35108, LVA.

Thursday, 24 February 1870

I spent a happy birth day on the 22nd. It is also Miss. Attwoods day to reckon her years by. We shared the honors and the plum pudding she had sent from home.

We all took a walk to the tunnel.[1] I carried an icicle home that was longer than myself. In boyish triumph I brought it home to the gate. Here it broke.

I made many good resolutions.

Yesterday I wrote Corson unfavorable to Mr. Varner.

Berry Reid called on me for a teacher, Miss. Ellen Wills will go there.[2] I wrote Jonathan.

This eve commenced with the ladies to read Bitter Sweet.[3]

1. JY may refer here to construction of a tunnel under Ninth Street, completed in Nov. 1872, that linked the Lynchburg and Danville Railroad (chartered in Feb. 1872) to the Orange, Alexandria, and Manassas Railroad. By the time the tunnel was finished, the two lines had consolidated into the Washington City, Virginia Midland, and Great Southern Railroad. Christian, *Lynchburg and Its People*, 293; Poor, *Manual of the Railroads of the United States, for 1878–79* (New York, 1878), 439.

2. Ellen Wills, who had been at the Allen Creek school in Bedford County, closed her school there in Dec. 1869 and reported her teaching activities from the New London School in Campbell County beginning on 1 Mar. 1870. JY to R. M. Manly, 3 Mar. 1870; JY to Robt. R. Corson, 13 May 1870, Yoder Letter Book, 3 Mar. 1870–1 Dec. 1870, pp. 5, 144, Acc. 35108, LVA; Ellen Wills, New London School, Campbell County, Report of Mar. 1870, in Teachers' Monthly School Reports, Feb.–Mar. 1870, Roll 19, Supt. of Ed., Va., BRFAL.

3. Josiah Gilbert Holland, *Bitter-sweet: A Poem*, originally published in New York in 1858, went through numerous editions thereafter.

Friday, 25 February 1870

Got book (Jefferson Manual of Parliamentary usages)[1] for McMahon. Took his watch to Jeweller. Examined two Etymologies. Examined price list of Books. Cleaned my room. Read papers.

1. Thomas Jefferson, *A Manual of Parliamentary Practice For the Use of the Senate of the United States*, first published in 1801, was reprinted many times. JY may have been using the 1865 edition "composed originally for the use of the Senate of the United States . . . with references to the practice and rules of the House of Representatives; the whole brought down to the practice of the present time," published in New York by Clark and Maynard.

Sunday, 27 February 1870

Was busy quite all the time reading, when not at service which was three times. Bitting preached a Sermon on immersion. He advanced many substantial arguments. I think he mentioned seventeen reasons why he thinks the Savior was baptized by immersion. A few he had better omitted—the case would be stronger. Miss Stevens was quite carried away with the argument. The sermon was good.

Monday, 28 February 1870

Cast up my accounts. Made form of society's expenses. Started General Report for February. Read "New Era" [and] in Synonyms. Read Bitter Sweet. Received Money collected in Ladies Schools.

Had letters from Wilson and Seay. Answered them. Gave explanations to Miss. Ellen Wills.

Stopped A few minutes at Debating Society.

Visited Rev. Foreman. Had numerous callers.

Monday, Tuesday,[1] 1 March 1870

Disappointed in not having received my reports. Visited Miss Attwoods school; also Miss Anna's; also the new school House.

Stayed the night with Brother Kenneday who was in racking pain most of the night. The tax upon my frame was severe. How thankless I am having so many blessings undeserved.

1.   JY wrote "Monday, Tuesday" although it was really Tuesday.

Wednesday, 2 March 1870

Blustering March weather. Called several times to see Brother Kenneday. O base ingratitude! I saw this fully displayed by parties that have been and now are the recipients of great, and not to be spared, favors.

Mr. Perkins has not been true to his engagements. He seems to be unappreciative of kindness bestowed on him. 7 letters. Still others are needed.

Thursday, 3 March 1870

Tried the copying aparatus.[1] It works well. Have accomplished little if anything. How dreadfully bad I have been. Carried away by appetite. What is to become of me? I have every inducement heaven and earth can offer and yet I fail, and fail so wickedly.

1. JY was referring to the new letterpress copybook and copy press that he was using. The bound copybook contained tissue-paper sheets and the letter itself was copied onto the tissue page by transferring the ink using moisture and pressure in a copy press. This was a customary way of copying documents between 1820 and 1920. Lewis J. Bellardo and Lynn Lady Bellardo, comps., *A Glossary for Archivists, Manuscript Curators, and Records Managers* (Chicago, 1992), 20.

Monday, 18 April 1870

Weather cold. This Easter Monday.

I did not write in this journal for upwards of a month. I can give no other reason for this omission than my wickedness. There was enough news all the time. The XV Amendment to the Constitution of the United States became a law [at] this time.[1] Great changes in the work I am engaged [in] have taken place. New schools have organized. McMahon resigned.[2] McGoldrick was discharged. Varner came near the same fate.[3] I have made my best efforts to conquer the enemy tobacco. I have failed though at times I abstained for four days.

1. The Fifteenth Amendment provided African Americans with the right to vote. Congress passed the amendment on 26 Feb. 1869 and required Virginia to ratify it as a prerequisite for readmission. The General Assembly did this on 9 Oct. 1869. The amendment became law on 30 Mar. 1870.

2. Charles McMahon was serving as a PFRA teacher at Plymouth Rock School House in Appomattox County at this time when he resigned and returned home. JY wrote to PFRA secretary, Robert Corson, early in Apr. to lament the loss of "such a man" who had "labored so faithfully for four years." He told Corson that McMahon had visited him to give the reasons for the decision and that JY had had to agree that his reasons were good. JY did not elaborate on those reasons, however. In mid-May, JY wrote to one of his other teachers that "McMahon is pleased with his new situation at Bristol, Pa." JY to Corson 5 Apr. 1870; JY to H. A. W. Wilson, 12 Apr. 1870; JY to Thos. J. Lythgoe, 10 May 1870, Yoder Letter Book, 3 Mar. 1870–1 Dec. 1870, pp. 72, 95, 123, Acc. 35108, LVA.

3. Regarding Varner, JY may have been referring to Varner's dispute earlier in the year over ownership of the Liberty School property where Varner had taught in 1866, and where J. E. McGoldrick was then teaching. The question of who actually owned the Liberty School arose in the winter of 1869–1870. McGoldrick wrote to Ralza Manly late in Dec. saying that Varner was in Liberty to make the last payment on the 1866 construction debt for the school and to "lift the deed." JY wrote to Manly the first of the new year that Varner was telling him that

two members of the PFRA held the deed to the property, and Varner himself wrote to Manly on 4 Jan. to say that the questions about the school's ownership were the result "simply" of "a misunderstanding. I have set that matter right among the people." He claimed that he was "not responsible for anything that was done after [he] left there," and repeated, "The whole matter was simply a *misunderstand[ing]*." J. E. McGoldrick, however, wrote to Manly late in Jan., reporting that Varner wanted the local black community to pay an additional $583 to obtain sole ownership of the Liberty School and its grounds. Although the BFRAL had supplied $250 in federal funds for building the school and a like amount had been given in money and labor by the black patrons of the school, Varner had sold the property to two members of the PFRA for an additional $583, according to McGoldrick. Varner then told the local black citizens that if they wanted to own the property, they must pay the new owners for their $583 investment. This would make the school cost $1,083, more than twice the sum actually spent on the building and grounds. McGoldrick told Manly that the black community "are very disheartened, at present and would like to hear from you what they should do."

Manly wrote to Varner on 3 Feb. 1870 and, without mentioning the disputed $583, asked Varner who actually held title to the property and how much the Bureau and the freedmen in the community had invested in it. Varner replied that the PFRA and the local black community were equal owners and went on to explain "the absurd rumour that the School house was to be sold simply because one of the parties 'shuffled of[f] his mortal coil' before the last payment came due,—got its end when I arrived in Liberty." McGoldrick to Manly, 31 Dec. 1869, 28 Jan. 1870; Varner to Manly, 4 and 10 Jan., 7 Feb. 1870; JY to Manly, 1 Jan. 1870, Unregistered Letters Received, Dec. 1869–Aug. 1870, Roll 10; Manly to McGoldrick, 3 Feb. 1870, and to A. Varner, 3 Feb. 1870, Letters Sent, Vol. 4 (54), pp. 473–474, 10 Nov. 1869–28 Mar. 1870, Roll 3, Supt. of Ed., Va., BRFAL.

Nothing further appears in Manly's letterpress book regarding this matter, but the Bedford County deed books show that in Jan. 1866 Varner and J. W. Shoemaker, then-superintendent of the Freedmen's Bureau schools for the Lynchburg area, bought thirteen acres on the east side of Liberty for $1,000 and made a deed of trust to secure payment for the land. In May they deeded in trust for $100 "two roods and Thirty four poles" to Stephen Caldwell, James R. Knight, and Francis R. Cape, of Philadelphia, trustees for the benefit of the PFRA, in order that a "school may be constructed for the mental and moral culture of Colored persons." No further transaction concerning the school is found in the deed books, but the deed of trust Shoemaker and Varner had made for the original thirteen acres was satisfied in July 1870, and in Sept. Shoemaker conveyed his interest in the thirteen acres to Varner for five dollars. Thereafter, Varner made various deeds of sale for portions of the land, mostly between 1870 and 1877, recording the final two deeds of sale in 1884 and 1892. Bedford County Deed Book 43, 1865–1868, pp. 66, 67, 117; Deed Book 44, 1868–1870, p. 481; Deed Book 45, 1870–1871, p. 87; General Index to Deeds, 1754–1930, Grantors, O–Z, letter V, p. 27, LVA.

Early in May 1870, JY reported to Corson that Varner had been in Liberty since 29 Apr. taking care "of his own business." Soon thereafter, JY revealed the conclusion of the Varner saga when he told his brother in a letter that Varner had recently shot a man who survived, but that Varner's career as a Freedmen's Bureau teacher was at end. Varner tried the next school year to get another teaching post, but JY wrote to Corson that "I know he will not do. I presume you know it." JY believed that both Varner and the PFRA would save "further annoyance" if the PFRA would write to Varner and "tell him that his services would no longer be needed by the Society." Evidently this was done as Varner's name does not appear on JY's 1 Dec. 1870 list of teachers requiring payment of their salary. JY to Corson, 5, 18 Apr., 6 May, 6 Nov., 1 Dec. 1870; JY to Varner, 12 Apr. 1870; JY to Jonathan Yoder, 9 May 1870, Yoder Letter Book, 3 Mar. 1870–1 Dec. 1870, pp. 72, 96, 107, 114, 120, 161–162, 164, Acc. 35108, LVA.

Tuesday, 19 April 1870

Called on members of City Council & prominent citizens of Lynchburg to ascertain the public sentiment in regard to public schools. All reports are favorable. But no one wished to act.

Wrote Varner, Corson, McMahon, and Forrest. Called on Perkins and Morgan.

Corson asks that Miss Harvey be offered McMahons school.

Played Presbyterian Dance.

Minister White[1] was lately deposed. Political fever or office fever runs high. Town election is approaching.

This world is not yet fit for a millennium. At least *I* am not.

1. It is not known why Sampson White, pastor of Court Street African Baptist Church, was asked to end his ministry there. The *News* reported that the congregation had "become dissatisfied with their pastor," and noted that the cause of that dissatisfaction had not been revealed, although the unhappiness was understood to be "very general with the members of the church." The church gave White a three-month grace period before his departure. He died a few months later on 20 Nov. 1870 at the age of sixty-nine and was taken home to Philadelphia to be buried by his late wife. Virginia Census, 1870, Campbell County, Lynchburg, 502; *Lynchburg News*, 6 Apr. 1870, p. 3; 22 Nov. 1870, p. 3.

Wednesday, 20 April 1870

One more war is at hand with tobacco. But no success. What can I do to be delivered? God give me a way!

Made reports. Read some. Attended prayermeeting at Baptist Church. Stayed last night with Brother Kennedy. He is so greatly afflicted. O God be gracious to him in Christ Jesus. I called on J. W. Wright.[1]

1. In 1870 James W. Wright was a forty-one-year-old white constable who had been appointed a commissioner in chancery for Campbell County by General E. R. S. Canby. His disabilities had been removed by Congress and he was not required to take the Test Oath. On 8 May 1871, he was appointed to the Radical Committee for the city's third ward and ran successfully for the office of alderman from that ward on the "People's Ticket." Of the various African American and white Radical candidates, only those white Radicals in the third ward were elected. U.S. Army, Department of Virginia, *Special Orders and Circulars, 1 January 1869–29 January 1870* ([Richmond, 1870]), Special Order No. 91, 6 May 1869, p. 2; Virginia Census, 1870, Campbell County, Brookville Township, 420; *Lynchburg News*, 9 May 1871, p. 3; 27 May 1871, p. 3.

Thursday, 21 April 1870

Visited Kelsoe's, Ada's, and Mrs. Ellis' school. Attended Emmas Ward's funeral.[1] Had a letter from Jesse. Wrote Isaac Oberholtzer.[2] Improved a rule for computing interest for Tinsley Watts.[3]

1. Emily Ward was buried on 21 Apr. 1870 as a debtor. JY originally wrote "attended Emily Wards school" and changed it to "funeral." The Lynchburg Overseers of the Poor paid for her burial. Diuguid's Burial Records, Book # 7 (1865–1875), 424, MS1949, Jones Memorial Library, Lynchburg.

2. The 1860 Pennsylvania census lists two possibilities for Isaac Oberholtzer: the first was an Isaac Oberholtzer who lived in Lancaster County, was thirty-two years old in 1860 and a farmer. He had a wife and three children. The other, and less likely, was a twenty-six-year-old expressman living in the household of Peter Henry, a bank watchman. Pennsylvania Census, 1860, Lancaster County, Salisbury Township, 735; ibid., Chester County, Phoenixville, 665.

3. Tinsley Watts is listed in the 1870 Bedford County census as being a twenty-seven-year-old farm laborer, with wife, Catharine, and year-old son, William. Virginia Census, 1870, Bedford County, Otter Township, 299.

Friday, 22 April 1870

Visited four schools. Perkins' is entirely without order. Weather is truly lovely. Called at Bitting's. He is gardening. Argued with Ambler on Carpetbaggers and Scalawags. I think I had the better of him.

Took a walk to "Lovers Leap" in company with the ladies. We did surely enjoy the scenery. We came late to supper.

Heard a powerful sermon by Williams of Petersburg.[1] It was 1¾ hours long— one hour too long.

1. Probably the Reverend Henry Williams Jr., African American pastor of the Gillfield Baptist Church in Petersburg. William Henry Johnson, *A Sketch of the Life of Rev. Henry Williams* (Petersburg, 1901).

Sunday, 23 April 1870

To day I have been informed that I can no longer watch with Mr. Kennedy a sick man, not because he objects, but because the lady he rents from objects to teacher of Cold. [colored] Schools coming on her premises.

Tuesday, 26 April 1870

Visited Miss. Martha Brent's school.[1] By so doing I walked 6 miles. Returned at 5 P.M. Then I walked to Holcombe Rock School meeting. Spoke about an hour. Walked home where I arrived at 1½ next morning. Thus walked 16 miles after five o'Clock.

1. Martha Brent had recently begun teaching a school at Sprout Spring in Appomattox County. Schedule of Schools Under the Pennsylvania Freedmen's Relief Association, Quarter Ending 30 June 1870, Letters Received, 1 Jan.–24 Aug. 1870, Roll 5, Supt. of Ed., Va., BRFAL; JY to Robert R. Corson, 4 May 1870, listing the teachers in his district; JY to Miss. Martha Brent, 10 May 1870, Yoder Letter Book, 3 Mar. 1870–1 Dec. 1870, pp. 110, 127–128, Acc. 35108, LVA.

Wednesday, 27 April 1870

Varner comes here to buy a pistol. Two citizens are after him being offended by an article published by him.[1]

To day Virginia is made sad by the news from Richmond stating that two hundred persons are killed and wounded by the floor over[2] the House of Delegates breaking down upon the Conservative caucus. The room above was densely crowded by the Court that was called to decide in regard to the Chahoon and Ellison case.[3]

1. JY received a letter that day from Corson who suggested that Varner be considered to take McMahon's school at Appomattox. In his answer JY informed Corson that Varner was involved in trouble with two local whites at Pamplin's Depot. The two men had planned to fight a duel, but were instead arrested. Soon after, Varner published an unsigned article about the matter. When one of the men demanded that Varner admit to writing it, he refused and was threatened with violence. Varner later shot and wounded the man. JY reported to his brother on 9 May that the bullet had been extracted, the "man is improving rapidly," and "Mr. Varner is no longer employed as a teacher." Corson to JY and JY to Corson, 27 Apr. 1870, Private Collection; JY to Jonathan Yoder, 9 May 1870, Yoder Letter Book, 3 Mar. 1870–1 Dec. 1870, p. 120, Acc. 35108, LVA.

2. JY originally wrote "the floor of" and then changed it to "the floor over the House of Delegates."

3. "The Chahoon and Ellison case" was an attempt to resolve Richmond's "Municipal War," a struggle between the supporters of Republican George Chahoon and Conservative Henry K. Ellyson. Governor Gilbert C. Walker, elected in 1869, appointed a new city council in 1870 under a bill known as the Enabling Act passed by the Conservative legislature. The council removed Chahoon and installed Ellyson as mayor, but Chahoon's supporters refused to give up control. Richmond in essence had two governments, and the opposing sides met in a series of clashes that left two dead. The Republicans turned to the courts for redress, and both sides eventually agreed to let the new Virginia Supreme Court of Appeals rule on the

case. On 27 Apr. 1870, as the justices took their places in the State Capitol to hand down their decision, the floor of the gallery caved in under the weight of the crowd of spectators who had gathered to hear the decision (which had been decided in favor of Ellyson), and landed in the hall of the House of Delegates below. Initial reports set the number of dead as high as 200, and even modern historical accounts conflict on the total casualties. Jack Maddex gives the number of dead as 58, while Michael Chesson claims that 60 died. *Lynchburg News*, 28 Apr. 1870, p. 2; Jack P. Maddex, *The Virginia Conservatives, 1867–1879: A Study in Reconstruction Politics* (Chapel Hill, 1970), 89–90; Michael B. Chesson, *Richmond After the War, 1865–1890* (Richmond, 1981), 112–114.

JY wrote to his brother Jonathan on 9 May 1870, reporting on the disaster, giving his views on local reaction to it, and chastising Jonathan for not having read about it in the newspapers. "Boy you must read the news of the day. Many of the people in Europe knew it two hours after it happened." JY estimated the death toll at about sixty-five people. Yoder Letter Book, 3 Mar. 1870–1 Dec. 1870, pp. 118–120, Acc. 35108, LVA.

Thursday, 28 April 1870

Visited J. D. Lanning's School. Walked sixteen miles. New[s] from Richmond state[1] that sixty are killed.

Had an Educational meeting.

The president insulted me. Miss. Attwood gave him a lecture for it.

1. The *Richmond State Journal* had been established in Alexandria in 1862 as the *Daily State Journal* and had moved to Richmond in Oct. 1868 as "the 'official paper for the U.S. government.'" A semiweekly edition begun in Mar. 1870 was considered "'the leading Radical paper in the State.'" Cappon, *Virginia Newspapers, 1821–1935*, 45, 187.

Friday, 29 April 1870

Travelled to Mrs. Smith's School. On my return a telegraph is awaiting me from Corson. Varner is also here. Last night he shot a man at Pamplins by the name of Couch[?] the wound is apparently not fatal.

Monday, 31 October 1870

This I can account a lucky day. I was assailed by strong temptations to drinking and other grievous sins. Had rather good luck in making bargains. Spent but little time in idleness. Wrote at night Corson, Wilson, & Bauman. Before the day ended I yielded to the "grievous sins."[1]

1. JY ended his diary 29 Apr. and resumed it with no break on the diary page on 31 Oct. 1870, presumably on his return from his summer vacation in Pennsylvania. The last sentence of the 31 Oct. entry is written is lighter ink and appears to have been added when he penned his 1 Nov. entry.

Tuesday, 1 November 1870

Anna Whitaker arrived.

Wednesday, 2 November 1870

I have seen the wisdom of being true to the conviction of principles.—Ada came. Miss Ellison[1] left for Fincastle. Made several purchases at auction. Bought wood for Polk St. School-house & for my room. Made extensive trips in search of a stove. Attended prayermeeting at Baptist Church. Temptations are pressing hard upon me.

Read in Clark's Commentary.[2]

1. M. E. Ellison, from Philadelphia, Pa., taught at Fincastle in the 1869–1870 and 1870–1871 school terms. From 1871 to 1875, she taught in North Carolina. Schedule of Schools Under the Pennsylvania Freedmen's Relief Association, Quarters Ending 31 Dec. 1869, 31 Mar. 1870, and 30 June 1870, Letters Received, 1 Jan.–24 Aug. 1870, Roll 5, Supt. of Ed., Va., BRFAL; JY to Robert R. Corson, 5 Apr., 4 May 1870, listing the teachers in his district, Yoder Letter Book, 3 Mar. 1870–1 Dec. 1870, pp. 78, 110, Acc. 35108, LVA.

2. JY may have been reading in Adam Clarke, *The Holy Bible, Containing the Old and New Testaments . . . With a Critical Commentary and Critical Notes*, published in eight volumes in London, 1810–1825, and in six volumes in New York, 1811–1825.

Thursday, 3 November 1870

Wrote a notice of colored schools. Took three stoves to school House. Read a Sunday School Paper sen[t] by Miss. Attwood. Read the Evening Press.

I told what I considered an innocent lie. It cost me forty five cents in Green Backs. Recd and Wrote letters. How often have I formed good resolution in regard to quitting the use of tobacco? How unavailable are they. Wrote J. P. Wickersh[am] for a copy of Pa. School Laws.[1]

1. The *School Laws of Pennsylvania* are a continuing series published in Harrisburg by the Pennsylvania Department of Public Instruction and begun in 1848.

Friday, 4 November 1870

Read new Era and the Lynchburg Republican. Put up my stove. Bought articles of furniture. Fitted stove pipe for three rooms at New School House. Had letters from Jonathan and Mrs. Chocklett. Thus was my time employed to night fall.

Saturday, 5 November 1870

Miss Stevens came to day. Rec'd Sewing machine from Depot & set up. Had stove pipe sold at auction. Bought Clarke's Commentary at Auction. Read Press and a portion of Harpers Magazine for Nov. Had a load of wood split for my room. Wrote Corson & Ellison. Had a letter Ellison.[1] I have not accomplished as much as I ought to have accomplished.

1. Miss Ellison wrote that when she arrived in Fincastle she found the school building in ashes and asked what should she do. The people there expected to decide the next Monday whether they could build a house, she said, but if they did it would not be large enough for the teachers. JY answered that she should have the people there rent a house until one could be built; and if that alternative failed, she should wait until she could be assigned another teaching post. A day later, JY wrote to Robert Corson that the Fincastle post had fallen through and that he hoped to send Ellison to Liberty in Bedford County. She clearly received some post as JY included her on his Dec. 1870 list to be paid her salary for Nov. JY to Robt. R. Corson, 5 and 6 Nov., 1 Dec. 1870, Yoder Letter Book, 3 Mar. 1870–1 Dec. 1870, pp. 159–160, 164, Acc. 35108, LVA.

Sunday, 6 November 1870

It was announced to start a bible class in Sunday School. None came. Some teachers joined in the class as there were few pupils present.

Heard Mr. Bitting preach on the words "Wether is easier to say thy sins be forgiven thee or take up thy bed and walk?"

In the Afternoon read a great sermon by Beecher on the heavenly state. At night went to the Colored Baptist Church, finding no room to sit I left it a[fter] I heard a part of Bitting's sermon. Had letters from Couch & Corson. Answered them. Wrote Ellison.

Monday, 7 November 1870

Rose early. Was out on a long trip before breakfast. Undertook to fix up stovepipe before opening school. But failed. Taught till twelve Oclock. Had some twenty eight pupils. Came very near whipping one scholar.

Afternoon took a stove from Baptist Church to School House. Set up four stoves. Had my room scoured. Fixed my coat at night. Had a letter from Wilson.

Tuesday, 8 November 1870

Election day, but not for me.[1] Had hard work with the boys at school. Wrote

& received letters. Heard a beautiful sermon by a Dr. Robinson of Louisville of Kentucky on "Come to the Savior" from 11th of Matth.

1. JY wrote to his brother in May 1870 that he had registered to vote but did not think he would do so. Evidently he did not want to get involved in the local political process. JY to Jonathan Yoder, 9 May 1870, Yoder Letter Book, 3 Mar. 1870–1 Dec. 1870, p. 117, Acc. 35108, LVA.

Wednesday, 9 November 1870

The result of yesterday's election i[n] this Congral Dist so f[a]r a[s] heard from is not as gratefying as was anticipated by the republicans.[1]

I have had a most trying experience in school with fifty three boys. Long ago I had learned that free Government was not intended for an ignorant people. To day the first time the question came up in my mind whether a people can be too ignorant for free schools?

1. The *Lynchburg News* announced on 11 Nov. 1870 that the congressional results for the state had reversed the number of Radicals and Conservatives in Virginia's delegation from five Radicals in the previous Congress to three in the upcoming session and from three Conservatives in the previous Congress to five in the new one. *Lynchburg News*, 9, 10, 11 Nov. 1870.

Thursday, 10 November 1870

No Election news definite. Was very busy in my school. Took my dinner at sunset.

Saturday, 12 November 1870

Bought at Auction what I do not need. This I do so often so that I can often not buy what I do need. Repaired a shirt. Had letters from McMahon & Gust Bauman.[1] Answered the latter. Have been busy generally.

1. The name Augustus Bauman is found on a list of unidentified names on the front end-papers of JY's 1869–1870 diary. Yoder Diaries, 1869–1870, Acc. 27680, LVA.

Sunday, 13 November 1870

An old man was 48 years a slave of tobacco—Wright.

Monday, 14 November 1870

15 New pupils. Much work. Interesting Church Meeting.

The front endpaper of this volume of JY's diary contains the following list of names:

Harry Bean, Royer's Ford [Pa.]
Daniel Endy
Jonathan East
L. S. Worman
Chas. Souder
Augustus Bauman
John W. Bauman
P. A. Attwood
Milton Gilbert
A. J. Mathias
Kate Yoder
Daniel Keck
J. W. Shoemaker
Jonathan Yoder
Corson
Tim Smith
Thomas J. Lythgoe
Martha Brent
Ellen Wills
G. W. Sisson

The last page of this volume of JY's diary contains the following receipts:

$21.50.[1]

 Received, New Glasgow Va. Jan. 18, 1870, of Rev. R. M. Manly Government Appropriation through J. E. Yoder Twenty one Dollars and Fifty cents for the repair of New Glasgow School House

His

Alex X Wharton

Mark

 1. JY originally wrote $24.50 and then wrote a "one" in the "four."

Jan. 28, 1870

Paid Mr. Smith $4 for Glass at Mount Airy Church.

$11.18[1]

 Rec'd New Glasgow Va., Jan. 29, 1870 of Rev. R. Manly Government appropriation through J. E. Yoder Eleven Dollars and eighteen cents for repair of New Glasgow School House.

His

Alex X Wharton

Mark

 1. JY originally wrote $11.28, and then made the last "two" a "one."

Index

The Fire of Liberty in Their Hearts: The Diary of Jacob E. Yoder of the Freedmen's Bureau School, Lynchburg, Virginia, 1866–1870 was designed by Paris Ashton-Bressler of the Virginia Department of General Services, Office of Graphic Communications. Page layout was produced by Paris Ashton-Bressler using Apple Power Macintosh 7600/120 and QuarkXPress 3.32. Text was composed in Berkeley Roman and Italic. Printed on acid-free Georgia-Pacific Valorum, natural vellum, 70-lb. text by Braun-Brumfield, Inc., Ann Arbor, Michigan.